English Catholicism 1558–

Newly revised and updated, the second edition of *English Catholicism 1558–1642* explores the position of Catholics in early modern English society, their political significance, and the internal politics of the Catholic community.

The Elizabethan Religious Settlement of 1559 ostensibly outlawed Catholicism in England, while subsequent events such as the papal excommunication of Elizabeth I, the Spanish Armada, and the Gunpowder Plot led to draconian penalties and persecution. The problem of Catholicism preoccupied every English government between Elizabeth I and Charles I, even if the numbers of Catholics remained small. Nevertheless, a Catholic community not only survived in early modern England, but also exerted a surprising degree of influence. Amid intense persecution, expressions of Catholicism ranged from those who refused outright to attend the parish church (recusants) to 'church papists' who remained Catholics at heart. *English Catholicism 1558–1642* shows that, against all odds, Catholics remained an influential and historically significant minority of religious dissenters in early modern England.

Co-authored with Francis Young, this volume has been updated to include recent developments in the historiography of English Catholicism. It is a useful introduction for all undergraduate students interested in the English Reformation and early modern English history.

Alan Dures is the author of nine textbooks and was a school head of History for 25 years, as well as a tutor for the Open University.

Francis Young is the author of 14 books, a Fellow of the Royal Historical Society, and a former Volumes Editor for the Catholic Record Society.

Seminar Studies

Introduction to the series

History is the narrative constructed by historians from traces left by the past. Historical enquiry is often driven by contemporary issues and, in consequence, historical narratives are constantly reconsidered, reconstructed and reshaped. The fact that different historians have different perspectives on issues means that there is often controversy and no universally agreed version of past events. *Seminar Studies* was designed to bridge the gap between current research and debate, and the broad, popular general surveys that often date rapidly.

The volumes in the series are written by historians who are not only familiar with the latest research and current debates concerning their topic, but who have themselves contributed to our understanding of the subject. The books are intended to provide the reader with a clear introduction to a major topic in history. They provide both a narrative of events and a critical analysis of contemporary interpretations. They include the kinds of tools generally omitted from specialist monographs: a chronology of events, a glossary of terms and brief biographies of 'who's who'. They also include bibliographical essays in order to guide students to the literature on various aspects of the subject. Students and teachers alike will find that the selection of documents will stimulate the discussion and offer insight into the raw materials used by historians in their attempt to understand the past.

Clive Emsley and Gordon Martel
Series Editors

English Catholicism 1558–1642

Second edition

Alan Dures and Francis Young

LONDON AND NEW YORK

Second edition published 2022
by Routledge
2 Park Square, Milton Park, Abingdon, Oxon OX14 4RN

and by Routledge
605 Third Avenue, New York, NY 10158

Routledge is an imprint of the Taylor & Francis Group, an informa business

© 2022 Alan Dures and Francis Young

The right of Alan Dures and Francis Young to be identified as authors of this work has been asserted by them in accordance with sections 77 and 78 of the Copyright, Designs and Patents Act 1988.

All rights reserved. No part of this book may be reprinted or reproduced or utilised in any form or by any electronic, mechanical, or other means, now known or hereafter invented, including photocopying and recording, or in any information storage or retrieval system, without permission in writing from the publishers.

Trademark notice: Product or corporate names may be trademarks or registered trademarks, and are used only for identification and explanation without intent to infringe.

First edition published by Pearson Longman 1983

British Library Cataloguing-in-Publication Data
A catalogue record for this book is available from the British Library

Library of Congress Cataloging-in-Publication Data
Names: Dures, Alan, author. | Young, Francis, author.
Title: English Catholicism, 1558-1642 / Alan Dures, Francis Young.
Description: Second edition. | Abingdon, Oxon ; New York, NY : Routledge, 2022. |
Series: Seminar studies | Includes bibliographical references and index.
Identifiers: LCCN 2021020318 | ISBN 9780367672324 (hbk) | ISBN 9780367672300 (pbk) | ISBN 9781003130376 (ek)
Subjects: LCSH: Catholic Church--England--History--16th century. | England--Church history--16th century. | Catholic Church--England--History--17th century. | Catholics--England--History--16th century. | Catholics--England--History--17th century. | England--Church history--17th century.
Classification: LCC BX1492 .D87 2021 | DDC 282/.4209031--dc23
LC record available at https://lccn.loc.gov/2021020318

ISBN: 978-0-367-67232-4 (hbk)
ISBN: 978-0-367-67230-0 (pbk)
ISBN: 978-1-003-13037-6 (ebk)

DOI: 10.4324/9781003130376

Typeset in Sabon
by Taylor & Francis Books

Contents

Acknowledgements vii

Introduction 1

1 Catholics in early Elizabethan England, 1558–1572 5

   Accession, religious settlement, and diplomacy 5
   The Northern Rebellion and Regnans in Excelsis *12*

2 Catholics in later Elizabethan England, 1572–1603 19

   The Anjou marriage and its consequences 20
   Government policy towards Catholics, 1580–1603 23
   Catholics and the regime: loyalty and resistance 27
   The Elizabethan Catholic community abroad 32

3 Catholic mission in early modern England 35

   The establishment of the Catholic mission 35
   The Archpriest Controversy 45
   The Approbation Controversy 47
   'A church under the cross': the success of the Catholic mission 49
   English mission beyond England 50

4 The Catholic community in early modern England 53

   The social composition of the Catholic community 53
   Devotion and ritual 60
   The Catholic community and English society 68

vi *Contents*

5   James I and the Catholics, 1603–1625   79

   The Gunpowder Plot 82
   Reactions to the Gunpowder Plot 83
   The Oath of Allegiance 86
   Increased persecution 88
   Hopes for toleration 90

6   The Catholics in Caroline England, 1625–1642   95

   Charles I and the Catholics 95
   Court Catholicism 100
   Anti-Catholicism 106
   Popish plots, the fear of popery, and the collapse of the
      regime 113

Documents   120
Guide to further reading   135
Bibliography   137
Index   146

Acknowledgements

I was much indebted to a number of people in the writing of the first edition of this book in the early 1980s. The late Patrick Richardson, founder editor of the Seminar Studies in History series, and a former colleague, encouraged me to contribute to it, while the late Professor Joel Hurstfield first stirred my interest in English Catholicism in the Tudor and Stuart period. While writing the book I received considerable help from Dr Alan Davidson, Dr Christopher Haigh, and the late Professor John Bossy, all of whom read the manuscript and made many helpful suggestions. I am particularly grateful to Dr Haigh for allowing me to read and use extensively two articles that were then yet to be published. My greatest debt was to my late wife for her practical help and constant encouragement.

Among those who have made a second and completely revised edition of *English Catholicism 1558–1642* possible after the passage of almost four decades, I am especially indebted to Professor Bill Sheils for reading and commenting in detail on the entire manuscript. Dr David L. Smith, Dr Adam Morton, and Dr James Kelly generously shared their work, and I acknowledge with gratitude the work of Jillian Macready, Aidan Dures, and Finlay Dures in assisting with typing the manuscript.

Alan Dures

I was delighted when Alan Dures (who taught me history at GCSE and A Level and first introduced me to the historiography of English Catholicism) invited me to co-author a revised edition of his *English Catholicism 1558–1642*. I share in thanking those whom Alan Dures has already mentioned, and I am especially grateful to Bill Sheils for casting his expert eye over the whole work. I thank Dr Liesbeth Corens, Dr Lucy Underwood, and Dr Eilish Gregory for sharing their work and offering insights on the text. Laura Pilsworth, Isabel Voice, and the production team at Taylor & Francis have guided the book efficiently and considerately towards publication in the difficult circumstances of a global pandemic. I gratefully acknowledge the permission of the Council of the Catholic Record Society to reproduce an extract from *Recusant Documents from the Ellesmere Manuscripts*, edited by Anthony Petti (1968) in Document 13. Every effort has been made to trace copyright holders of other material reproduced in the book that remains in copyright, and to obtain their permission for the use of copyright material.

Francis Young

Introduction

This subject of this book is English Catholicism in the crucial period between the accession of Elizabeth I and the outbreak of the Civil War in 1642. Originally published in 1983, *English Catholicism 1558–1642* was intended as a single integrated introduction to the political and social history of Catholicism in early modern England. Clearly, the historiography of Catholicism has been completely transformed in the intervening decades, and while the aim of this second edition remains the same, it has been thoroughly revised to take account of the transformation of a historical field that was once obscure but now attracts considerable attention. The first edition stressed the innovative work of John Bossy. Prior to this, English Catholicism had been seen mainly in terms of heroic resistance, and martyrdom took centre stage in Catholic narrative. Bossy attributed Catholic survival to the emergence of the English Catholic community, defined as 'the body of Catholics as a social whole and in relation to itself with its internal constitution and the internal logic of its history' (Bossy, 1975: 5).

According to Bossy, this community became a separatist dissenting body with recusancy at its heart. In the last few decades historians have moved away from almost exclusive emphasis on recusancy in favour of a more complex understanding of who might be considered a Catholic in early modern England. Alexandra Walsham's book *Church Papists* (1999) was especially important in drawing attention to a hitherto overlooked group, those Catholics who reluctantly attended their parish church in order to avoid recusancy fines. As Michael Questier has noted, English Catholicism 'was not a neat, simple and unproblematic religious category' (Questier, 2000: 260), and 'Catholics' included nostalgic crypto-Catholics, the 'Nicodemite' Church Papists (who remained Catholics at heart while attending church) and occasional conformists ('fair-weather recusants' who went to church when penalties loomed), hardened recusants, converts, and foreign visitors. This book adopts a broad understanding of who counted as part of the English Catholic community, including those English Catholics who lived abroad.

The English Catholic community was far from being totally separated from wider English society. This revised edition builds on the insights of Michael Questier and Peter Lake that English Catholics continued to be engaged in English politics and endeavoured to influence public opinion throughout the period, and that this engagement increased further under the Stuarts. Divisions with the regime

DOI: 10.4324/9781003130376-1

and especially within the established church enabled loyalist Catholics to push for an accommodation with the English state. The culmination of this process came in 1638–40 when Catholics came close to establishing an alliance with Charles I, which meant that Catholics were part of the Royalist attempt to defeat the presbyterian Scots and their 'godly' supporters led by John Pym. For Catholics to achieve a secure and comfortable position within the English state, some defeat or curbing of the 'godly' was essential, as these Puritans defined themselves in terms of their anti-popery – opposition not only to Catholicism, but to any hint of Catholic sympathy.

Recent work has also brought out the extent which English Catholicism was connected to and shaped by Counter-Reformation Europe. Early modern England was unusual as a country where, in spite of a largely successful Protestant Reformation, Catholics continued to exist as a religious minority who exercised ongoing local influence and sporadic influence in national affairs. This survival was in contrast to the Scandinavian nations, where Catholicism was virtually wiped out by the Lutheran Reformation. It also contrasted with the Netherlands, where certain areas continued as predominantly Catholic, and with Scotland where Catholicism was more common in the Gaelic-speaking Highlands; in England, Catholics were concentrated in no single region and were represented by no particular linguistic or ethnic group. Furthermore, English Catholics existed in a country where the Reformation was broadly a success, in contrast to Ireland – a nominally Protestant kingdom where the Reformation failed significantly and the majority remained Catholic.

The focus of this book is on England, and to some extent on English Catholics outside England, but the phenomenon of English Catholicism after 1558 cannot be viewed in isolation from the wider Reformations in Britain and Ireland; England was one of two kingdoms under the English crown and one of two kingdoms occupying the island of Great Britain. England's centrally directed Reformation under Henry VIII, Edward VI, and Elizabeth (and the centrally directed Counter-Reformation under Mary) was, according to the still influential historiography of Geoffrey Elton, a 'Reformation from above' (Haigh, 1982: 995), but this was true to an even greater extent of the Reformations imposed on reluctant Wales and Ireland. In Scotland, by contrast, a popular Reformation pushed the Catholic Mary, Queen of Scots, out of the kingdom and into England in 1567. Mary's dynastic proximity to the English throne (and her Catholicism) rendered her a destabilising force in Elizabethan England, and when a Catholic revolt broke out in the north of England two years later, rebels were able to take refuge across the border in Scotland. Even before the prospect of King James VI's accession to the English throne, therefore, Scottish affairs were of great importance to the course of the English Reformation.

English attitudes to Ireland – claimed as a kingdom by Henry VIII and his successors from 1541 – were informed not only by a desire to repress Catholicism but also by longstanding colonialist prejudices against the 'wild Irish'. However, events such as the papal and Spanish invasions of Ireland in 1579 and 1601 informed government attitudes to Catholics in England as well – especially since Catholic insurgencies in Ireland were often supported not only by the Gaelic Irish but also by the 'Old English' of the Pale. Ireland was an unstable theatre of war that, as far as the English government was concerned, displayed the fullness of Catholicism's dangerous potential. Any concessions granted to Catholics in either England or Ireland were likely to have repercussions for the other kingdom. As the Irish rising of 1641 would eventually show, Irish Catholicism was potent enough to overthrow the Reformation altogether, a fear that also became attached to English Catholics.

The Scottish religious policy of James VI attracted particular attention in England in the 1590s once it became clear that James was the most likely successor to Elizabeth. As the son of a Catholic mother, baptised as a Catholic, and renowned for his opposition to extreme Calvinists in Scotland, James became a figure of hope for English Catholics. As Chapter 5 of this book will explore, the dashing of those hopes on James's English accession catalysed the Gunpowder Plot. Furthermore, as Chapter 6 will explore, Charles I's plan to use Irish Catholic troops to quell the Scottish Covenanters – and even his opponents in England – was a profoundly destabilising factor in the last years before the outbreak of Civil War in England. While this book deals with Catholicism in England, the wider British and Irish context of English Catholicism ought to be borne in mind; English Catholics were part of a wider North Atlantic community of British and Irish Catholics.

The structure of the book is partly chronological and partly thematic, with the first two chapters covering the political history of Catholics (and government attitudes to Catholics) in the reign of Elizabeth: first in the uncertain early years after the Elizabethan settlement of 1559 (Chapter 1) and then in the last three decades of the reign when Catholics faced a determined legislative onslaught (Chapter 2). Chapter 3 examines the theme of the Catholic mission, those measures and structures that enabled the continuation of organised Catholic life in the extremely challenging circumstances of Elizabethan and Stuart England. The focus of Chapter 4 is on the Catholic community itself: who were the Catholics of early modern England, how did they express their faith, and how did they relate to their non-Catholic neighbours? Chapter 5 returns to the chronology by dealing with the reign of James I, a period that saw both great Catholic expectations of toleration and some of the severest persecution of Catholics in the aftermath of the Gunpowder Plot. The subject of the book's sixth and final chapter is the reign of Charles I to the outbreak of the English Civil War in 1642, a period that saw both the development of a court Catholicism at the heart of power as well as the emergence of virulent forms of anti-Catholicism.

In spite of their small numbers in early modern England, Catholics – and the idea of Catholics – were disproportionately influential in English history. While the conscious political rejection of Catholicism shaped many aspects of early modern England (and, through it, present-day Britain), the continued existence of a Catholic community persistently challenged the idea of a reformed, godly England. England's ongoing need to engage diplomatically with powerful Catholic nations, the government's perpetual need for money, the high noble status of some Catholics, and the resilience of the Catholic community ensured that a policy of annihilating Catholicism was never truly a viable option between 1558 and 1642.

England's popular memory was shaped by set-piece confrontations with Catholicism, such as the Spanish Armada of 1588 and the Gunpowder Plot of 1605, but the relationship between Catholics and politics was in reality more complex. The Catholic community was itself divided: between those Catholics willing to attend Protestant services and those who refused; between those whose priority was survival and those whose priority was the re-conversion of the nation; and between those willing to compromise in order to secure some civic rights and those willing to undergo martyrdom for the Catholic faith. Successive governments exploited these divisions among Catholics, while Catholics struggled to negotiate their own position as a dissenting religious minority unable to agree on issues of leadership and governance – while the wider Catholic world, including English Catholics, underwent the process of 'Counter-Reformation' through the implementation of the decrees of the Council of Trent (1545–63).

This book analyses the crucial period between the accession of Elizabeth I and the outbreak of Civil War in 1642. These were the decades that determined whether English Catholicism would survive or not, when the government's treatment of Catholics oscillated at various times from intense and lethal persecution to accommodation, and even indulgence. The very existence of post-Reformation English Catholicism arguably challenged the foundations of the early modern English polity as a nation that defined itself against a Catholic past and the Catholic world, yet Catholics proved a resilient minority of religious dissenters. Ultimately, governments were forced to compromise in various direct and indirect ways with this reality.

1 Catholics in early Elizabethan England, 1558–1572

Elizabeth I's decision to abandon the religious policy of her half-sister Mary I in favour of a Protestant religious policy was the act that created a minority of English people who chose to identify themselves as Catholics. However, the piecemeal enforcement of the Elizabethan Religious Settlement in the 1560s enabled many Catholics to practise their faith with the assistance of priests ordained in the reigns of Henry VIII and Mary. Nevertheless, some of the early contours of English Catholicism emerged at this period, such as the appearance of both recusants and church papists. However, events in the late 1560s and early 1570s hardened the government's attitude towards Catholics and made it increasingly difficult for Catholics to practise their faith. The period 1558–72 was a crucial, formative yet uncertain time for England's Catholics.

Accession, religious settlement, and diplomacy

At the beginning of Elizabeth's reign in November 1558 England was a divided nation, but almost certainly one in which the majority was attached to traditional religion. Nicholas Sander, an early Catholic exile in Louvain, claimed in 1561 that less than one per cent of the population was 'infected with heresy', although this seems well wide of the mark. Despite the successful Catholic restoration under Mary, there were strong pockets of Protestantism in London and the southeast, soon to be invigorated by the return of Protestant exiles from Europe; these exiles brought with them the reformed theology from radical centres such as Frankfurt, Strasbourg, or Geneva. It was clear from the early weeks that Elizabeth would opt for a form of Protestantism, but even the committed Protestants advising the queen recognised the problems of a divided nation. Nicholas Throckmorton advised Elizabeth that while authority was being established 'it shall not be meet that either the old or new [religion be] fully understood'. William Cecil was bolder in pushing a Protestant agenda, but, recognising the twin threats of foreign Catholic powers and domestic conservative religion, he appreciated that skilful political manoeuvring would be required. The imperial ambassador, Count Helffstein, reported in March 1559 that Elizabeth 'seems both to protect the Catholic religion and at the same time not entirely to condemn or outwardly reject the new Reformation' [Doc. 1, p. 120].

DOI: 10.4324/9781003130376-2

The queen was key to the future religious character of the country and all historians now accept that Elizabeth was a Protestant. In fact, she was a devout Protestant who had translated the psalms and was a reader of the vernacular Bible. Her major influences came through her childhood education in the household of Katherine Parr and, under Edward VI, the spiritual guidance of her chaplain, Edward Allen. These experiences shaped Elizabeth as an evangelical Protestant, whose doctrinal beliefs are best described as Lutheran. Of course, given her parental background, she was going to reject any notion of papal authority and indeed she was no lover of 'popery', although she did not see her Catholic subjects as agents of the Antichrist. The queen signalled her Protestant preferences early in the reign when, on Christmas Day 1558, she departed from the chapel royal before the adoration of the sacrament because the bishop of Carlisle had insisted on the Catholic ritual of elevating the host. By her coronation on 15 January 1559, the host was no longer elevated, demonstrating a Protestant view of the Eucharist. Despite her obvious commitment to Protestantism and her denunciation of superstitions, Elizabeth continued to display a crucifix in the chapel royal, where throughout her reign she also showed a taste for elaborate church music, mainly composed by Catholics, and the liturgy remained in Latin (Doran, 2011: 38–42; Sheils, 2011: 254–7; Marshall, 2017: 422–4).

The Parliament of 1559 brought in a new religious settlement with the Acts of Supremacy and Uniformity. The former restored the royal supremacy, although Elizabeth became 'Supreme Governor', not 'Head' of the Church of England, while the latter laid down 'one uniform order of common service' based on the Prayer Book in use in 1552, but with some modifications. The denunciation of the bishop of Rome and all his detestable enormities was omitted. So too was the 'Black Rubric', explaining how kneeling at communion did not imply adoration. For the administration of the communion itself the words of 1549 (which implied a real presence of the body and blood of Christ) were coupled with those of 1552 (which implied a memorial of Christ's death), producing total ambivalence. This final settlement was probably close to Elizabeth's own preferences, though Doran has argued that the queen would have opted more clearly for the communion service of 1549 with its belief in the corporal presence (Doran, 2011: 40). The Latin Prayer Book used in the queen's own chapel owed more to 1549 than to 1552 (Jones, 1984: 174–86). The settlement was unambiguously Protestant, but nodded towards moderation through the inclusion of elements of the 1549 Prayer Book, for example. It was not a return to the Edwardian Reformation of 1550–3 and fell well short of the hopes of more radical Protestants. Nevertheless, there was opposition in the Commons, while a majority in the Lords was only secured by the exclusion of two bishops and an abbot; even then the Act of Uniformity was only passed by three votes, with all the bishops and seven peers opposed (Marshall, 2017: 424–34; Sheils, 2011: 254–5).

Opposition in Parliament was quickly followed by the resignation of all Marian bishops except for Kitchin of Llandaff. Eamon Duffy has spoken of 'a dramatic stiffening of spine and principle' under Mary I that contrasted with the supine attitude of clergy to the reformations of Henry and Edward (Duffy, 2009:

197). A number of cathedral clergy also resigned, but most of the parochial clergy remained in place. However, the oft-quoted figure of 300 resignations is too low; the true figure by the mid-1560s of resignations or deprivations was closer to 800. This figure is still low, but part of the explanation lies in the reluctance of the authorities to deprive the parochial clergy, especially after the high death toll following the influenza epidemic in 1557–8 and the subsequent shortage of clergy. Conformity was made easy as the clergy had to agree only to a simple summary of the new ecclesiastical settlement of 1559 and not to the Oath of Supremacy itself. Nevertheless, only a minority subscribed to the Northern Commissioners in 1559, with little or no evidence of deprivations. According to John Aveling there were relatively few deprivations in the West Riding of Yorkshire over the next 30 years, and even some 40 clergymen who were prosecuted for 'Catholic practices' were never deprived (Marshall, 2017: 442–4; Questier, 2019: 22n69).

Given the continued presence of Catholic-minded clergy, it is not surprising that many parishes in the North retained conservative features in the 1560s. In Holderness in the East Riding of Yorkshire several parish priests continued masses for the dead. At Ripon three priests not only continued in their use of banned images but offered masses in the chancel to rival official services. The bishop of Hereford, John Scory, lamented the neglect of preaching and services by the clergy of Hereford Cathedral, who merely 'mutter against' the religious settlement *[Doc. 2, p. 120–1]*. Most spectacularly of all, the vicar of Bonnington in Lincolnshire provided all seven sacraments until 1576 (Sheils, 2011: 255). Lancashire was strongly Catholic. Strype, in his *Annals of the Reformation*, complained that in the 1560s 'mass [was] commonly said, priests harboured, the Book of Common Prayer and the service of the Church established by law laid aside'. Catholic practices continued strongly well beyond the Northern Counties, especially in the Welsh borders and the West Country, but also parts of Hampshire and Sussex. Even in areas of greater Protestantism some churches were slow to eliminate all vestiges of traditional worship; it was only in 1571 that Great St Mary's, Cambridge, sold its holy water stoup, banners, vestments, and crosses (Marshall, 2017: 480–1; Haigh, 1975: 255–65; Dickens, 1943: 161).

Given the conservative nature of many parishes, few Catholics saw any reason to challenge the Elizabethan church openly, so continued to attend their parish church. There was little papal leadership on the issue of attending Protestant services; it was only in 1562 that the papacy made an authoritative statement prohibiting attendance, and even then it took no steps to publicise it. Throughout the early 1560s the Elizabethan government remained in contact with the papacy, and Pope Pius IV seems to have held out hope England would accept the decrees of the Council of Trent (Bartlett, 1992: 643–59). However, a group of Catholic exiles at Louvain in the Low Countries began to insist on Catholic separation and generally to adopt an aggressive stance against the new Elizabethan church. The Louvain community, eventually an estimated 300 former university fellows, struck a very different note to their English counterparts. One of the most prominent members, Nicholas Sander, was an early advocate of recusancy and worked closely with the ex-cathedral clergy who led the English insistence on recusancy. According to John

Morren, a cathedral clergyman who visited Louvain, Sander explained simply and clearly that attendance at Protestant service was wrong, that 'if ye associate yourself at sacramente or servise that is contrarie to the unitie of Chryste his churche ye fall into scysme' (Smith, 2017: 311). Other Louvain scholars such as Thomas Harding and Thomas Stapleton launched an all-out attack on the legitimacy of the Elizabethan church, contrasting the universal and ancient character of Catholicism with the novel and insular nature of the new Elizabethan religion.

In England too, there was a small group of clerics who were advocating separation from the Elizabethan church. They were headed by some ex-cathedral clergy who, apart from the Marian bishops, showed most resistance to the 1559 religious settlement. They maintained close contact with the Louvain exiles and had their greatest impact in Lancashire, where, along with the Marian recusant priests, they laid the foundations of early recusancy. The two most prominent clerics, both deprived cathedral prebendaries, were John Morren and Laurence Vaux. In 1561 John Morren was circulating a broadsheet echoing the Louvain writings, which argued that 'the Religion now used in the Church was not heard of before Luther's time, about 40 years ago' (Haigh, 1975: 249). At the same time Morren also began to advocate recusancy. Vaux, on his return from Louvain in 1566, brought with him instructions to publicise the papal prohibition on attending Protestant services. By 1568, when eight Lancashire gentlemen were charged with recusancy, it was apparent how much work Morren, Vaux, and others had done to insist on non-attendance. The duo, along with nine other priests, had been working as a team to promote recusancy among the gentry, some of whom had even taken a vow pledging recusancy and support for papal supremacy. The influence of the group spread across the North, particularly in Yorkshire. In the 1570s it appears that Morren and Vaux were operating alongside Robert Copley, a former parish priest, who had been at the residence of the earl of Northumberland at Ripon before 1569 (Smith, 2017: 317–18).

The ex-cathedral clergy were part of a larger group of 'Marian' priests, mainly parochial clergy who resigned or were deprived after 1559; the Marian priests had made an important contribution to Catholic survival in the 1560s and beyond. Their numbers were considerable; 75 were known to have worked in Lancashire, and over 150 in Yorkshire (Haigh, 1975: 255–7; Aveling, 1966: 34). The Marian priests were able to provide an alternative ministry, both to those not attending their parish churches and to those conservatives who were. They worked closely but not exclusively with the gentry, and on occasion had access to concealed liturgical instruments once used in the parish church. The early Elizabethan bishops considered the Marian priests a danger to the new church. Edwin Sandys, bishop of Worcester, complained in 1564 of 'popish and perverse priests which, misliking religion, have forsaken the ministry and yet live in corners, are kept in gentlemen's houses in great estimation with the people' (McGrath and Rowe, 1984: 105). The bishops of Ely and Peterborough expressed similar points about the impact of the Marian priests. In Hereford it appears that there was a degree of organisation; Bishop Scory complained of a number of Marian clergy 'going from one gentleman's house to another' and also being protected by his own cathedral clergy (McGrath and Rowe, 1984: 111). A limitation on the effectiveness of the Marian priests was a high rate of imprisonment, especially in southern England (McGrath and Rowe, 1984: 103–18; Sheils, 2011: 257).

Notwithstanding the activities of the cathedral clergy, the Louvain exiles or the Marian priests, there was little recusancy or serious Catholic challenge to the regime before the late 1560s. This was due, in part, to Elizabeth's policy. Formerly historians tended to describe this policy as lenient, but more now describe it as cautious; we have seen that in 1559, even advocates of Protestantism accepted the need for caution. For Elizabeth, the Reformation was achieved in 1559 and she sought no further Protestant measures to upset her conservative subjects. Her aim was to achieve weekly attendance at the established church, not to extract any declaration of Protestant beliefs or demand subscription to theological doctrines. In the 1560s the queen was largely achieving her aim. The regime, however, was quick to punish overt Catholic activities, especially in southern England where enforcement was easier. A Marian priest, Nicholas Bush, was sent to the Fleet Prison for administering the sacraments according to Catholic rites to Lady Hobblethorne of Essex. A number of the former cathedral clergy operating in the southern counties were quickly imprisoned, compelling others to move northwards. The Elizabethan authorities were sensitive to the use of embassy chapels by English Catholics. In 1560 a number were arrested for attending mass at the French embassy; for diplomatic reasons, no action was taken against those attending mass at the same time in the Spanish embassy (Trimble, 1964: 20–2).

Government policy was restrained by the problems of enforcement, so there were differences across the country. Rigorous enforcement was difficult in areas such as the North Riding of Yorkshire where some 75 per cent of leading families were Catholic. In Sussex the leading aristocracy were Catholic, so the lieutenancy of the county was in Catholic hands. The wider problem of officeholding was revealed in 1564 episcopal reports to the Privy Council on the religious affiliations of justices of the peace. The bishops classified the JPs into those who were 'favourable', 'unfavourable' or 'neutral' towards the Elizabethan settlement. Such categories are vague and subjective, and some bishops sent out more detailed reports than others. Nevertheless, even after all these reservations the 1564 returns show a strong religious conservatism among officeholders, even after commissions of the peace had already been remodelled to reduce the Catholic element. In Lancashire only 6 out of 24 justices were considered 'favourable' to the settlement. Before 1581 religious enforcement was in the hands of the ecclesiastical authorities, and all the bishops were new appointments in 1559, including a number of 'godly' Protestants among the Marian exiles. Nevertheless, it was no easy task to directly confront Catholic gentry, as Bishop Pilkington of Durham found; his aggressive promotion of Protestant policies in the 1560s contributed significantly to the Northern Rebellion in 1569 (Trimble, 1964: 26; Marshall, 2017: 464; Cliffe, 1969: 166–88).

There were other factors that weighed with government policy beyond Elizabeth's caution and the policy of enforcement. The need to maintain Habsburg friendship was recognised, as Philip II could check papal aggression towards England. At times, such as in the marriage negotiations with the Archduke Charles of Austria or in attempting to establish more friendly relations with France in 1564, it was essential to project a conservative image of English religion. When the French ambassador visited Archbishop Parker at Canterbury in 1564, Parker stressed the similarities to Catholicism of the new Elizabethan religion with its days of abstinence and church music. The French ambassador concluded that the English 'were in religion very nigh to them'. Moreover, in the 1560s the Council consisted of more than just Cecil and Leicester, important though these two were. There was a strong conservative element on the Council, with the likes of the duke of Norfolk and the earls of Arundel and Pembroke. On occasion, most notably in 1568 and early 1569 over the projected marriage of the duke of Norfolk and Mary, Queen of Scots, Leicester supported the conservatives. This led to a degree of fluidity and uncertainty as to the direction of religious travel, which in turn encouraged Catholics not to challenge the regime or to break away immediately from the new Elizabethan church (Younger, 2018: 1061–92).

In 1563 Elizabeth showed that she was prepared to check parliamentary attempts to make failure to subscribe to the 1559 settlement much harsher. Alexander Nowell, dean of St Paul's, set the tone in his opening sermon in Parliament, by demanding the death penalty for the deprived Marian bishops [*Doc. 3*, p. 121]. An act 'for the Assurance of the Queen's Majesty's Royal Power' made the denial of the supremacy a treasonable offence and the second refusal of the oath was punishable by death. The list of those required to take the oath was widened to include MPs, but peers were exempt. Elizabeth ignored requests for the Marian bishops to be executed, and she ensured that no-one suffered the death penalty for refusing the Oath of Supremacy by instructing Archbishop Parker not to administer the oath twice.

The issues in 1563 were wider than a cautious queen negating the demands of an anti-Catholic Parliament. Parliament, in fact, was far from unanimous; there was strong criticism in the Lords and no less than 83 MPs voted against the act. Moreover, the main focus in Parliament was the queen's marriage and succession. The more aggressive demands for Elizabeth to settle these issues came from the Protestant element in Parliament. This included a failed bill, drafted by Cecil, which proposed that were the queen to die suddenly, sovereign power would pass to the Privy Council until Parliament was able to nominate a successor. Such a discussion of succession was anathema to Elizabeth, who saw it as a challenge to her prerogative. According to Questier, in these circumstances the queen could not afford to alienate Catholic support, as 'Catholics could pose, if not as proponents of an absolutist monarchical authority, then at least as critics of parliamentary claims to define and alter succession' (Questier, 2019: 43). The argument that Viscount Montague used in the Lords to attack the anti-Catholic measures may well have been special pleading; it clearly stressed that Catholics, more than the queen's Protestant critics, were loyal subjects: 'they [the Catholics] disobey not the queen … so that no man can say that thereby the realm doth receive any hurt or damage by them' (Questier, 2006: 138; Marshall, 2017: 354–7).

From the beginning of the reign, the Elizabethan regime, or most of it, recognised that good relations with the pope were essential in order to prevent a strong papal denunciation of the new queen and her church, which might encourage Catholic resistance in England. As we have seen, the failure of Pope Pius IV to provide strong guidance to Catholics on the issue of attendance at Protestant services did indeed contribute to near total conformity in the early 1560s. Initially, papal policy, encouraged by Philip II of Spain, was based on the assumption that England could be won back to Catholicism by diplomacy. There were plans for England to send representatives to the reopening of the Council of Trent; Nicholas Throckmorton, a firm Protestant, told the Venetian ambassador that the English would attend if the Council were 'free' – that is, more in line with historic General Councils than the previous sessions of Trent. Although one English bishop did attend the Council (the exiled Marian bishop of St Asaph, Thomas Goldwell), the possibility of any broader English participation effectively ended in May 1561 when the papal nuncio Martinengo was refused entry to England. This was the work of William Cecil, who conveniently discovered a popish conspiracy involving Sir Edward Waldgrave, a privy councillor under Mary, and the papal nuncio himself. Cecil later confided that 'he thought it necessary to dull papist expectations' (Marshall, 2017: 452; Questier, 2019: 32).

Despite this affront to the pope, Anglo-papal diplomatic ties continued in the early 1560s. Pius IV generally favoured diplomacy over action. Even in 1563, when the pope, under pressure from the Louvain exiles, considered excommunicating Elizabeth, he eventually responded to the pleas of Philip II and Emperor Ferdinand that such an action would inflame religious tensions in the Netherlands and Germany as well as England. By 1565, however, Pius IV had come to realise that, if England was to return to papal jurisdiction, a military solution had to be considered. This met with a positive response from Philip II who declared himself sympathetic to the English claims of Mary, Queen of Scots, as the granddaughter of Margaret Tudor, the eldest daughter of Henry VII. In the eyes of some Catholics Mary was the only legitimate queen of England, given that the papacy never ratified the annulment of Henry's marriage to Katherine of Aragon – with the result that his marriage to Anne was a sham and Elizabeth was illegitimate.

In October 1565 Philip wrote that 'when the time comes to throw off the mask and bestir ourselves ... the Pope and I will consider the manner in which we may aid and promote that cause of God which now the queen of Scotland upholds, since it is manifest that she is the gate by which religion must enter the realm of England, all others being now closed' (Haugaard, 1968: 308). The letter was cautious and conditional and does not signal immediate action on Mary's behalf; it is nevertheless significant. Papal policy hardened further with the election of Pius V, a stridently orthodox Dominican friar, in late 1565. The new pope ensured that the ban on church attendance was publicised in England by Laurence Vaux, and the printed attacks on the Elizabethan church by the Louvain exiles were stepped up (Marshall, 2017: 481–2).

In contrast to deteriorating Anglo-papal relations, the marriage negotiations between Elizabeth and Archduke Charles of Austria, son of the Holy Roman Emperor Ferdinand, kept England close to one branch of the Habsburgs between 1563 and 1567. It also offered Catholics the hope that the Elizabethan church might shift in a more Catholic direction. Elizabeth encouraged such hopes as she made immediate concessions and then signalled to the emperor that the new Elizabethan church was essentially quite conservative. In September 1563 Elizabeth released the imprisoned Marian bishops into comfortable house arrest at the emperor's request. On Ash Wednesday 1565, when Dean Nowell preached against images, Elizabeth walked out. A few weeks later Bishop Guest of Rochester gave a sermon in which the real presence in the Eucharist was asserted (Doran, 1996: 76; Marshall, 2017: 478–9).

Between 1565 and 1567 the marriage was a dominant political issue, raising Catholics' expectations and heightening Protestant fears. In the spring of 1566 the archdeacon of Essex felt compelled to combat rumours that the queen intended to restore popery, while the earl of Sussex thought that the negotiations were endangered by criticisms from Calvinist preachers. The religious divisions in England were sharpening. The issue of religion finally ended the negotiations, as Elizabeth refused to allow Archduke Charles access to a private mass in England. The failure of the negotiations was a blow for the Catholics and for conservatives at court such as Norfolk and Sussex, its major backers. Relations with the Habsburgs were damaged; the Austrians were angered, and Spain, which had been more sceptical of Elizabeth's intentions, now realised that the last hope of England returning to Catholicism by peaceful means had gone (Doran, 1996: 76–7, 95–6; Marshall, 2017: 478–9).

The Northern Rebellion and *Regnans in Excelsis*

The Northern Rebellion of 1569 was arguably the closest Elizabethan England came to a religious civil war, and showed how it was possible for Elizabeth's religious settlement to unravel. The rebellion proved that English Catholics were willing to use military force against the regime and, along with the papal response to the rebellion in the bull *Regnans in Excelsis*, informed later official attitudes to the danger posed by Catholics. It was a critical juncture in relations between the regime and Catholics at home and abroad, and thus deserves detailed examination (Duffy, 2020: 46–65). The original catalyst for the rebellion was the person of Mary Stuart, who received close attention from the English government throughout the 1560s. Mary was seen as a constant threat to Elizabeth; the Scottish queen had the strongest of claims to the English throne and possible support from some Catholics, both English and foreign. Firmer friendship between the two queens, based on Elizabeth's recognition of the legitimacy of Mary's claim, might well have lessened the threat, but Cecil cautioned against such recognition (Guy, 2004: 187–99).

Mary's unexpected arrival in Cumberland in the spring of 1568 brought a new dimension to an ongoing problem. The failure of the Habsburg marriage had again brought the succession issue into focus and the weakening of Anglo-Spanish ties increased the possibility of Philip II's support for Mary Stuart and of Spanish intervention in the rebellion in Ireland (Kesselring, 2007: 38–44). For Cecil, all problems facing England in the later 1560s crystallised in the person of Mary Stuart. Mary's presence threatened to encourage 'all papists and discontented persons ... whereof the consequence is overdangerous to be mentioned'. Cecil was convinced of an existing Catholic threat in England and feared that 'the secret and great numbers of discontented subjects in this realm, that gape and practice for a change by her means, to be rewarded by her' (Kesselring, 2007: 25). Cecil arranged for Mary to be tried at York for her alleged crimes in Scotland, but his ultimate plan was not clear. During the trial at York in October 1568, a long-term proposal, not of Cecil's making, did emerge: namely that Mary should marry the duke of Norfolk and be restored to the Scottish throne.

The marriage plan appeared to offer the best solution, not only to the immediate problem posed by Mary's presence in England, but to the wider issues of Anglo-Scottish relations and even the succession. Mary could be restored to Scotland, more acceptable with an English Protestant peer as her consort; England would be likewise safeguarded by Norfolk's presence in Scotland. The proposal has recently been described as coming from 'the centre ground of early modern politics' (Younger, 2018: 1066). It had the support of not only the leading conservatives Arundel and Pembroke, but Protestants such as Leicester and Throckmorton. However, the political context in which the plan evolved was complex and difficult. The conservatives were soon engaged in a bitter dispute with Cecil over what they perceived was a dangerous anti-Spanish policy which had culminated in the English seizure of Spanish bullion in December 1568. Spes, the Spanish ambassador, soon tried to exploit the anti-Cecil sentiment, telling the Spanish king that he thought that Elizabeth was losing power and that Norfolk and his friends were ready to support Philip: 'they will all rise to serve you' (Questier, 2019: 76). Spes's comments are scarcely reliable, but significantly they are close to some later Protestant assessments of Norfolk's motives. According to these writers, Norfolk was a papist whose ambition was to use his power as Mary's consort to lead a Catholic uprising against Elizabeth (Alford, 1998: 199).

In the course of 1569 the Norfolk-Stuart marriage plan encountered increasing difficulties. By May, Cecil's position on the Council appeared secure, which made the marriage less likely. In July, in the absence of Cecil from the Council, Norfolk secured Mary's release from captivity. More or less simultaneously, the earl of Moray, the linchpin in the whole plan, withdrew his support; Moray was the Protestant regent in Scotland without whose backing Mary could not return to her native country. In addition, there had always been a near fatal flaw in the plan throughout; none of Norfolk's supporters had been willing to present the queen with their proposals. With the plan already failing, on 8 September Leicester told Elizabeth and sought her forgiveness. The queen, now sensing a conspiracy, summoned Norfolk to the court, but the duke chose instead to return to his East Anglian estates, a move many took to be a sign of impending rebellion.

Norfolk soon changed his mind, returned to court and pleaded for mercy from the queen. By 8 October he was in the Tower (Kesselring, 2007: 38–9).

The link between the Norfolk-Stuart marriage and the Northern Rebellion is neither clear nor direct, although there were connections. The earl of Northumberland, who along with the earl of Westmorland led the revolt, was a longstanding supporter of Mary Stuart, though not initially of the proposed marriage. By late 1568 and early 1569 there was already considerable support for Mary in the North. During the trial at York in October 1568, Richard and Francis Norton along with Thomas Markenfeld, all significant players in the Northern Rebellion, offered to kill the Scottish regent Moray on Mary's behalf. With the marriage proposals collapsing in early 1569, Norfolk contacted Northumberland and Leonard Dacre to seize Mary as a backup plan. In the end it was Elizabeth's summons to court of the two earls following Norfolk's retreat to his East Anglian estates that prompted the rising, despite the duke's belated call to his brother-in-law Westmorland not to rebel (Kesselring, 2007: 46–53; Questier, 2019: 78–9).

The origins of the Northern Rebellion went beyond the Norfolk-Stuart marriage. The leaders of the revolt were strongly Catholic. Thomas Percy, 7th earl of Northumberland, showed a particular commitment to traditional religion. Already deemed a 'rank papist' in 1559, he had been formally reconciled to Catholicism by 'master Copley', a Marian priest. According to the earl's own testimony, he was influenced by the Louvain writer Nicholas Sander, who had shown 'how enormously the Protestant did misconstrue the word of God and abuse and falsify the ancient writers' (Kesselring, 2007: 53). Charles Neville, 5th earl of Westmorland had been an ardent supporter of Mary I and continued in his traditional faith after 1558; his children, too, were brought up Catholic. Leading gentry in the rebellion showed similar religious commitment. John Swinburn had been fined for maintaining a Catholic priest, and Thomas Markenfeld had just returned from exile, invigorated by contact with Counter-Reformation Europe; and the Norton brothers, Thomas and Richard, were noted Catholics.

The earls, their supporters and the wider Catholic population had suffered at the hands of Bishop James Pilkington of Durham since 1561. Pilkington, a Marian exile, has been judged probably the most radically Protestant of all the bishops appointed by Elizabeth (Kesselring, 2007: 21). The bishop surrounded himself with likeminded Protestants such as William Whittingham, who became dean of Durham Cathedral in 1563 and had previously worked closely with Calvin in Geneva. Throughout the 1560s this new Protestant establishment zealously set about their task, displaying a particular insensitivity in doing so. Matters were compounded by the fact that the bishop of Durham exercised both temporal and spiritual jurisdiction over the County Palatine of Durham. Pilkington wrote of his flock: 'I know not whether they like me worse or I they'. In 1567, when Whittingham began a concerted attack on remaining images and altars, Pilkington appeared to take particular delight at the distress of parishioners: 'Our poor papists weep to see our churches so bare' for 'there is nothing in them to make curtesy unto, neither saints, nor yet their old little god' (Kesselring, 2007: 22). Whittingham went beyond official directives in attacking funerary monuments excluded by Elizabeth. His wife, Katherine, supervised the burning of the banner of St Cuthbert, a saint who had come to represent Durham itself. As Marcombe notes, 'if the Dean was hated for anything in Durham, it was surely this' (Marcombe, 1987: 134). Despite his zealous determination to implant Protestantism in the diocese, Pilkington found a continued attachment to conservative religion, made stronger by the presence of Scottish Catholic priests and an underground Catholic organisation linked to Louvain (Kesselring, 2007: 22).

The rebels, who first appeared in Durham Cathedral on 14 November, doubtless had a range of motives for joining the rising beyond resentment at the attacks on traditional religion by Pilkington and Whittingham (Fletcher and MacCulloch, 2008: 110–16). Both Northumberland and Westmorland had political and personal grievances, as did some of the supporting gentry. It was, however, religious issues that evoked the greatest popular response. The main focus of attack was against recent Protestant changes. Married clergy were denounced, often violently; one rebel, Christopher Jackson, swore 'a vengeance upon all fuckbeggar priests and the errant whores their wives' (Kesselring, 2007: 68). Protestant books were destroyed in 73 Yorkshire churches and more than 20 in Durham. The destruction of Protestant books was matched by a restoration of Catholic objects. Altar stones and holy water stoops were retrieved from quarries and dunghills where they had previously been hidden and restored to Durham Cathedral and parish churches. At Sedgefield they burnt Protestant books at the town cross while stones for the altar were being extracted from their hiding places. These activities culminated in mass celebrated by Richard Hartburn, who preached that as the parishioners had freed the holy stones from the earth, they had also removed themselves from the erroneous faith of Queen Elizabeth (Kesselring, 2007: 71–2; Duffy, 1992: 583–4).

From Durham the rebellion quickly gathered pace, and with new recruits Ripon was taken on 18 November. By the end of November the rebels had occupied Barnard Castle and Hartlepool. Despite this promising start, the rising was effectively over two weeks later. November was a bad time to raise a rebellion, especially as the earls lacked the necessary supplies and money to fight a winter campaign. It is possible that a sustained campaign might have encouraged wider resistance from people like Henry Clifford, earl of Cumberland (who was equivocating) or Leonard Dacre of Gisland, Cumberland, who finally engaged government troops once the main rebellion had collapsed. The earls of Northumberland and Westmorland capitulated quickly and easily, escaping to Scotland on 16 December. They had singularly failed to raise the Catholic North, while rebels paid a heavy price with widespread confiscation of land and 600 executions (Kesselring, 2007: 64, 118–43; Questier, 2019: 79–81).

In early November 1569 the Northern earls had written to Rome asking for support. The papacy had already attempted, without success, to gain Spanish and French backing for an invasion of England, so Pius V was ready to excommunicate Elizabeth in support of the northern rising. The bull of excommunication, *Regnans in Excelsis*, against Elizabeth was promulgated on 25 February 1570, over two months after the rebellion failed. The bull of excommunication deprived Elizabeth of 'her pretended title' of Supreme Head of the Church, a title which she neither possessed nor claimed. It commanded English Catholics not to obey the queen; if Catholics failed to withdraw their obedience as instructed, they would incur the penalty of excommunication. The papal pronouncement was an act of great political radicalism, deposing the queen and inviting her subjects to rebel. It was also impractical, with no provision for enforcement. Catholic monarchs had not even been officially informed. Philip II of Spain thought the bull would drive Elizabeth and her ministers 'the more to oppress and persecute the few good Catholics still remaining in England', and the Emperor Maximillian requested the pope to withdraw the excommunication. The papal publication served Protestant interests in England more than Catholic. The Protestant writer Thomas Norton soon had the bull in England, before the Northern Rebellion, and claimed that 'the original bull was among the rebels, brought by Markenfeld or some such other … [and] kept close to be publicized so soon as they should have been able to get in their company such a head as they desired to set up' (Kesselring, 2007: 159). By 1571 the Louvain writer Nicholas Sander gave Catholic backing to this new chronology, by apparently showing that the rebels were acting in response to the bull. Sander thought that this gave the rebellion greater legitimacy (Kesselring, 2007: 158–78; Marshall, 2017: 493–4).

Elizabeth anticipated that the 1571 Parliament would propose anti-Catholic measures beyond her liking, so she sent an opening message that the Commons 'should do well to meddle with no matters of state but such as be propounded to them'. Much of the legislation was uncontroversial and meant to protect Elizabeth from papal denunciation. The treason acts made it treasonous to signify in any way that Elizabeth was not the lawful queen. Another act prohibited the bringing in or executing of any bull from Rome; anyone who reconciled an English subject by means of a papal bull was guilty of treason. A bill proposing a £12 fine for not attending church at least once a quarter and a 100 mark (£66) fine for not receiving communion at least once a year passed both houses but was vetoed by the queen. The papal bull had made it clear that the Protestant Eucharist was heretical and participation a damnable matter, so the bill would have compelled religious conservatives to choose between complete recusancy or full Protestantism. This was not Elizabeth's way; even after the 1570 bull the queen expressed her intention not 'to have any of them [Catholics] molested by any inquisition or examination of consciences in the cause of religion', as long as they did not overtly break her laws (McGrath, 1967: 104; Marshall, 2017: 498).

While the 1571 Parliament was in session, the web of another plot was being woven round Mary, Queen of Scots. The plot was coordinated by Roberto Ridolfi, who had close connections to the papacy and over the previous two years had been intriguing on Mary's behalf. The Norfolk-Stuart marriage was revived, although Norfolk needed persuading. Ridolfi unrealistically promised Spanish help and widespread aristocratic support in England. The plot was so unrealistic that some historians have doubted its authenticity and it is certainly possible that by 1571 Ridolfi was working for Cecil. The plot failed to materialise. Nevertheless, the dangers from Mary were widely perceived as real. When

Parliament assembled in May 1572, there was a chorus of demands for the deaths of both Mary and Norfolk. The duke's fate was in effect already sealed and he was duly executed; the main argument against him was that from the beginning the proposed marriage to Mary Stuart was a means of prompting a Catholic uprising and deposing Elizabeth. Elizabeth instructed Parliament to drop its attainder bill against Mary, despite the warning that 'her majesty must needs offend in conscience before God if she do not punish her [Mary] according to the measure of her offence'. The queen allowed a bill to exclude Mary from English succession to proceed, but when royal assent was required, Elizabeth replied, 'she is not yet fully resolved' so it failed to become law (Marshall, 2017: 503–4; Questier, 2019: 90–2; MacCaffrey, 1993: 135–44).

It is difficult to assess the exact impact that the events of 1568–72 had on Catholics and their standing in English society. Younger has pointed out that although the balance of the Council was altered by 1572 with the inclusion of Protestants such as Francis Walsingham and Henry Sidney, the conservative influence was not eliminated despite the execution of Norfolk, the death of Pembroke, and the retirement of William Howard from active political life. Arundel was rehabilitated, the earl of Sussex joined the Council, and so did Sir James Croft, who has been described as a 'Catholic willing to accept a royal supremacy' (Younger, 2018: 1067). So there was a continuity of some 'middle ground' within the regime, but the reactions in print to the 1569 rebellion do suggest a growing difference in the way that Catholics and Protestants viewed one another, at least among elements within each confession.

The immediate official reaction to the rebellion played down religion, as Elizabeth did not wish to be seen carrying out mass executions against people for their religious beliefs. By contrast, Thomas Norton placed religion centre stage, albeit within a political context. Norton was a client of William Cecil, so his work represents 'something like (pseudo-)official propaganda' (Lake, 2016: 23). He used the rebellion to point out that the threat from popery was immediate and widespread, as papists were to be found at every level in the church and society: 'Cathedral churches are stuffed with them, as dens of thieves'. So the 'bottom of [the] late treason had to be discovered which would involve shaking papists' out of the structures of Elizabethan government. In a criticism directed towards Elizabeth, he argued that papists had managed to survive within government because of a mistaken policy of clemency; the regime should realise that 'no clemency, gentleness, benefits, or loving dealing can win a papist'. The solution to this immediate Catholic danger was for the queen to rely on her true subjects, whom Norton called 'gospellers'; these were zealous Protestants like himself: 'her majesty may be assured of us as we stand for her, our loving sovereign, our mother, our country' (Lake, 2016: 26). So consistent loyalty and love of monarchy and country could only be found among true Protestants (Lake, 2016: 23–32; Kesselring, 2007: 153–9).

The strongest riposte to the denunciation of Catholicism by Thomas Norton was the 1572 *Treatise of Treason* by John Leslie, bishop of Ross. Leslie offered a defence of both Mary, Queen of Scots, and the Northern Rebellion. The northern earls had rebelled as a result of being outmanoeuvred by the Machiavellian exploits of 'evil counsellors'. There was a conspiracy against the queen, but it was not fostered by the northern earls or Mary Stuart; the conspiracy was formed by William Cecil and Nicholas Bacon, who attempted a Protestant seizure of power. The ultimate aim of the conspirators was to exclude both Elizabeth and Mary, 'all the blood royal of England', and replace them with someone they could easily manipulate (Questier, 2019: 98–100). Moreover, the 'rebels' of 1569 could never be disloyal to the queen: Catholicism was inherently loyal, while Protestantism was rebellious, as recent events in the Netherlands, Scotland, and France showed. This ties in with Viscount Montague's assertion in the 1563 Parliament that Catholics were loyal while Protestants challenged the monarch. The earl of Northumberland had attributed his political difficulties in the 1560s to the growth of Protestantism, which was endeavouring to undermine the traditional aristocracy. The idea that Catholics were the upholders of the traditional hierarchy and monarchical rights became the main element of Catholic royalist argument throughout the Elizabethan period (Kesselring, 2007: 173–4), but from the Protestant point of view such claims were fatally undermined by Pope Pius V's radical claim to a deposing power that potentially threatened all royal authority.

2 Catholics in later Elizabethan England, 1572–1603

The execution of the duke of Norfolk in 1572 marked the end of the crisis that had engulfed the country over the previous four years. However, the failure of Parliament to persuade the queen to formally exclude Mary Stuart from succession (let alone execute her) meant that Mary was always likely to figure in Catholic intrigues unless a new settlement with Elizabeth was reached. Nevertheless, the Treaty of Blois with France in 1572 and better relations with Spain seemed to offer a period of greater diplomatic stability for the Elizabethan government; good relations with the major Catholic powers were generally seen as essential to internal religious peace. However, the prospect of religious calm was upset by news from France in late August of the St Bartholomew's Day Massacre of French Huguenots in Paris. Catholics, believing they had the blessing of the French monarchy, turned on their Protestant neighbours, killing 2,000 in Paris alone and many thousands across the country.

The news from France immediately stirred English Protestant fears: might the papists, so recently involved in the Ridolfi Plot, try to follow the French Catholics? In September 1572 Archbishop Parker wrote to Burghley that 'the imps' (priests) of the English papists were 'rejoicing much at this unnatural and unprincely cruelty and murder' (Marshall, 2017: 509). There was fear that France and Spain might unite to ensure Catholic ascendancy across Europe, while papists in England, who 'owe more obedience to a higher power', would respond to calls for a Catholic uprising. Parker thought that the number of papists was growing fast, a fear soon confirmed by a report on gentlemen and nobles in Hampshire; 97 of 247 were described as either 'papist' or 'earnest papist'. Special prayers were ordered to be read in churches to seek the protection of the Lord, with emphasis on Psalm 22: 'the wicked conspireth against us'. Yet the reaction to events in France, which prompted this strong anti-popery, did not result in new measures against Catholics, perhaps due to the realisation that English Catholics had offered no support to their co-religionists in France, and that Catholicism in England was quite containable. In late 1572 Parker even blamed some resurgence of Catholicism as a reaction to militant Protestant preachers. By 1573 Bishop Horne of Winchester confidently described England as 'having secured tranquility at home and peace abroad' (Marshall, 2017: 510).

For much of the 1570s there were reasons to support Horne's judgement. Despite the St Bartholomew's Day Massacre England maintained good relations

DOI: 10.4324/9781003130376-3

with France, partly through the possibility of a marriage between Elizabeth and François, duke of Alençon (who became duke of Anjou in 1576). After the recall of the brutal Alba from the Netherlands, England was less concerned that the Spanish occupation there would be followed by an invasion of England. By the mid-1570s 'this was probably about as stable as Elizabethan politics could get' (Questier, 2019: 105). In late 1574 the exiled Catholic Sir Francis Englefield heard rumours of possible toleration for Catholics in England, and that even Burghley was not opposed. Allegedly the Spanish ambassador in Rome was aiding the process by lobbying for the cancellation of the 1570 bill of excommunication; nothing materialised, however, so perhaps they were no more than rumours (Questier, 2019: 105). In the second half of the 1570s the 'secured tranquility' appeared to be endangered. This was due in particular to renewed Spanish successes in the Netherlands, although by 1579 rebellion in Ireland and increased Catholic influence in Scotland all added to the sense of crisis. It was decided that England would be better able to confront these dangers, especially in the Netherlands, if Elizabeth married the duke of Anjou. So negotiations, which had formed background diplomacy for much of the 1570s, became more active and urgent in 1579 (Doran, 2015: 130–94).

The Anjou marriage and its consequences

The Anjou match proved to be a seminal event in the relationship between English Catholics and the Elizabethan regime. For the regime the aims of the marriage were political, but most contemporaries saw likely religious consequences. For English Catholics it offered the hope of a new position within the state, and for Catholic loyalists the opportunity to acquire some significant power within the regime. As already noted, however, the match took place against a background of increasing Catholic threats from Ireland and Scotland, and the arrival of a new, more aggressive, Jesuit mission. The regime's response in the early 1580s was to initiate policies of unprecedented ferocity which marked a turning point in Elizabethan persecution. The Catholic Throckmorton and Babington plots were in part the expression of failed Catholic hopes, in part a reaction to persecution. We can only speculate on the differences an Anjou marriage might have made, but it seems highly likely that had Elizabeth acquired a Catholic consort, albeit a somewhat 'politique' (religiously and politically pragmatic) Catholic, the experience of English Catholics in the 1580s would have been different.

The marriage proposal, like the earlier Norfolk-Mary Stuart match, came from deep within the Elizabethan establishment. The conservative earl of Sussex was a major backer, and Burghley, after initial scepticism, was a supporter; Leicester and Walsingham were the leading opponents in the Council. The main purpose of the match was to solve foreign policy problems, not to deal with the succession, although of course it was likely to have implications for the succession issue. It was hoped that the match would cement Anglo-French relations and thereby enable Anjou to aid Dutch rebels without England being directly involved in a dangerous religious war. The prospects of the match, however, meant different things to different people, and Anjou, as a Catholic but also a politique who had supported both Huguenots and Dutch rebels at times, drew different responses from different groups in England (Lake, 2016: 96–8).

For Catholics, the Anjou match offered more than improved stability in England's foreign relations. It promised the possibility of a 'major shift in the ideological and factional composition of the Elizabethan establishment', as well as improved conditions for all Catholics. A group of Catholic or crypto-Catholic aristocrats, including Henry Howard (brother of the executed duke of Norfolk), Charles Arundell, and the somewhat unstable earl of Oxford, supported the marriage and sought political rewards in return. In late 1579 it appeared that a wider circle of Catholics would find favour with Elizabeth. When the queen was faced with opposition to the match from within the Council, she considered admitting four leading Catholics, including Viscount Montague and Sir William Cordell, although in the end no appointments were made (Lake, 2016: 97; Bossy, 1959: 2–16; Younger, 2018: 1069–70; Questier, 2006: 153–6).

Opposition to the marriage in the country was widespread. Preachers of the Lenten sermons in 1579 'spoke very violently against the match'. Puritans such as John Stubbs, possibly with the support of Leicester and Walsingham, articulated the radical Protestant case against the marriage. In his 1579 treatise *Discoverie of a Gaping Gulf*, Stubbs ignored the political aims of the match and stressed its disastrous consequences for a Protestant nation. Any royal marriage to a papist was a heinous sin, inviting the vengeful judgement of God. It was a betrayal of England, which he compared to the kingdom of Israel. Through the match England would become 'a principal prop of the tottering house of Antichrist' (Marshall, 2017: 525). Stubbs drew on the memories of the massacre of St Bartholomew's Day by alluding to 'the exquisite torments and infinite numbers there put to death' (Lake, 2016: 99). Lord Henry Howard soon gave the Catholic answer to Stubbs. Howard stressed his nationalism, so he wrote out of 'dutiful affection to my native country'. The marriage was necessary to solve the issue of succession, an issue which Parliament had constantly raised, and which it was generally agreed was necessary for 'peace and tranquility, and the sole safeguard and defence from civil tumults and sedition' (Lake, 2016: 103). Religion was not really a problem, as Anjou was not a zealot. Finally Howard suggested that those who opposed the marriage had their own sinister agenda. This clique wanted to seize power by gaining control of the queen once she had married one of their own instead of Anjou (Lake, 2016: 103–11).

It is difficult to pinpoint the exact reasons or even the point when the marriage negotiations collapsed, but it happened quite some months before Anjou left England in February 1582. The main reason for the failure, according to Elizabeth, was the opposition of her subjects. It was not just the vitriolic attacks by the likes of Stubbs; more moderate Protestants, including some of the bishops, opposed the match. In the spring of 1580 foreign diplomats were reporting that the ecclesiastical authorities were endeavouring to undermine Catholic confidence in the match by increasing persecution, and thus demonstrating that Anjou could do little to protect Catholic interests. Elizabeth tried to counter this; she told her bishops that they 'were oppressing the Catholics more than she desired' (Questier, 2019: 126). Early in 1581 the main aristocratic Catholic backing for the marriage collapsed. This was largely down to the earl of Leicester, who persuaded the ever-unreliable earl of Oxford to denounce Henry Howard and Charles Arundell for a supposed conspiracy dating back to 1577 involving the French ambassador; they were both immediately dismissed from court.

A final factor contributing to the marriage collapse was the arrival of the Jesuit mission, which not only heightened religious tensions in England with its high-profile presence, but also focused on the marriage as a means of Catholic advancement (Lake, 2016: 109–10). The arrest of Francis Throckmorton in November 1583 revealed that some Catholics had moved from ambitions of power in the Elizabethan regime to plotting, within a short period following the collapse of the Anjou marriage. Henry Howard and Charles Arundell were hoping to free Mary Stuart by negotiating to restore her to Scotland in association with her son James, but such plans were subsumed in an international conspiracy involving Allen and Persons, the French Catholic League, led by the duke of Guise, and Philip II of Spain. Francis Throckmorton, a Warwickshire Catholic gentleman who had been radicalised in the Low Countries in the 1570s, acted as go-between. The aim was to assassinate Elizabeth and replace her with Mary Stuart.

The initial scheme was ambitious, involving an invasion of Scotland, the north of England, and the English south coast. Philip II withdrew his support and the Scottish and northern plans were jettisoned. The final plan envisaged an invasion of the Sussex coast by a strong Catholic League army, and this force would be supported by a number of prominent Catholics in the area, which was noted for its Catholic strength. John Bossy argued that the plot represented a serious threat to the regime: 'it was a fairly near thing' (Bossy, 2001: 75–81). In the event, the Elizabethan regime was never tested, as the Guise troops never left Normandy, and once Throckmorton confessed under torture the plot unravelled. The consequences of its collapse were significant. It finally signalled the demise of the Catholic 'loyalist' group, who had fervently backed the Anjou marriage. Henry Howard was arrested and Charles Arundell fled the country. Henry Percy, 8th earl of Northumberland was also arrested. Northumberland, living at Petworth in Sussex, was suspected of being one of the 'principal gentlemen' designated to help the invading force, but he was also on the fringe of that 'loyalist' group involved in the Anjou marriage. From the regime's point of view an important plot had been thwarted, but problems remained. The ongoing issues of succession and Mary Stuart had been further highlighted, so until more direct evidence of Mary's guilt could be established she remained as dangerous as ever (Lake, 2016: 111–16; Bossy, 1996: 145–6; Questier, 2006: 164–6; Questier, 2019: 141–56.)

The Babington Plot, which was revealed by Walsingham in July 1586, had Mary Stuart at its centre. The leader, Anthony Babington, a Derbyshire gentleman, was aided by John Ballard, a secular priest, and a number of Catholic gentlemen linked to Edmund Campion and the early Jesuit mission. The Jesuit connection was strong enough for Elizabeth to claim that 'the design rose up from the wicked suggestion of the Jesuits' (Questier, 2019: 167). Certain claims made by the former Spanish ambassador that the plot was supported by leading Catholics, such as Viscount Montague, have been dismissed as 'pure fantasy', and the Jesuit Robert Southwell thought the conspiracy was fabricated by Walsingham. The plot was real, however, and involved a number of English Catholic gentlemen, and had the backing of Philip II. However, Walsingham knew of its existence from an early stage so it was never a serious threat to Elizabeth; rather, it served the purpose of effectively sealing the fate of Mary Stuart (Marshall, 2017: 557–8; MacCaffrey, 1993: 346–8; Questier, 2019: 166–7).

Government policy towards Catholics, 1580–1603

A new level of draconian persecution was initiated in 1581 by 'an act to retain the queen's majesty's subjects in their due obedience'. This was a response, in particular, to the newly arrived Jesuit mission, but also to the growth of recusancy, which had been clearly revealed by the 1577 survey undertaken by Bishop Aylmer. The backcloth of a papally sponsored Irish rebellion and the recent dominance of Guise influence at the court of James VI in Scotland doubtless contributed to this more ruthless approach from the Elizabethan regime. It did, however, sit uneasily with the ongoing negotiations in the Anjou match, though the ejection from court of Howard and Arundell in early 1581, at the instigation of Leicester, might have been significant in this respect.

The 1581 act aimed to check the growth of recusancy. One part of the statute was straightforward in levying punitive fines of £20 a month on recusants. The main clauses were far from straightforward; indeed, because of their ambiguity, historians have long differed over their interpretation. The ambiguity concerned the issue of 'reconciling' conformist Catholics 'to the Romish religion', which meant converting conformist Catholics to recusancy. The act prohibited such reconciliations, but did this mean all newly converted recusants were guilty of treason? Or did the act of 'reconciliation' also have to involve the rejection of the political authority of the queen before the process was treasonous (Dures, 1983: 29)?

The latest historian to examine the statute, Lucy Underwood, agrees that it is 'deeply ambiguous', but she also offers some penetrating insights on what constituted treason (Underwood, 2016: 246–67). She shows that contemporaries as well as historians were aware of the central issues of interpretation. For example, a tract entitled 'a plea for a priest', written between 1593 and 1603, attempted to argue that reconciliation did not involve political disobedience to the queen. This was also the defence pleaded by John Rigby in 1600 before the Lord Chief Justice. Rigby admitted that he had indeed been reconciled 'to god almightie' but he 'was never reconciled from anie obedience to my Prince [Elizabeth] for I obey her stil' (Underwood, 2016: 256). Rigby was nevertheless executed, although the fact that only 17 individuals in Elizabeth's reign suffered a similar fate suggests that such an interpretation was not widely applied.

There was a further ambiguity in the 1581 statute. The process of reconciliation involved absolving the individual from the sin of being a 'schismatic' (a conformist Catholic), so the sacrament of penance was a key element in the process; and the power to forgive sin ultimately came from papal authority. So did the statute outlaw confession as well as reconciliation? Henry Garnet feared it did, and in 1594 lamented that 'the heretics can by English law condemn all Catholics to death', though he conceded that the usual interpretation of the law penalised reconciliation, not absolution (Underwood, 2016: 254).

The clause introducing the fines for recusancy was, in the long term, possibly even more significant. The state rather than the ecclesiastical authorities was now the main instrument for reporting and punishing recusants and the act was the centrepiece of anti-Catholic policy of Elizabethan and Stuart regimes up to the Civil War. The £20 per month fine was levied on 'every person over the age of 16 years which shall not repair to some church, chapel or usual place of common prayer'. It was, however, the 1587 statute, with its crucial administrative changes, which made the financial penalties such a formidable weapon against recusants. Few recusants had actually paid the £260 (for the purposes of setting fines, a year was deemed to contain 13 months of 28 days each); debt had accumulated in the Exchequer. Under the 1587 statute recusants could be convicted by proclamation in their absence to ease pressure on the courts. Fines levied on recusants were no longer limited to a specific conviction but were cumulative. But the greatest change was the provision that two-thirds of a recusant's land could be seized by the Exchequer if the recusant failed to pay the fines. The land was 'sequestrated', which meant that the recusant did not forfeit his legal right to the land, but to two-thirds of its annual value, as assessed by a local jury, which went to the Exchequer.

As the 1580s progressed, new Catholic dangers emerged which further threatened the security of the Elizabethan regime. By 1584 the Throckmorton plotters had all been duly punished, but two European deaths, that of the duke of Anjou in June and the assassination of William of Orange in July, presented unprecedented dangers to England. Anjou's death meant that Henry of Navarre, a Huguenot, was next in line to succeed the childless Henry III of France; but the Catholic League was determined to prevent this. Some of the Catholic exiles in France had already been active during Anjou's last illness. The English ambassador in Paris reported that 'great councils were had at Dr Allen's house and other places' to support Charles Bourbon of the Catholic League 'in order to deprive Navarre of the French crown'. The possibility that the Catholic League might seize the French throne, with its close ties to Spain as well as English Catholic exiles such as Allen, alarmed the Elizabethan regime (Questier, 2019: 153–4; Lake, 2016: 150).

The assassination of William of Orange was even more alarming to the Elizabethan regime. On a political level the impact of Orange's death paralleled developments in France, in that it appeared to signal the collapse of resistance to Spain in the Southern Netherlands, bringing the possibility of a western Europe dominated by Spain a step closer. But above all, the assassination brought home the personal dangers to Elizabeth, especially given the fear that some papists favoured killing the current English queen and replacing her with Mary Stuart. The regime's response came in the form of the Bond of Association, which was both immediate and radical. In October 1584, a document was drawn up by the Privy Council which bound signatories to resist to the full extent of their power 'any act counsel or consent to anything that tend to harm of her majesty's royal person'. The role of the bondsmen was to protect the life of Elizabeth. If they failed in this and the queen was assassinated, then they swore to kill any 'pretended successor', which meant Mary Stuart, whether she had been party to the killing of Elizabeth or not. The bond was to be signed by all the leading gentry and officeholders, by means of an oath sworn on the Bible. Many across the country signed, including Mary Stuart herself.

When Parliament met in late 1584, one member's gloss on recent developments across Europe was that the pope was 'knitting together all the papist princes and states to the overthrow of the Gospel in all places, but especially in this kingdom'. In addition to putting the Bond of Association on a statutory basis, the regime's main response was an 'act against Jesuits, seminary priests and such other like disobedient persons'. This act followed Burghley's 1584 publication *Execution of Justice* in arguing that seminarists came to England solely for political reasons, to 'stir up and move sedition, rebellion and open hostility'. Henceforth, any priest entering the country after ordination abroad was *ipso facto* guilty of treason; any layperson assisting such a seminarist was guilty of felony and might be sentenced to death. This removed the ambiguities of the 1581 statute, although, as we have seen, John Rigby was executed under that 1581 law as late as 1600. The 1585 statute was the most severe of Elizabeth's reign; out of 146 Catholics executed between 1586 and 1603, no fewer than 123 were indicted under this law. It might have been even more draconian if a Commons amendment making it treasonous to teach the 'Romish religion' had been accepted. This threatened to equate heresy with treason, so would have undermined the oft-repeated argument of the regime that no person was executed for their religious views, only for their treasonous political behaviour (Marshall, 2017: 555; McGrath, 1967: 192; Questier, 2019: 158).

The execution of Mary Stuart in 1586 following the exposure of the Babington Plot removed a major threat to Elizabeth, but it did little to ease internal and international tensions. The failure of the Armada in 1588 ensured the immediate survival of English Protestantism, but it did not eliminate the Spanish threat, as further Armadas were planned. As a result, 1588–92 was a period of ongoing insecurity for the regime and maximum suffering for English Catholics. Immediately before and after the Armada the number of Catholic executions, mainly for treason under the 1585 statute, reached its peak; between 1586 and 1591 there were 86 Catholic deaths, 31 in the Armada year of 1588. The severity of persecution was endorsed by Jesuit reports in the years around the Armada. According to Robert Southwell, the defeat of the Spanish invasion bought little relief; in fact, the hatred that had been directed against Spain was now turned exclusively on Catholics: 'the asps' eggs have burst … the poison has begun to be poured out and to spread violently far and wide'. Garnet too expressed near despair 'for when we thought that there was an end to these disasters … our hope was suddenly turned to sorrow' (McCoog, 1996: 256). If the 'hope' had been the Armada, he did not support any further Spanish attempts. All Garnet could do was lament the fate of so many priests facing execution and prison and the fact that 'nearly all of us can be said to be in prison because we dare not go around the city but at night' (McCoog, 1996: 256).

Government persecution in terms of new proclamations and statutes continued in the early 1590s. The queen issued two proclamations in 1591. The first, in April, aimed to stop any English Catholic aid reaching the Catholic League in France. The League was involved in a civil war to prevent Henry of Navarre, still a Protestant, ascending the French throne, while Elizabeth was sending military support to Navarre. The second proclamation, in October, was aimed directly at seminarists and recusants. As always there was a propaganda dimension to the proclamation. It explained that the regime was forced to take severe measures against English Catholics because of the nature of the seminaries at Douai, Rome, and Valladolid and the activities of their backers, the pope and Philip II. These latter two gathered round them 'dissolute young men', while the seminaries were propaganda centres, dedicated to teaching the theory of the pope's power to depose monarchs (Houliston, 2007: 50–1).

The proclamation also laid down the precise measure that in every parish a committee of eight persons was to be nominated to examine parishioners on their religious beliefs and their attendance at church. Catholics had never before been so closely interrogated at a parochial level and in Questier's judgement this proclamation 'set up a quasi-police state surveillance machine to be used against those whose loyalty was potentially in question' (Questier, 2019: 196). The resulting reports showed extensive Catholic beliefs and significant recusancy. This prompted calls for further action, which came in the form of the 1593 'act against popish recusants', which limited recusants to within five miles of their dwelling place. This was moderate compared to the statutes of the 1580s, though this would not have been the case but for alterations to the original bill. Among the measures dropped was perhaps the most radical proposal of any in the period, that children of recusant parents should be taken away at the age of seven to be brought up in the Protestant faith (Dures, 1983: 31).

It appears that by 1593 there were at least some within the regime who were beginning to think that ever-increasing penalties against Catholics had served their purpose. Bishop Bancroft was one of a group of senior clerics who began to see the Puritans as more threatening than Catholics to the stability of both the Elizabethan church and state. It is significant that Puritan nonconformists were included in some of the measures in the 1593 statute, and in the same year the prominent separatists Henry Barrow, John Greenwood, and Welshman John Perry were executed (Questier, 2019: 200). There had already been some signs of a Catholic loyalist response, while Bancroft's stance foreshadowed his later support for the loyalist Catholic Appellants when archbishop of Canterbury. Certainly by the mid-1590s (or even earlier) the intense blanket persecution which Catholics had endured for more than a decade appeared to be abating, with severe persecution limited to particular areas in the north still suffering at the hands of the earl of Huntingdon (Caraman, 1964: 167).

From the 1581 statute onwards the aims of the regime were clear: to check the growth of recusancy and to limit the impact of the mission in its ability to sustain Catholicism. It appears that the regime failed in these objectives, as the mission continued to expand and recusancy increased. However, important qualifications need to be made. Although the mission grew in size and improved in its organisation, the persecution left its mark; priests were constantly lost through execution and imprisonment, recruitment was more difficult, and mobility was often limited. In the more tolerant conditions under the Stuarts the mission flourished much more easily. It is certainly true that recusancy increased, but so too did church papistry. Contrary to the judgement of historians in the 1960s, the 1587 statute appears to have been very successful. In London and Middlesex half the recusants indicted in the 1590s conformed before they suffered a financial penalty. In Lancashire the 1590s also saw an increase in church papists, and church papists overall became a vital component in the Catholic community; in 1592 even William Allen accepted the presence of church papists within the Catholic body.

The severe persecution of the 1580s and 1590s was at least a partial success. For the regime's critics, however, it was close to a total failure and still tougher measures were needed. Lord Chief Justice Popham, writing in 1599, addressed the issue: 'I see no waye to reduce these [recusants] to a better conformytie and obedyence unless it may seeme good to Lords [of the council] eyther to have them detayned in close prison … or to have the othe ministered to some of them first and so second tyme'. For Popham, only more imprisonment and executions would achieve the regime's goal, but by 1599 this was not the direction in which the Elizabethan government was travelling (Dures, 1983: 31–4; Haigh, 1975: 269–94; Walsham, 1999: 73–99).

Catholics and the regime: loyalty and resistance

The issue of Catholic loyalism did not surface in the conformist decade of the 1560s until the accommodation between Catholics and the regime was challenged by the Northern Rebellion and the bull of excommunication, *Regnans in Excelsis*. Although the suppression of the rebellion was followed by a period of relative calm throughout the 1570s, the rebellion and the bull had left a legacy. The bull had deprived Elizabeth of all political authority, and in 1571 the Louvain exile Nicholas Sander's *De visibili monarchia* justified the papal right to depose monarchs. By 1574 Richard Bristow's 'Motives' aimed to reconcile the papal bull with loyalty to the queen. It was true, wrote Bristow, that Catholics earnestly prayed for the conversion of their prince [Elizabeth] but 'neither in the meantime denying him such love and worship as we may' (Holmes, 1982: 32). The first seminarists arrived in England in 1574 on a mission that was strictly spiritual, even if Douai's founder William Allen was involved in plots to depose Elizabeth from 1572 and throughout his career (Duffy, 2017: 134). Overall, there was little advocacy of resistance to Elizabeth throughout the 1570s.

Elizabeth's progress to East Anglia in 1578, an area where recusancy and occasional conformity were rife among the gentry, marked the beginning of a tightening in policy (Collinson, 2006: 33). Elizabeth's Privy Council used the opportunity to round up gentry recusants, with one of them, Edward Rookwood, even being publicly humiliated in the queen's presence for attempting to hide a statue of the Virgin Mary (Rowe and Young, 2016: 44–6). The 1580s would go on to raise the issues of Catholic loyalty or resistance to the regime in an acute form. The Jesuit mission, with its stress on avoiding political engagement, followed the established seminarist tradition; indeed, it came with a modification of the 1570 bull by Pope Gregory XIII. The pope declared that Catholics were not obliged to carry out the 1570 bull's instructions to depose Elizabeth under present circumstances, 'but only when public execution of the same bull becomes possible' (McCoog, 1996: 140). Despite the continued emphasis on the purely spiritual goal of the mission, the measures taken by the regime in the first half of the 1580s made it well-nigh impossible for the seminary priests to pledge total loyalty to Elizabeth while also fulfilling the aims of the mission. The lay supporters of the mission faced similar issues of allegiance. Moreover, the level of persecution was such that the future of the Jesuit mission appeared to be in doubt at one time (McCoog, 1996: 177).

According to the missionary leaders Allen and Persons, the Elizabethan regime was making it impossible for Catholics to maintain their faith, so the overthrow of the regime was a moral imperative. Both became deeply embroiled in the Throckmorton Plot to assassinate Elizabeth and place Mary Stuart on the throne. For Allen and Persons the use of force to achieve a Catholic England was just as legitimate as depending on spiritual means; the difference was merely a matter of tactics. Francis Throckmorton defended his role in the plot by allegedly refusing to ask pardon of the queen, declaring that she should 'ask pardon of God and the State for her heresy and misgovernment in allowing innocent men to be killed every day unjustly' (Questier, 2019: 150; Houliston, 2007: 46–50).

The failure of the Throckmorton Plot entailed a change of tactics, so from mid-1584 Allen and Persons became engaged in a print debate with Burghley. If the Elizabethan regime could not be overthrown, it was important that Catholic opinion should be heard. In particular, Burghley's argument in his 1583 *Execution of Justice in England* that the regime never persecuted Catholics for their religious beliefs, only their political threat to Elizabeth, needed to be challenged. Allen's 1584 *True, Sincere and Modest Defence of English Catholics* attributed any current 'disorder' in England not to any action by Catholics, but to the regime's policies. In turn these policies were not the queen's, but those of 'evil counsellors'. Such counsellors 'abused her weak sex' and went against 'her own natural inclination' (Lake, 2016: 136–7). Moreover, in supporting sedition by the likes of William of Orange and the heretics acting against James VI in Scotland, these evil counsellors were undermining monarchical authority, which could rebound against Elizabeth. Persons' 1584 *Leicester's Commonwealth* was similarly framed in the ideas and language of Catholic loyalty to make a devastating attack on the regime. Persons particularly focused on the Anjou marriage, which, had it materialised, would have provided 'a most sovereign and present remedy, all our maladies both abroad and at home had at once been cured'. Moreover, the match had been supported by the 'wisest and faithfulest Protestants of the realm' but jeopardised by one 'evil counsellor', the earl of Leicester. So England did indeed have widespread troubles in 1584, but these stemmed not from Catholics, but from the monstrous personality of the earl of Leicester (Lake, 2016: 116–22).

Historians have tended to place these publications in the category of 'resistance' to the Elizabethan regime, but labels are less important than understanding the purpose of these texts. It is also important to note that in 1584 Allen and Persons both stressed the need for seminarists not to be politically involved and for English Catholics to be loyal to the Elizabethan regime. However, the situation had changed dramatically by 1588. Allen's *Admonition to the Nobility and People of England and Ireland* urged Elizabethan Catholics to rise up in support of the Spanish Armada, whose landing Allen believed was imminent. Allen defended the Armada on the basis of papal support, which in turn rested on the pope's legitimate right to depose rulers. In a companion tract Allen launched a vicious personal attack on the queen in anticipation of another papal bull against Elizabeth, which never in fact materialised. This broadside was scurrilous, describing Elizabeth as 'an incestuous bastard, begotten and born in sin of an infamous courtesan'. Her carnal lust for Leicester was one of the root causes of English tyranny, and the major reason why Elizabeth never married. This built on *Leicester's Commonwealth* and other earlier publications, but loyalty to the queen is replaced by an unprecedented vitriolic attack on Elizabeth. It is difficult to gauge the impact of these publications on English Catholics, but the second one, in particular, might well have been counterproductive (Pritchard, 1979: 12–13; Holmes, 1982: 134, 152, 193; Questier, 2019: 182–4).

English Catholic reactions to the Armada provide a good gauge of loyalty, but evidence of that reaction is limited. Burghley, in a pamphlet designed to counter Allen's *Admonition*, claimed that during the attempted Spanish invasion English Catholics had shown total loyalty. In the pamphlet, Burghley's fictional Catholic mouthpiece declares 'there was no difference to be seen betwixt the Catholic, and the heretic' (Lake, 2016: 316). Even the areas of greatest Catholic sympathy such as Lancashire, Cheshire, and parts of Sussex were united behind their aristocratic leaders in support of Elizabeth. Burghley's account of such loyalty cannot be dismissed, but it would have been more convincing if the regime had not reacted to the Armada and subsequent Spanish threats with mass imprisonment of English Catholics, and the highest rate of executions in the whole period. Burghley's insistence that the prisoners in Ely enjoyed 'large walks in the garden' scarcely counterbalances such persecution.

Philip II is a more reliable witness to Catholic loyalty to Elizabeth, in the sense that he consistently refused to give credence to the protestations of the exiles that English Catholics would join an invading Spanish force. In early planning in September 1586, Philip insisted that the Spanish knew best how to manage an invasion and that Catholics would be of 'small advantage to us'. The Spanish king's opinion had not changed by February 1587 when he warned Olivares, his ambassador in Rome, not to mention the planned expedition to Allen and Persons, as if information spread to English Catholics it would diminish Spanish chances of success. A further memorandum to the Spanish Council was similarly downbeat about English Catholic support. One author thought that Catholics had been overawed by the brutality of the suppression of the Irish rebellion in the early 1580s and the severity of the persecution in

England itself. Another report simply warned that Catholics in England were not well disposed to foreigners. This point might well have been right, as there was a strong strand of anti-Spanish sentiment in Counter-Reformation English Catholicism reaching back to the last years of Mary I (Edwards, 2013: 263; Loomie, 1996: 389–92).

A number of leading Catholic peers and gentry made protestations of loyalty at the time of the Armada. Lord Vaux declared his loyalty, even though in 1585 he had declined to furnish a levy of horse to support Elizabeth's campaign in the Low Countries, when he was named as a 'friend' of Philip II. Viscount Montague was loyally mustering men to fight the Spaniards in late July 1588. It is possible that the Council accepted Montague's troops, but he was not allowed to lead them; indeed, it appears that in late August Montague was placed under house arrest (Questier, 2006: 168n91). The most vociferous protestation of loyalty came from Sir Thomas Tresham, who offered to go naked into battle to defend England and the queen (Childs, 2014: 161–2). In a letter to the Council, Tresham expressed his resentment and shame that he and fellow nobles and gentlemen 'who daily go around with weapons as a badge of our vocation' were not allowed to fight the Spanish (Pritchard, 1979: 50–1).

Tresham provided more evidence of his loyalty than most English Catholics, and historians have generally endorsed his own self-projection. Sir Thomas denounced his brother William when in 1582 he left England without licence. In 1585 Tresham led a group of nobles and gentry who presented a petition of loyalty to the queen, hoping in return for some measure of toleration. The petition denounced the recent 'damnable' Parry Plot, and promised to hand over any treasonous seminary priest should one ever appear. There is no reason to doubt Tresham's sincerity, even though in 1605 (in frustration at James's renewal of recusancy fines) he spoke with 'small reverence towards the late Queen Elizabeth' as well as the new king. However, in 1581 at his trial in Star Chamber for harbouring Campion, Tresham had made a fundamental challenge to the regime. His defence was one of individual conscience as part of a positive freedom which the individual should enjoy in order to obey the law of God. In effect Tresham argued that conscience trumped the laws of England. The judges rejected the conscience argument and fined Tresham the huge sum of 1,000 marks. Moreover, despite his protestations of loyalty, he spent many years in prison, obviously at odds with the regime. The fact was that owing to the legislation of the 1580s many Catholics recusants who were actively involved in supporting the mission were open to charges of treason. In that sense the Catholic laity did not have to plot against the queen or support the Spanish Armada before the regime cast serious doubts on their loyalty (Kaushik, 1996: 48–62; Underwood, 2016: 246–67).

Nevertheless few, if any, of the Catholic laity in England appear to have endorsed the Allen-Persons line of armed resistance. Moreover, according to Houliston, the standing of Allen and Persons suffered internationally after the Armada, with the failure of English Catholics to support the invasion as they had confidently predicted (Houliston, 2007: 48–51). Their continued backing of the Spanish after 1588 was not always fully endorsed even by the Jesuits in

England. Garnet complained in 1590 that every rumour of another Spanish Armada brought greater persecution. In 1591 Robert Southwell's *Humble Supplication* reverted to the 'evil counsellor' argument, although there was a strong emphasis on the duty of obedience that Catholics owed their monarch. According to Southwell the queen was not responsible for the current intolerable persecution; this was the work of counsellors like Francis Walsingham, who in 1586 had fabricated the Babington Plot. However, despite his stress on Catholic loyalty, Southwell refused to condemn the stance of Allen and Persons, saying only that their politics could be safely ignored as they were bound to be ineffectual (Pritchard, 1979: 68–72). Other Jesuits, however, continued to support armed resistance; Gerard's reaction to the defeat of the Armada was the hope that the next 'enterprise may be effected with greater ease and safety' (McCoog, 1996: 261–2).

Support for armed resistance and another Spanish invasion continued to come from exiled clergy such as Joseph Creswell and Thomas Stapleton, although by the mid-1590s the changing politics in both England and Europe began to shift the parameters of the debate on loyalty and resistance. In England some in the regime were advocating a lessening of persecution in the hope of encouraging greater Catholic loyalism. The first writer to respond to this changing situation was the former Jesuit turned secular priest, Thomas Wright, who returned to England in 1595 and immediately circulated his recent tract. Wright argued against the theory advocated in 1588 and in the early 1590s that Catholics had a moral duty to support a papally backed Spanish invasion. He suggested that Spanish motives were political rather than religious. Moreover, if the pope backed such an invasion this was a temporal matter, not an issue of faith, and the pope could err in temporal matters, so it was lawful for English Catholics to take up arms to protect Elizabeth (Pritchard, 1979: 61–3). In the same year, Persons' *Conference* again argued for the right to resist monarchy, albeit on very different principles from his earlier works; the power of monarchy was not based on the hereditary principle but on the people. However, this publication was also a response to changing political circumstances. For Persons the key to a Catholic England was now royal succession, although he had no particular candidate in mind. Persons was clear, however, that James VI of Scotland had to be excluded from English succession because his personal religion was 'puritanism', so the aim of the *Conference* was to undermine the claims of the Scottish king (Questier, 2019: 217–21).

Persons' *Conference*, it has been argued, was the last of the 'resistance theory' publications, so in many respects the second half of the 1590s marks a new Catholic politics, reflected in the loyalist Appellants at the end of the decade (Holmes, 1982: 149–52). However, the earl of Essex's disastrous rebellion of 1601, when Essex attempted unsuccessfully to seize control of London and overthrow Elizabeth's advisors, merits a brief comment in the context of Catholic loyalism. Predictably, Essex's enemies on the Council denounced the rebellion as supported by both papists and separatist Puritans. There were, however, some Catholic connections. Thomas Wright, the priest we have just discussed, was part of the Essex circle and claimed that his master was a Catholic who concealed his religion to broaden his appeal. This is scarcely compelling evidence, but there were some Catholics on the fringes of the Essex entourage, and the future Gunpowder plotters, Robert Catesby and the Wright brothers, were part of the rebellion. This is not to suggest that the Essex rebellion was Catholic; but, for all the Catholic loyalty we have demonstrated, some disaffected individuals remained. Famously, these surfaced again in the Gunpowder Plot of 1605, but they were also apparent in the 1603 Bye Plot, led by William Watson, a prominent member of the loyalist Appellants.

The Elizabethan Catholic community abroad

The option of emigration or exile was not a new one for those unwilling to accept the Elizabethan settlement in 1559; during the reigns of Henry VIII and Edward VI, over 200 religious conservatives had already gone into exile, including Cardinal Reginald Pole. Many of these exiles returned on the restoration of Catholicism under Mary in 1553 (Smith, 2018: 806–34), but after 1559 exile was to become a way of life for a large number of Catholics. Although the numbers leaving England were small at first, the creation of English seminaries and religious houses on the Continent was drawing many exiles by the 1570s (Gibbons, 2011: 15–16).

The English Catholic émigré community was more than just a group of suffering exiles longing to return to an imagined future Catholic England. Émigrés had many and complex reasons for choosing to leave England and remain on the Continent, and 'exile' was a fluid status as many émigrés continued to move to and fro between England and other countries. Furthermore, not all English Catholics travelled to and lived in Continental Europe for explicitly religious reasons. Catholics moved to the Continent to worship freely, to train for the priesthood, to enter religious life, to gain an education, to teach in Catholic universities, to go on pilgrimage, to serve in foreign armies, or simply to see the sights. Furthermore, many Catholics had links with the Continent and travelled there because other members of their families had moved there (Corens, 2019: 17–19). A number of English-born Catholics formally ceased to be exiles in the true sense when they became naturalised subjects in the countries where they settled.

The English College at Douai was founded by William Allen in 1568, followed by other seminaries at Rheims, Rome, Valladolid, Seville, and elsewhere, while the first house of female religious, a house of Benedictine nuns in Brussels, was founded in 1598 (Corens, 2019: 4). The Bridgettine nuns of Syon Abbey, refounded by Mary I, never surrendered their house or accepted its dissolution, maintaining a continuous existence as a monastic community in exile, settling in Lisbon by 1594 (Walker, 2010: 157). In other cases, individuals who had professed in pre-Reformation religious houses resumed their religious life abroad – such as Elizabeth Woodford, an Augustinian canoness of Burnham in Buckinghamshire, who joined St Ursula's Priory at Louvain as early as 1548 (Bainbridge, 2020: 27). Furthermore, from the late 1580s Englishmen began joining Benedictine monasteries in Spain, France, and Italy, predating efforts to re-establish an English Benedictine Congregation in 1607, whose existence was ratified by Rome in 1619 (Lunn, 1980: 11–36).

Some of the most prominent English clerical exiles in Counter-Reformation Europe included the Cardinal Protector of England, William Allen (1532–94), the theologian and Louvain professor Thomas Stapleton (1535–98), the moral theologian Gregory Sayer (1560–1602), and the Capuchin mystic known as Benet of Canfield (1562–1610). These were influential scholars and educators of wider European as well as merely English or expatriate significance. However, influential lay figures – particularly noblewomen – were central to the expatriate Catholic community. Jane Dormer, duchess of Feria (1538–1612), one of the most senior peers of Spain, was an Englishwoman who patronised other English expatriates and encouraged Spanish plans for an invasion of England in the late 1570s (Rodriguez-Salgado, 2006). Anne Percy, countess of Northumberland (1536–91) went into exile in 1570 after the failure of the rising of the northern earls against Elizabeth in 1569. The countess of Northumberland petitioned on behalf of other exiles and corresponded with Mary, Queen of Scots – for which the English government kept her under close surveillance (Scott, 2015). Similarly, in the next generation, Anne Cornwallis, countess of Argyll (d. 1635) acted as a benefactor and focal point for the expatriate English Catholic community (Marshall, 2008).

For some, the Continent presented opportunities for military adventure – such as the Catholic Sir William Stanley (1548–1630), who initially fought in the Low Countries on behalf of Elizabeth's government but defected to Spain in 1587, becoming governor of Deventer and living out the rest of his days under Spanish rule (Rapple, 2008). Similarly, Oliver Starkey (1523–88), who had served in Parliament in Mary's reign, became the most prominent English member of the Knights Hospitaller, helping to defend Malta against the Turks in 1565. In 1578 he was appointed Prior of England (the head of the Order in England), in spite of the Order's exclusion from the kingdom and the dissolution of its preceptories (Bindoff, 1982: 378).

As these examples show, the English Catholic émigré experience was not a wholly negative one, and as it became clearer that a Catholic restoration was not imminent in England (or could only be effected with overwhelming military force), more and more Catholics settled permanently abroad. The Continent offered forms of Catholic life that were simply unavailable to men and women in England, such as membership of a vowed religious community and the opportunity to teach at Catholic universities. While there was a shifting community of visitors to and from the Continent (such as missionary priests), there was also a permanent settled community of English émigrés, some of whom chose to become naturalised subjects of foreign princes. This issue came to a head when a former commissary of Bishop Bonner, notorious for his cruelty towards Protestants in Mary's reign, was kidnapped from Bergen-op-Zoom by English agents in 1570. John Story was a hated figure in England, but at his trial for treasonously plotting Elizabeth's death he refused to recognise the court on the grounds he was a Spanish subject. The court, however, deemed that no one could renounce their allegiance to the prince of the land in which they were born (Young, 2017: 111–16). For this reason, it was futile for missionary priests to renounce their allegiance to Elizabeth and become naturalised subjects, since the statute forbidding an Englishman from receiving orders under the authority of the Bishop of Rome still applied.

3 Catholic mission in early modern England

While the early Elizabethan Catholic community was served by priests ordained in the reigns of Henry VIII and Mary I, the dwindling numbers of such priests and the zeal of Catholic exiles for the implementation of a true Counter-Reformation mission resulted in the establishment of English seminaries abroad. The first 'seminary priests', trained in the foment of the European Counter-Reformation and vowed to minister in England, arrived in the 1570s, and the seminary priests were soon followed by the earliest Jesuits in the 1580s. However, although the efforts of missionary priests were undoubtedly heroic, the English mission was beset by problems and division from the start. These problems were, to some extent, structural; the English mission had to solve the problem of how clergy of a hierarchical and administratively complex church should operate in a context where the maintenance of an ordered hierarchy was simply impossible under draconian penal laws. However, disagreements soon developed into animosities between different groups of clergy, offering the English government an opportunity to weaken the Catholic community by exploiting internal divisions. Yet while the mission did not succeed in its avowed aim of restoring England to the Catholic faith, it did succeed in its more basic goal of sustaining the Catholic minority in many parts of the country and making recusancy possible by giving people access to a priest. Furthermore, English seminaries and colleges recruited students in sufficient numbers for England to become an exporter of Catholic missionary clergy to the wider world.

The establishment of the Catholic mission

The original purpose of the foundation of the English College at Douai by William Allen has been the subject of debate. By 1580 Douai was accepted as the first 'Tridentine seminary' (inspired by the counter-reforming decrees of the Council of Trent), whose purpose was to provide priests for a mission to combat Elizabethan Protestantism. John Bossy questioned whether this was Allen's original intention, suggesting that the clear goal of producing missionary priests emerged slowly under the influence of individuals such as Gregory Martin, Edmund Campion, and Robert Persons (Bossy, 1975: 14–15). Eamon Duffy has argued that Allen and his fellow exiles were aware from an early stage of a missionary dimension to Douai's founding. The clearest expression of this came from Allen's close associate, the Frenchman Jean de Vondeville, who in 1568 told the Spanish authorities in the Netherlands that the college would have an explicit missionary dimension; students were to be trained in religious controversy before being sent back to England to promote Catholicism. From the beginning Allen had a sense that the religious situation in England required urgent action, as he lamented 'the great desolation of Christian comfort' brought about by the Elizabethan settlement. Allen set out to attract the best students from the English universities, especially Oxford, and soon both the calibre of student and numbers were impressive. Between May and September 1576 student numbers increased from 80 to 120 (Duffy, 2017: 132–67; Duffy, 2020: 68–70).

Allen made a number of innovations to the preparation of priests for the English mission. There was a great emphasis on the study of the Bible, as Allen believed that the English Bible had been instrumental in the spread of Protestantism and the missionary priests needed to be equipped to refute Protestant interpretations. So between three and five chapters of the Old and New Testaments were read out at each meal, followed by weekly lectures and disputations. This great emphasis on the Bible can be seen in Gregory Martin's translation of the New Testament, the Douai Bible, in 1582. The students studied the decrees of the Council of Trent and the Catechisms of Trent and of Peter Canisius, the renowned Dutch Jesuit; English Catholicism would now be drawn back into the European Counter-Reformation that had been pioneered there in Mary's reign. Allen stressed the urgent need to promote recusancy. The English laity must see the necessity of making a clean break with the parish, tainted by Protestantism, otherwise Catholicism would simply decline. This was expressed with great intensity. Catholics should 'hold the heretics in perfect detestation' and 'feel sorry in heart' that any 'Catholic' should be so 'reckless of their salvation' as to attend services at their parish church (Duffy, 2017: 152). There was also a focus on the pastoral for the mission, and in the decade from the mid-1570s there was a huge increase in devotional books for the English market.

The geographical location of Douai was significant for the future pattern of the English mission. It was in the extreme southwest of the Netherlands in a French-speaking area, almost equidistant from Paris and Brussels. Although students occasionally travelled via Antwerp or Bruges, the better route to England went through St Omer to Calais, Gravelines, or Dunkirk. Moreover, in 1578 the situation in the Netherlands forced the seminary over the border to Rheims so that between 1578 and 1590 the vast majority of priests came to England from French ports. Spain was only used to host English seminarians on any scale after the outbreak of the final civil war in France in 1589. The importance of Spain was reinforced by the founding of a seminary at Valladolid in 1589 and another at Seville three years later. Priests going from Spain to England often made use of intermediary ports such as Waterford and Cork in Ireland or Nantes and La Rochelle in France.

The ports of departure usually dictated the priests' point of entry into England. Those coming from the Netherlands were likely to arrive in Hull,

Newcastle, or other ports along the east coast. Consequently, reception places sprang up on that coast, such as Grosmont Priory near Whitby, well known as a shelter for priests by the early 1580s. Priests who used Calais or Dunkirk landed on the south coast and frequently made for London; after 1580, with the establishment of the Jesuit mission, London became a base and the place the Jesuits generally made for, even when landing elsewhere. The sea route from Spain was never as popular as other routes even in the 1590s, but when it was used it landed priests on the southwest or the northwest coasts.

By 1575 eleven priests had arrived in England from Douai, and by 1580 the number was a hundred. John Paine, one of the early arrivals, remarked that 'the heretics were as much troubled at the name of the Anglo-Douai priests as the Catholics are consoled'. Allen also made optimistic comments about the mission, asserting in 1577 that 'the number of those who were daily restored to the Catholic church almost surpassed belief'. However, Allen realised that returning England to the status of a fully Catholic country was an enormous challenge and one that might require the support of foreign Catholic powers. For Allen, the spiritual and political were part of the same process, so in 1576 he had discussed the prospect of a joint papal-Spanish invasion of England with other Catholic exiles. Although the scheme did not materialise, by July 1579 there was a papal force in Ireland; this consisted of some 700 Spanish and Italian troops supporting the Irish rebel James Fitzmaurice Fitzgerald, accompanied by Nicholas Sander, one of the keenest advocates of Catholic political action. The spiritual needed to support the political, so Allen renewed his efforts to involve the Jesuits in the English mission (Duffy, 2017: 134–5; Marshall, 2017: 527–9).

Allen had a great regard for the Jesuits and from the mid-1570s had sought their help. According to Allen, the Jesuits were 'especially raised by God at this time to fight heresy' and he argued that they could play a crucial role in England, a country that was needier and nearer than India (the Jesuits had a considerable presence in India) (McCoog, 1996: 130–1). Initially, the Jesuit general Everard Mercurian was reluctant to accede to Allen's request. Mercurian was concerned about the order being drawn into politics; by 1580 he was concerned that a Jesuit mission to England, following the papal invasion of Ireland, would provoke a hostile reaction from the English government, endangering the missionaries. Despite Mercurian's reservations, Allen achieved his goal and was even able to choose the first two Jesuits for the mission, Edmund Campion and Robert Persons. However, the fears of the Jesuit general immediately materialised. Catholics had enjoyed a period of relative calm thanks to the negotiations towards the Anjou marriage, but the English government, hearing that Campion and Persons were on their journey, acted before their arrival. On 8 May 1580 a commission was sent out from the Council 'to examine and punish the papists of Lancashire, Cheshire and Yorkshire for such abuses as they have committed in hearing of masses and other misdemeanours' since the arrival of the duke of Anjou (Questier, 2019: 126).

By late June, with both Campion and Persons on English soil, the Spanish ambassador lamented that 'for the last few weeks they [the authorities] have proceeded with much more rigour than formerly against the Catholics' (Questier,

2019: 126). Moreover, it was not just the English government that viewed the Jesuit mission as a political danger. At a meeting in Southwark in July 1580 some secular priests expressed concern. The seculars had heard a rumour that the arrival of Campion and Persons was part of a wider invasion; Persons felt compelled to emphasise that they were not part of the Irish rebellion and that their mission was entirely spiritual, not political (McCoog, 1996: 144).

Mercurian had sanctioned the sending of Campion and Persons to England on the assumption that they would maintain a low profile, minister to the English Catholics, and avoid, if possible, confrontation with heretics. This was not the style of the two Jesuits. Within a week of arriving Campion had preached to a large congregation in the house of Thomas Lord Paget in Smithfield. Campion and Persons both wrote defences of their mission and challenges to the authorities, including an invitation to public debate. Initially meant to be used only if one of them were captured, 'Campion's Brag' (as it came to be known) was immediately circulated in mid-1581. This was a direct challenge to the Elizabethan government; according to the 'Brag', nothing could prevent the success of the Jesuit mission, not torture, prison, or even execution: 'The expense is reckoned, the enterprise is begun; it is of God, it cannot be withstood. So the faith was planted, so it must be restored' (McCoog, 1996: 147). Soon Campion was a Catholic champion and probably the most wanted priest in England. Within a month Campion was captured at Lyford Grange in Berkshire; on 1 December, along with two other priests, he was executed at Tyburn (McCoog, 1996: 143–47). Campion's death was quickly followed by Persons' flight to the Continent. The mission appeared to be in ruins, and if Mercurian had not died in August 1580, it could well have signalled the end of Jesuit involvement in England.

Did this amount to total failure? This was not the view of either Allen or Persons, who were as one in celebrating the martyrdom of Campion; in Persons' words nothing could have such a positive impact on the mission as 'brief but glorious death agony' (McCoog, 1996: 174–5). Leaving aside the issue of whether martyrdom was a positive goal – and the new General Acquaviva insisted that Campion had been sent to England to 'toil' not to endure 'torture' – the two Jesuits had made a positive impact on the English mission. This involved using London as a base and developing more formal cooperation between priests and gentry in the capital. Persons had immediately worked with a group of leading Catholic gentry led by George Gilbert, who had already established a fraternity to help incoming priests arriving from the Continent. Thanks to the financial assistance and careful planning of Gilbert, Persons was able to travel through Gloucestershire, Herefordshire, Worcestershire, and Derbyshire, and Campion through Berkshire, Oxfordshire, and Northamptonshire. Both priests were escorted through each county by a number of young men of 'gentle birth' before meeting up again in London (McCoog, 1996: 151).

Campion and Persons made other significant contributions. In July 1580 they held a meeting in Southwark with the seculars, important in itself, in which they discussed a range of issues including the overall organisation of the mission. Persons stressed the necessity of recusancy for all Catholics, and although this was not new, the force of Persons' argument and its immediate publication gave it a greater impact than earlier pleas for recusancy. Both Jesuits used the printing press to great effect; it was Persons who had set up a press, first in the house of a Leicestershire Catholic, Robert Brookesby, in Greenstreet, East London, and then in Southwark in the house of Francis Browne, brother of Viscount Montague. Over the course of the next 20 years the secret presses in England would produce pamphlets and treatises on issues of religion and theology for both clergy and laity (McCoog, 2017: 39). In their brief period on the mission, Campion and Persons had certainly raised its profile, but at considerable cost. Peter Lake has argued that the very public nature of the Jesuit mission contributed to the failure of the Anjou marriage (Lake, 2016: 110). As we have already noted, the Jesuit arrival was greeted by increased persecution and the situation soon worsened. In late 1580 Campion lamented 'where I am there is no talk but of death, flight or prison' [*Doc. 4*, p. 121–3]. In many respects, therefore, 'the reckoned expense' was considerable, not only for Campion but also for the other seminarists and the Catholic laity, resulting in 'immeasurable suffering' [*Doc. 5*, p. 123–4].

One of the most important consequences of Campion and Persons' brief involvement with the mission was the adoption of a leadership role by the Jesuits. As the Appellants later bitterly protested, this was more of a takeover than an agreement with the seculars; there were tensions from the beginning and a spectacular flare-up in Wisbech Castle in the early 1590s over the Jesuit William Weston's leadership claims. The Jesuits, however, acting under the direct authority of their general and with a designated superior in England, brought an embryonic clerical structure to the mission which the seculars lacked until the seventeenth century. In some respects, therefore, it was both natural and beneficial for the Jesuits to assume the leadership role, and Persons continued to have a strong influence over the mission years after leaving England. By 1584 he had established a scheme for sending priests from Europe to England. Rouen was the centre of operations as it was close enough to the sea 'that ... some can make trips for boats to convey people across'. Rouen was also fairly close to the seminary at Rheims; Allen sent the priests, and Persons (or his assistants) arranged their crossing. London continued to be used as a base, as Persons explained to Acquaviva in 1584: 'one of them [Jesuits] will have to live mostly in London or near it in order to direct the others'. This was the itinerary Persons followed to transport William Weston and the Jesuit brother Ralph Emerson to England in 1585. They landed on the Norfolk coast, but only Weston made it to London 'where there were many houses' ready to receive him (Basset, 1967: 71–2; McCoog, 1996: 171).

One of Weston's first tasks was to hold a conference in Hoxton at the house of the Kentish Catholic gentleman William Wilford, between a number of gentry and seminarists. The meeting had been prompted by recent legislation against Jesuits and seminary priests and their helpers. It was agreed that in the short term the priests should endeavour to stay in inns rather than gentry residences. To finance this the gentry present – William Lord Vaux, Sir Thomas Tresham, Sir William Catesby, and Thomas Wilford – all agreed to contribute 100 marks each to a common fund; it was hoped that this would be supplemented by money from other Catholic gentry. Lord Vaux was chosen to administer the fund, his son Henry to launch the wider appeal; Father Weston was the intermediary between Lord Vaux and the seminary priests. In effect the Jesuits now had a key role over the finances of the mission, a role that would be greatly extended by Henry Garnet (McCoog, 1988: 103–23).

In spite of the work of Persons and others in the early 1580s, the mission was still precarious, with priests being lost at an alarming rate. Between 1581 and 1586 more than 30 had been executed and 50 were in prison, more than half of those who had entered the country. Although London appeared to be working well in receiving incoming priests, the distribution across the country was still defective. In July 1586 Weston complained that 'there are three or four counties together yet unfurnished with priests'. A fellow Jesuit regretted that 'in many counties, containing no small number of Catholics, there is not a single priest' (Caraman, 1964: 35), although this may have been special pleading on his part.

The mission experienced severe difficulty in the late 1580s as Henry Garnet and Robert Southwell took over after Weston's imprisonment in 1588. There was a constant refrain, especially from Garnet, that more priests were needed. The severe persecution was limiting the priests' ability to widen their audience: 'the fruit would certainly be more abundant if we were able to preach from the roofs what we can now say into the ears only of a few' (McCoog, 1996: 237). At times Garnet was concerned that his emphasis on the problem caused by the persecution might be deterring potential recruits to the English mission, so he resorted to the upbeat: 'there is still life and spirit among the Catholics' (McCoog, 1996: 237). However, by 1590 Garnet was so despondent about the level of persecution that he appeared to break rank with the Allen-Persons support for the Armada. In May, on the rumour of another Spanish Armada, Garnet complained that it was he and his fellow missioners who would suffer: 'it is we who are tortured and torn apart, we who are not plotting but hiding at home giving ourselves to prayer and devotion' (McCoog, 1996: 263).

Despite such difficulties, the organisation of the mission continued to improve. Until his execution in 1592, Southwell was based in London to assist new arrivals, while Garnet toured the country while meeting with Southwell twice a year in London. Regional missions were being established. John Gerard was put in charge of East Anglia until his arrest in 1594, after which the secular priest John Bavard seems to have taken over. Garnet tried to supervise the East Midlands himself, but after 1592 he was increasingly in London. In the West Midlands Edward Oldcorn, another Jesuit, made Hinlip Hall in Worcestershire the centre of local operations from 1589 until 1606. The Yorkshire mission began early in 1582 with Thomas Bell, a secular priest in charge of the Yorkshire clergy. Bell was 'one of the most active and influential priests working in the north of England'; however, in 1592 he clashed with Garnet over the issue of Catholics occasionally conforming and soon afterwards apostatised to the established church (Walsham, 2000: 218). John Mush, the future Appellant, and the Jesuit Richard Holtby replaced Bell. They both did similar work in improving the route from the Netherlands to the northeast of England. The existing Middelburg to South Shields run was developed and newly arrived priests were passed from South Shields to Holtby's refuge at Thornley, Durham, and from there to Grosmont Priory (Bossy, 1975: 204–9; Aveling, 1976: 158–9). The national coverage was still somewhat patchy, but by 1596 Garnet was expressing his satisfaction at progress made: 'the result now is that many persons who saw a seminary priest hardly once a year, now have one all the time' (Caraman, 1964: 45; Dures, 1983: 24).

The mission coincided with the changing pattern of Catholicism in England, with the emergence of widespread recusancy in the 1580s and 1590s. Recusancy was not new; prompted by the work of the Marian priests, eight gentry were presented in Lancashire in 1568 and 86 recusants were listed in 1574 (Haigh, 1975: 262). This trend of increased recusancy continued across the country in the 1570s before the seminarists had made any significant impact. In the 1580s, however, the seminary priests brought a new insistence on recusancy and were highly successful in preventing Catholic conformity, which was still largely the norm at the time of their arrival.

A major motive for Allen's foundation of the Douai seminary was the recognition that Catholics were in danger of losing their identity by attending Protestant services; Allen believed that recusancy was essential. Even in the early 1560s Allen launched a vigorous campaign to persuade fellow Lancastrians 'to abstain altogether from the communion, churches, sermons, books and all spiritual communication with heretics' (Duffy, 2017: 139). The first published work insisting on recusancy came from Rheims (the Douai seminary had moved there in 1578), *A Treatise of Schisme* by Gregory Martin. In 1580 Robert Persons published *Reasons why Catholiques refuse to go to church*, which stressed that non-attendance at Protestant services was not an act of rebellion but simply an unwillingness to abandon their faith; attendance risked 'infection and scandal'. Moreover, spiritual perfection, for which all Catholics should strive, could not be achieved without recusancy (McCoog, 1996: 152; Duffy, 2017: 169–70). Yet even Allen, faced by the weight of penalties against Catholics, had conceded by 1592 that confessors could be lenient to Catholics who fell away from recusancy [*Doc. 8*, p. 125–6].

Although this insistence on recusancy certainly made its mark on Catholic commitment, it did not go unchallenged among the Catholic clergy and not all the Catholic laity opted for recusancy. A significant number of gentry became church papists, which generally amounted to occasional attendance at Protestant services. The most common pattern of church papistry was for the head of household to attend his parish church, while his wife, children, and servants were recusants. The most likely reasons for such conformity was to avoid the financial penalties of recusancy, which were particularly punitive after 1587, and the need for prominent gentry to retain office, either local or national. Two priests in particular, Alban Langdale (a priest ordained in Mary's reign, and chaplain to Viscount Montague) and Thomas Bell (a seminarist), offered similar defences of church papistry. One justification was that Catholics were acting out of 'just fear'; they also argued that such conformity came into the category of 'adiaphora' or 'things indifferent'.

A point that bears emphasising is that church papists had a strong Catholic identity: they were as likely to maintain priests, send their children to be educated in Catholic Europe, and finance the mission as their recusant colleagues. Langdale suggested that separation, which he obviously considered important to Catholic identity, could be achieved without recusancy. He argued that the church papist could identify himself by refusing to take communion, refusing to repeat the required liturgical responses, and generally showing a measure of dissent in Protestant services. In fact, almost all church papists refused communion until new legislation in 1606 (Walsham, 1999: 52). Church papists were often objects of suspicion, or the butt of satire, for Protestant neighbours who distrusted their motives and sometimes considered their dissembling more dangerous than recusancy [Doc. 9, p. 126].

The changing commitment of Catholics is evident in a number of areas. In Sussex in the 1560s there were probably some 30 Catholic families among the leading gentry; by 1580 this had been reduced to 25, but of these, 15 were recusant. This trend continued into the 1590s, which saw a further reduction in the number of Catholic gentry, but a slight increase in recusancy (Manning, 1969: 52). Yorkshire showed a similar pattern; by 1604 there were 112 recusant families, probably double the number of the early 1580s. However, as in Sussex, this represented a process of polarisation rather than a Catholic increase. As J. T. Cliffe observed, 'If the number of recusant families was growing, this does not mean there had been significant gains from Protestantism. What we are witnessing is a polarisation process within the Catholic gentry; one section going over completely to Anglicanism, while another was becoming fully and irrevocably committed to the old religion' (Cliffe, 1969: 189). Cliffe may have been underestimating the degree of fluidity between Catholic and Protestant, but the drift was clear. In a totally contrasting area, London, there was a dramatic tenfold increase in recusancy from 1587 to 1603, when the figure was about 600. In part this was due to an influx of gentry from outside the capital, but there was also a significant non-gentry recusancy emerging.

Lancashire also showed an increase in recusancy in the 1580s and 1590s. In his study of the county, Haigh argued that greater detection in these decades needs to be taken into account, but concluded that 'it is nevertheless true that there was a considerable expansion after 1578' (Haigh, 1975: 289). By 1604 there were 3,500 recorded recusants, a tenfold increase since 1590. However, this figure needs to be put in context, and was doubtless due in part to the toleration that Catholics enjoyed at the accession of James I. John Gerard had already noticed that Lancashire Catholics openly showed themselves only in times of relative calm: 'People of this kind come into the [Catholic] church without difficulty, but they fall away the moment persecution blows up. When the alarm is over, they come back again' (Walsham, 1999: 76). The number of church papists also increased in Lancashire, especially in the 1590s. This suggests that they were emerging as a distinct category of committed Catholics, but Catholics who felt the need to attend Protestant services at least occasionally in order to avoid the harsh financial penalties of the 1587 statute. Nevertheless, a degree of fluidity remained between recusant and church papist identities.

Whether this increased recusancy was a direct consequence of the Douai mission drew sharply different judgements from John Bossy and Christopher

Haigh some 40 years ago. For Bossy the increased recusancy was the outcome of the mission, which laid the foundations of a new Catholic community, separated from the Elizabethan parish, and which continued to grow in numbers. For Haigh there was no significant break in the 1570s with the emergence of a new Catholic community; continuity characterised Elizabethan Catholicism. So the seminary priests had a limited impact on English Catholicism, and in the end they failed to halt the overall decline of Catholicism, leaving 'a rump community and decline in which whole regions and social groups were neglected' (Haigh, 1981: 132). This failure was due to the missionary bias in favour of the southeast and an over-dependence on the gentry.

There are undoubtedly strong elements of continuity in Elizabethan Catholicism. There was a geographical continuity; the areas of greatest conservatism in the 1560s, the North and the Welsh borders, were the areas of greatest recusancy in 1603. Lancashire remained the most Catholic county up to the Civil War, and indeed beyond it and perhaps even into the present day. Moreover, the key process of separation – the move towards recusancy – was already apparent in the late 1560s and early 1570s; this was due to the work of the remaining Marian clergy. Furthermore, the emergence of church papistry, which Haigh was one of the first historians to appreciate, shows that the process of separation was not total. Catholics generally had a strong sense of the continuity of their church. The Louvain writers in the 1560s contrasted the ancient origins of Catholicism with the recent foundation of Elizabethan Protestantism. Recusants were schooled to answer their Protestant interrogators by stressing that they were only following the religion of their forefathers [*Doc. 6*, p. 124]. Lady Cecilia Stonor declared in 1584 that she 'was born in such a time when the holy mass was in great reverence, and brought up in the same faith ... I hold me still to that wherein I was born and bred' (Sheils, 2011: 257–8).

The fact that there were strong elements of continuity in Elizabethan Catholicism does not mean that the Douai mission was not significant or successful. Thomas Bramston, a Benedictine novice at Westminster Abbey before the dissolution, became a schoolmaster in the employ of Sir Thomas Tresham, but eventually travelled to the Continent to be ordained priest, thus embodying the strange mixture of pre-Reformation continuity and Counter-Reformation ingenuity in English Catholicism [*Doc. 7*, p. 124–5]. By the mid-1570s, when the seminarists began to arrive, the long-term survival of Catholicism was under pressure, despite the work of the surviving Marian priests. Catholics were feeling more uncomfortable within the parish as conservative practices were suppressed and Catholic imagery or objects of worship were removed. Catholicism had to operate outside the parish; a new structure was needed and that had to be focused on the gentry. By the end of Elizabeth's reign the seculars would be arguing for a Catholic parochial structure, overseen by bishops, on the basis that England remained part of evangelised Christendom, as opposed to a mission territory that required complete conversion anew. But if that was ever practical, it was not possible in the 1580s and early 1590s. Gentry households were needed as bases; they could provide protection for priests and the physical space in which mass and the sacraments could be administered. The gentry were essential to finance the priests. This did not mean that the impact of the seminaries was limited to the gentry households. In 1580 a number of gentlemen had conducted Persons and Campion across several English counties, as we have seen. In the late 1580s and early 1590s John Gerard operated from the home of the Wiseman family near Saffron Walden (and later from the Drury family's home in Lawshall, Suffolk), but conducted a nationwide ministry, including Lancashire. In the 1590s the household of Lady Magdalen Montague, served by a number of seminary priests, became a Catholic centre with an impact across the neighbourhood. The chapel had a congregation of over a hundred and pilgrims prayed in the holy well in the grounds. The result was, according to one commentator in 1597, that '[Protestant] religion in that country and especially in that towne is gretely decayed' (Sheils, forthcoming).

The close relations with the gentry was bound to lead to more seminarists working in southern England, as the gentry were more numerous and wealthier in the south. Nevertheless, this should not be exaggerated, as Haigh himself points out that in the last two decades of Elizabeth's reign 'Lancashire attracted more than its quota of seminary priests because the area was a fairly safe one' (Haigh, 1975: 279). Moreover, the focus in the south should not be seen merely as a weakness in the mission. John Gerard's work in East Anglia contributed to a gentry Catholicism that was stable and long lasting in an area that was strongly Protestant, and aggressively so in parts. A small but significant body survived in Kent, despite the county's well-deserved reputation for Protestantism. The choice of London as a base, pioneered by Persons, was logical. In the crucial early decades it was a major entry point for priests and a natural meeting place for priests and gentry, especially given the number of important gentry in London from across the southern counties in the 1580s and beyond. Foreign embassies and the royal court were in the capital, both essential channels for Catholic lobbying. London prisons were important Catholic centres and by 1603 a vibrant Catholic community was establishing itself in the capital.

This is not to say that the Elizabethan mission was entirely successful. It never led to the reconversion of England; the scale of that challenge was soon recognised as Allen and Persons developed a parallel strategy of supporting foreign Catholic invasions alongside the spiritual goal of the mission. In the 1580s and 1590s there was a shortage of priests, as the persecution took a heavy toll in executions and imprisonment. Despite these weaknesses there were some essential achievements which laid the foundation for greater success in the seventeenth century as more tolerant conditions prevailed under the Stuarts. There was something approaching a Catholic structure across the country thanks to the work of Garnet in particular. By 1603 English Catholicism was part of the wider Catholic reform movement across Europe, no longer simply the church of their forefathers, and the seminary priests were the major instrument of this transition. The seminarists, especially Southwell and Garnet, had begun to address the problem of how to support those Catholics who did not have regular access to the mass and the sacraments. This was a major challenge for 'a church under penalty'.

The Archpriest Controversy

The arrival of the Jesuits in England in 1580 had a profound impact on existing efforts at Catholic revival already underway by both the Douai seminarists and the Marian priests. The Jesuits saw England, along with certain parts of Europe and the New World, as 'missionary territory'. In such areas Protestantism could be reversed and Catholicism re-invigorated only through a radical approach based on the distinctive evangelising qualities of the Jesuits. The seminarists shared the central objective of reconverting England to full Catholicism, but were more likely to envisage the restoration of a traditional ecclesiastical structure.

The potential for a clash between the Jesuits and the seculars probably existed from the arrival of Campion and Persons. This was the view of Thomas Bluet, though as an Appellant writing in 1601, he cannot be trusted to reflect exactly opinions in the early 1580s; nevertheless, it seems likely that some seminarists saw the arrival of the Jesuits as disruptive. Bluet complained that Campion and Persons, with their 'sundry such great brags and challenges', provoked the English government to initiate the persecution that characterised the 1580s and beyond (Lake and Questier, 2019: 147). Persons' plan, before leaving England, to provide some organisation for the mission was necessary and entirely beneficial, but it still amounted to a Jesuit take-over.

In 1584 the Jesuit William Weston arrived in England as Jesuit Superior, but he was captured in August 1586 and imprisoned at Wisbech (Harmsen, 2004). While Weston took a leading role in the community of incarcerated priests and was initially a unifying figure, some of the seminary priests eventually began to question why Weston should have authority over them. The death of Cardinal Allen, the 'cardinal protector' of England, in October 1594 left the secular clergy without even nominal leadership and brought matters to a head. Weston became increasingly dictatorial in his government of the 'college' inside the prison, encouraging the priests to adopt a rule of life. In a deliberately provocative act at Christmas 1594, a secular priest called Christopher Bagshawe arranged for a group of traditional mummers, accompanied by a hobby horse, to perform in the castle's Great Hall. Weston had specifically banned festivities of this kind as unfitting for men of the cloth, and from that time onwards Weston and Bagshawe were at loggerheads, with Weston leading the pro-Jesuit party and Bagshawe leading the anti-Jesuit party. While Bagshawe's party aimed to persuade the government to tolerate Catholicism and provide Catholics with an oath of allegiance they could swear in good conscience (in order to safeguard Catholics' right to practise their ancient faith), the aim of Weston's party was the out-and-out conversion of England, by any means possible (Renold, 1958: xi–xxiii; Lake and Questier, 2019: 37–53).

The issues at Wisbech erupted in full intensity and bitterness in the Archpriest Controversy in 1598. There had been something of a crisis since the death of William Allen in 1594. As prefect, Allen had supervised the mission itself, overseen the Continental seminaries, and approved secular clergy. After a failure to appoint a successor, everyone, including the Jesuits, expected Rome to appoint a bishop to supervise the Catholic church in England. Instead, Enrico Caetani, Cardinal Protector of England in Rome, appointed George Blackwell as an archpriest. Blackwell was given the support of 12 assistants from among the secular clergy, and he had disciplinary control over the seculars, including the authority to punish through suspension any disobedient seculars or ultimately to revoke their faculties. However, the archpriest had no power over the Jesuits or the laity. There was an immediate outcry against the appointment among the seculars, some of whom immediately appealed to Rome. The seculars considered the office of archpriest to be an anomaly and against proper ecclesiastical order. Blackwell was also perceived as pro-Jesuit, which further fuelled secular ideas of expanding Jesuit influence. This was the case not only in England but across Europe, following the establishment of new Jesuit colleges at Seville and Valladolid. This led to the greatest internal crisis yet faced by the post-Reformation Catholic church in England.

The issue of the archpriest soon moved into the 'Appellant Controversy', as between 1598 and 1602 a number of secular clerics appealed to Rome against Blackwell. The papacy was slow to respond but gave its final ruling in 1602. Blackwell's appointment was confirmed, but the Appellants won concessions. The archpriest was ordered not to exceed his authority, and not to consult with the Jesuits but to report directly to Rome, and to take three Appellants as assistants. In the course of the crisis hostilities sharpened and became more political. By 1599 some of the Appellants were working closely with the English government, especially with Bishop Bancroft, behind whom stood Sir Robert Cecil, who appeared to be sympathetic to the view that English Catholic loyalism should merit some form of toleration. These issues were soon entangled in the English 'succession crisis', with one of the leading Appellants, William Watson, negotiating with James VI of Scotland. Watson sought to gain promises of toleration in return for Catholic support for James's bid for the English throne. At the same time the Appellants sought to stigmatise the Jesuits as major obstacles to Catholic harmony and peaceful relations with the English monarchy. Parsons appeared to support their case by working assiduously against the Appellants in Rome, and up to 1603 opposing James as Elizabeth's successor (Lake and Questier, 2019: 1–36, 81–8).

By the early seventeenth century the seculars had established a position that changed little up to 1640; they constantly claimed that the appointment of an English bishop with traditional episcopal powers would solve all the major problems in the English Catholic church. Birkhead, appointed archpriest in 1608 after Blackwell's dismissal for taking the Oath of Allegiance, petitioned Rome for the restoration of the full hierarchy. This was necessary, he claimed, to resolve the conflict between the seculars and the Jesuits, and regularise almsgiving to the mission. Birkhead complained that alms were going to individual priests, especially among the religious orders, and lack of accountability meant that 'scarcely any thing comes from the general needs of the poor who cry in vain for bread' (Haigh, 1981: 129–47; Questier, 1998: 1–39). However, it was not until three archpriests later, in 1623, that William Bishop was appointed as bishop of Chalcedon. This appointment, however, was not the restoration of the normal regime of bishops that had ended in 1599; it was a kind of halfway house. William Bishop was in full episcopal orders but lacked 'ordinary jurisdiction' – that is, territorial jurisdiction over the see or diocese.

William Bishop spent only a few months in England, but before his death he established a new administrative structure for the secular clergy (Bossy, 1975: 53–4). He set up a dean and chapter, supported at a local level by vicars general, archdeacons, and rural deans. The dean and chapter, in particular, were a concrete expression of continuity with the pre-Reformation church, as the right to elect future bishops was vested in it. It was, however, a top-heavy structure. The chapter consisted of a dean and 18 canons, while the rest of the hierarchy amounted to some 50 people, all to control about 400 secular priests (Schofield, 2017: 156–68). The new bishop of Chalcedon immediately turned his attention to the Benedictines, who had re-established an English Congregation in 1619 and numbered about 60 in the 1620s. The Benedictines agreed to accept the position of a loosely supervised autonomy, although some monks continued to claim that the Benedictines had the exclusive right to govern themselves (Lunn, 1980: 110).

The Jesuits had continued to expand, and by 1623 formed a separate English province under the government of Richard Blount. The number of priests had risen from 9 in 1590 to over 100 (by 1642 the number was nearly 200) and the number of districts had increased to 12. The provincial continued to live in or near London, kept in touch with local supervisors, and handled the finances. The duties of the local supervisor were to oversee the physical and spiritual needs of the Jesuits in his district, to place them as the mission required, and to see that they spent a week every year doing their spiritual exercises. Although the Jesuit districts were called 'colleges', they were not physical buildings but a body of priests. Nevertheless, some gentry houses such as Holbeck House in Nottinghamshire, Cwm in Herefordshire, and perhaps Coldham Hall in Suffolk were used as Jesuit colleges (Dijkgraaf, 2003; Thomas, 2014: 572–88; Young, 2016: xlviii–xlix).

The Approbation Controversy

The arrival of Bishop's successor, Richard Smith, in England in 1623 initiated a number of measures that led to yet another crisis, the Approbation Controversy. This controversy, according to Questier, 'reignited all the fury and antagonisms of the appellant dispute' but with even more serious issues involved (Questier, 2006: 438). Smith claimed that, according to the decrees of the Council of Trent, no priest had the power to hear confession unless he had received the approval of the bishop of the diocese. Smith probably had in mind the eventual construction of a parochial system controlled by bishops, but in the context of the English missions of the 1620s, such a pronouncement could only be interpreted as an attack on the Jesuit confessors. Moreover, this action agitated many of the laity by casting doubts on the validity of their confessors (Bossy, 1975: 54).

The second issue Smith raised, that of missionary finance, was equally significant and contentious. Echoing Birkhead in 1611, Smith was concerned about funding. The giving of alms to individual priests encouraged resident chaplains and the concentration of priests in areas of existing Catholicism at the expense of poor remoter areas. Centralised control of finance would overcome this problem, and in 1627 Smith applied to Rome to authorise such a move, which would enable archdeacons to distribute funds according to local needs.

The attempt to control the Jesuit confessors and missionary finances significantly aggravated the ongoing bitter dispute between the seculars and the Jesuits. For Smith's supporters such measures were essential to bring order and discipline to the mission. Moreover, this was timely as the English Catholic Church could claim to be pursuing a similar policy to that of the avant-garde bishops in the Church of England, and could equally claim, along with the Laudian bishops, to be upholders of the monarchical principles of authority and hierarchy. Smith's opponents, who included the Jesuits and a significant number of the Catholic gentry, saw things very differently. A fully episcopal church would transgress the royal supremacy and bring revenge from the state on the Catholic clergy. Smith's bid for financial control brought him into conflict with the gentry as well as the Jesuits. It was impractical to channel all alms through the archdeacons, as bequests made by Catholics had to be secretive, often involving complicated legal trusts [*Doc. 17*, p. 132. The gentry also feared that Smith's attempts at financial control would ultimately lead to the establishment of Catholic church courts to supervise wills, matrimonial issues, and the like. Such courts would have created huge problems for the gentry, with the potential for clashes with existing common law and ecclesiastical courts (Bossy, 1975: 57; Allison, 1982: 111–45; Questier, 2006: 436–52).

Gentry opposition to Smith went beyond the issue of bequests, as most were opposed to the restoration of a full pre-Reformation church structure; the seigneurial nature of the mission ensured the independence of the laity. Smith, however, retained some support among the Catholic elite, even though it was leading gentry who petitioned the Privy Council against the bishop in 1628. Smith's subsequent arrest and imprisonment in 1629, however, probably owed more to the king's final attempt to appease an anti-Catholic Parliament than to the action of the Catholic gentry. In 1631 Smith left England and subsequently resigned his bishopric, but his supporters continued to petition Rome for a replacement (Questier, 2005: 1–37).

The potential for clerical conflict on the English mission was further enhanced by the refounding of the English Benedictine Congregation in 1619. Even before the formal foundation, the Benedictines had clashed with the seculars in 1608; both argued George Gervase, a martyr executed at Tyburn, was one of their own (Kelly, 2018b: 257–64). The Benedictine claim for jurisdiction over any diocese whose pre-Reformation cathedral had been Benedictine hardly pleased the seculars, though it was scarcely a practical issue. For historic reasons the Benedictines were more opposed to the Jesuits. William Gifford (1557–1629) had been a vigorous opponent of Robert Persons and his politics. Another eminent Benedictine, Thomas Preston, also denounced aggressive political Catholicism, denying even the Pope's right to issue political directions to Catholics. Leander Jones was a leading advocate in the 1630s of the idea of reunion between the Church of England and Rome.

The disputes among the different clerical groups also split the Catholic laity. The 2nd Baron Petre was one of the Jesuits' greatest supporters. Moreover, he built up an alliance of Jesuit-supporting families through marriage, starting with the 2nd baron's marriage to Katherine, daughter of Edward, 4th earl of Worcester. The Somerset clan was firmly on the Jesuit side throughout the approbation affair. By contrast, the 2nd Viscount Montague generally supported the seculars, though he also patronised the Benedictines. Family allegiances were not totally constant; John Southcote, a leader of the pro-episcopal group in the 1630s, was from a strongly Jesuit family. The split in the laity, however, was significant, even influencing the choice of convents for Catholic families. Women who came from the Petre-Jesuit county of Essex generally entered convents at Louvain, Bruges, or Antwerp, all with reputations for strong Jesuit influence (Kelly, 2018a: 23–38).

'A church under the cross': the success of the Catholic mission

The impact of these splits within the clergy and laity on the strength of the Catholic community is difficult to assess, although we have already argued that the splits weakened attempts of English Catholics to align themselves more closely with the regime. The impact on the mission itself, however, was probably not significant. As Lake and Questier stressed in relation to the Archpriest Controversy, the struggle represented 'two rival versions of Counter Reformation Catholicism in England'. All the seminarists shared the objectives of converting Protestants and sustaining existing Catholicism, while attempting to revitalise that Catholicism in line with the reforms of Counter-Reformation Europe.

The final critical issue to be addressed is whether the mission can be deemed a success. By 1642 English Catholicism was a minority religion. Bossy's original estimate of some 40,000 Catholics in England in 1603 might be on the low side, given the now accepted prevalence of church papistry (Bossy, 1975: 192). It is now generally accepted that Catholics were more numerous among the gentry and aristocracy than in the overall population. There is some consensus too on the continued expansion of Catholicism between 1603 and 1642, apparent in areas as diverse as the North Riding of Yorkshire and London. For Haigh this represented more of a failure than a success for the English mission. He criticised the seminarists for settling in the houses of the gentry, failing to proselytise widely, and neglecting the poor. This resulted in a decline of popular Catholicism, especially in parts of the North not well served by the seminarists. It is true, of course, that both William Allen and Robert Persons aimed for a fully Catholic England. However, without a significant political change within England or more feasibly foreign Catholic intervention, such an aim was always unrealistic.

Recent work has tended to be more positive on the achievements of the mission. Michael Mullett has argued that the seminarists did indeed operate from within gentry homes but used them as a base from which to make contact with a wider social range. The Jesuits insisted that while some fathers lived in gentry houses they were also 'occupied in instructing the poor … in a perpetual round of labours'. It was reported that in Yorkshire in the 1620s a collection of 120 gold crowns had been made in alms for poor Catholics, while in Co. Durham it was noted that 'the richest harvest was gathered in excursions taken for the instructions of poorer classes ... on long pedestrian journeys and a very poor diet' (Mullett, 2009: 36–7). This pattern reflects our analysis of the social structure of Catholicism; the gentry or richer yeomen were generally crucial for sustaining a Catholic community, but the majority were of lesser social standing.

The range of challenges facing the missionary priests in developing a 'church under the cross' in a Protestant country was immense. This went beyond the traditional priestly duties of saying mass and administering the sacraments. The Jesuits, in particular, provided extensive guidance and help to establish rosary sodalities, innovative spiritual approaches for the laity in the use of sacred spaces, and the promotion of reliquaries, Catholic books, and paintings. The seminarists were also a major channel of distribution for such objects, most of which originated in Europe. What is also significant is the degree to which the priests maintained control of a process which inevitably gave greater freedom and independence to the laity, and indeed depended on the laity's great involvement. The rosary, for example, which could simply be a private devotion, became in Jesuit hands a means of evangelising significant numbers, a method they employed on other missions including Japan. The status of the seminarists was enhanced by their willingness to exploit martyrdom and encouraging relic collection. In the case of Ann Vaux, we saw John Gerard redefining an image of female sanctity to suit the needs of the Jesuit mission. Valued objects such as the *Agnus Dei*, the rosary, books, and pictures were all held in higher regard if they came with a clerical blessing or clerical approval.

A number of historians have also shown that seminarists did not simply concentrate on sustaining an existing Catholicism; conversion was always a significant part of the missionary aim, though conversions went both ways. (Questier, 1996; Underwood, 2014). Moreover, many converts mention the influence of priests, though friends, relatives, and books also played a part. A number of youths appear to have been converted by contact with the Catholic priests in Wisbech prison in the 1580s and 1590s, and indeed prisons were often centres of conversion. One of today's leading scholars, Alexandra Walsham, is in no doubt of the overall success of the mission: 'It is necessary to re-emphasise the critical part played by mission in the creation of post Reformation Catholicism in Britain' (Walsham, 2014: 29). For Walsham, the success of the mission came from 'the intensity, emotion and energy' that underpinned the Counter-Reformation in England, across Europe, and even beyond (Walsham, 2014: 31).

English mission beyond England

While the settlement of emigrant English Catholics in the Low Countries, France, Spain, and other European countries began as early as 1559, English Catholics abroad were missionaries as well as exiles. Early modern English Catholics were part of a newly globalised Counter-Reformation world and travelled both to the New World and the Indian subcontinent. The Jesuits, in particular, were renowned for their willingness to travel beyond the usual geographical boundaries of trade and diplomacy, and Englishmen who joined the Jesuits were bound under obedience to go anywhere their superiors told them. While the vast majority of English Jesuits returned to England on the perilous mission there, some went elsewhere. A number of English Jesuits found themselves in Vienna, Prague, Poznán, Kraków, or Vilnius, while John Mead (c. 1572–1653), known in Portuguese as João D'Almeida, ventured even further afield to Brazil in 1588 and spent most of the remainder of his life at the Jesuit College in Rio da Janeiro (Worthington, 2012: 151–86; Murphy, 2004). Another English Jesuit, Thomas Stephens (1549–1619), arrived in India in 1579 and spent the rest of his life evangelising southern Goa, publishing the first catechism and grammar in the Konkani language as well as writing Konkani epic poetry (Borges, 2004).

The idea of an English Catholic colony in the New World was first mooted in 1582 by William Catesby, as a place where Catholics could enjoy 'liberty of conscience'. With other Catholic gentlemen he drew up plans for a colony at Norumbega in present-day New England, but the project never came to fruition (Childs, 2014: 273–4). In spring 1605 an expedition funded by Lord Arundell of Wardour and led by George Waymouth landed at Allen's Island in Newfoundland and planted a cross (Rice, 2005: 234), but no successful colony was established, and it was not until 1621 that another Catholic, Sir George Calvert (later Lord Baltimore), established a colony on Newfoundland's Avalon Peninsula. In 1623 Calvert obtained a charter from Charles I that granted him the powers of lord palatine (along the lines of the bishops of Durham) over the new territory, but by the 1620s the colony was struggling and Calvert began seeking a grant of land much further to the south, along Chesapeake Bay (Krugler, 2010).

Although George Calvert died in 1632 before the new colony of Maryland could be settled, his son Cecilius took forward the idea of a New World colony where English Catholics might enjoy liberty of conscience and, in March 1634, two ships carrying English Catholic settlers and Jesuit priests, the *Ark* and the *Dove*, arrived in Maryland. The Jesuit Andrew White set about converting the indigenous Piscataway and Yaocomico peoples to Catholicism (Cooper, 2004), but the Jesuit Superior in the colony, Thomas Copley, fell out with Cecilius Calvert, the lord proprietor, over the status of Catholicism in Maryland. While Copley insisted Maryland was 'a Catholic country', Lord Baltimore envisaged Maryland as an experiment in religious toleration where anyone would be free to practise their religion (Gillett, 2019: 246–7). However, this freedom was not shared by the enslaved Africans on whom the colony became increasingly dependent for the harvesting of tobacco, and the Jesuits themselves soon became slave owners (Debe and Menard, 2011: 129–41).

Although Maryland did not remain an exclusively Catholic colony for long, the Catholic community of Maryland retained its connection with the English Catholic community until the American Revolution and beyond. The Maryland colony and the other colonial endeavours of English Catholics are a reminder that English Catholics were involved in the same missionary endeavours as other Counter-Reformation Catholics, and in the same colonial projects as non-

Catholic English people. Indeed, it suited Charles I's government to make use of the Calverts and their Catholic settlers to further establish English dominance of Atlantic North America, which may explain the extensive powers granted to the barons Baltimore as lords palatine. Catholics were an inconvenience within the body politic of England, but not, perhaps, in the context of England's colonial ambitions.

4 The Catholic community in early modern England

The focus of this chapter is the internal dynamics and character of the Catholic community itself, including its social composition, the role of devotion and ritual in sustaining English Catholicism, and the organisation and structure of the Catholic church in England. The chapter examines the internal tensions and conflicts within the English Catholic church as well as the broader influence of English Catholicism beyond England's borders. Finally, the chapter considers the continued involvement of Catholics in English society alongside their Protestant neighbours at both local and national level.

The social composition of the Catholic community

The aristocracy played a vital role in the Catholic community. Lawrence Stone estimated that about a fifth of the 121 peers in 1641 were Catholic, although these were perhaps the least important 20 per cent (Questier, 2005: 1). The Catholic peers certainly suffered a loss of political power over the period, but as Questier and others have shown, this was far from absolute, and they provided leadership and protection to the Catholic community. We have already seen the differing contributions of the Brownes in Sussex, the Petres in Essex, and Lord William Howard in the northern counties. To these we can add the ability of the 4th earl of Worcester to sustain Catholicism in Hereford and the Welsh Borders, in conjunction with the powerful gentry Morgan family, and the success of the earl and his successors in helping the Jesuit mission in Wales. The 9th earl of Shrewsbury provided the Jesuits with a house in Clerkenwell, London, for use as a novitiate. In the conflict between seculars who favoured the appointment of a bishop and their Jesuit opponents, it was the support of peers that both sides constantly canvassed (Questier, 2006: 477). Significantly, a list of Jesuit missions in 1609 shows that they were based not on geographical areas but on aristocratic families and their kinsmen.

As John Bossy showed, the gentry were essential to Catholic survival in local communities. In Derbyshire, for example, recusancy can be explained largely in terms of tenants and servants of the leading gentry – the Langfords, the Eyres, and the Fitzherberts. The strength and continuity of the Catholic landlord can be seen in Lincolnshire, where even in the late seventeenth century a third of the

DOI: 10.4324/9781003130376-5

recusants in the Kesteven division of the county came from the parish of Irnham, where the staunchly Catholic Thimelby family had been landlords since the mid-sixteenth century. In Little Crosby in Lancashire the Blundells produced a small Catholic enclave: 'William Blundell is the lord or owner of one small lordship or manor consisting of forty houses or thereabouts, and there are not ... any other but Catholics in it, except peradventure one or two day labourers, which being born in other places, are come to live there for work' (Bossy, 1975: 174–5). The Catholic gentry were of particular importance in those areas, such as East Anglia, where Protestantism was making significant progress by the late sixteenth century. Small Catholic enclaves built up around the gentry homes of Catholics, but the presence of townhouses of Catholic gentry in provincial towns had an even more significant effect on the development of urban Catholicism. Encircled by the homes of Catholic families at Hengrave, Lawshall, and Stanningfield, the Suffolk town of Bury St Edmunds became home to a persistent and resilient Catholic minority consisting of gentry, professionals such as physicians, and 'plebeian' Catholics (Young, 2008: 188–94).

Aveling concluded that non-gentry Catholics made up one-third of Catholics between 1580 and 1603 in Yorkshire, rising to two-thirds by 1615. Of the non-gentry, the richer yeomen farmers were the most important. In the chapelry of Egton in North Yorkshire the leadership of the community fell to the substantial Catholic farmers of the area by the early seventeenth century, as the gentry Cholmley family conformed to the established church. From the 1590s a recusant core of non-gentry had emerged in Egton, such as the farmer John Hodgson, members of the Simpson family of cordwainers, and the widow Burton, all of whom forged links with local recusant gentry throughout the county. The relationship between yeomen and gentry was not one of dependency, but in the isolated communities in the North Yorkshire Moors the only access to mass and Catholic services was likely to be via gentry households. Nevertheless, there were some close-knit yeoman communities. The Hodgsons, mentioned above, were recusant from 1580, most of the marriages in the family were Catholic, and godparents were chosen from a small circle of Catholic neighbours; from the mid-seventeenth century the sons of the family were being sent to Douai for education (Rowlands, 1999: 29–30; Sheils, 1999: 131–52).

A number of Catholics were described as poor; a 1595 return to the Privy Council recorded 223 in the diocese of York and 212 in the archdeaconry of Richmond. It is difficult to know exactly what is meant by 'poor', although some were categorised as vagrants. However, this seems to have included those who were deliberately itinerant such as Robert Young of Wycliffe, Yorkshire, described as a vagrant but 'a conveyor of seminaries from place to place and a persuader to popery' (Hilton, 1999: 117–19).

In York there was still strong religious conservatism among the governing elite in the early years of the new regime. As late as 1573 there was a performance of the medieval Paternoster plays, although the fact that it caused a major dispute was evidence of growing reformist strength on the city council. Furthermore, by the 1570s Catholics were feeling the impact of two strongly Protestant appointments:

Edmund Grindal as archbishop of York (and later Canterbury) and Henry, earl of Huntingdon, as president of the Council of the North. A return of the 90 recusants in the city in 1576 probably reflects the zeal of Huntingdon's investigation rather than any recent increase in Catholic strength. In the 1580s more Catholics were removed from civic office, while in the 1590s there was a more rigorous enforcement of weekly church attendance. By the seventeenth century recusant numbers were declining, despite more lenient presidents of the North. The social composition had changed little since the late 1570s. All social classes were represented, including women, but the most important were the professionals and prosperous tradesmen. A small number of gentry were significant, but now living in the suburbs not the city (Aveling, 1970: 1–76; Sheils, 2009: 77–9).

Catholicism in London shows a different pattern to York. There were few Catholics among the city elite in the 1560s; indeed there was little Catholicism within the walls of the city at any time. Numbers were small, with some 600 recusants between 1580 and 1603, out of a probable population of 200,000. Numbers probably doubled in James's reign, and in the 1630s 3,000 'papists' were said to be in the capital. In the early decades of Elizabeth's reign the Inns of Court were the main focus of Catholic activity, but the situation changed significantly in the 1580s and the 1590s. In these decades, the Elizabethan government brought some of the most prominent Catholic gentry from across the southern counties to London. Many were imprisoned, some suffered house arrest, while others had to confer with Protestant dignitaries.

As a result, geographical clusters of Catholic gentry appeared in the capital. Sir John Arundell was the most prominent of the West Country gentlemen, while Lord William Vaux and Sir Thomas Tresham headed a Midland group. East Anglians included Sir Thomas Cornwallis from Suffolk and members of the Essex Wiseman family. There were prominent Sussex Catholics closely linked to the Browne family and a number of Kentish Catholics. Even when in prison most maintained London households and they tended to live in the same suburbs, especially Clerkenwell and Holborn, although a Midland group converged on Hackney, Hoxton, and Shoreditch in East London. Following the Jesuit mission in 1580, the Thames became a major entry point for seminarists and London a Jesuit base. It was the cooperation between the gentry in London and the seminarists that placed the mission on a sounder footing in the 1580s. That cooperation also laid the foundation for a vigorous Catholic community in London, despite the Elizabethan persecution, and also contributed significantly to a wider community across southern England (Dures, forthcoming).

London Catholicism consisted of more than gentry; indeed, between 1603 and 1630 non-gentry were roughly equal to gentry numbers. Among the non-gentry the largest class, the yeomen, appear to be generally poor, but professionals and tradesmen were relatively wealthy, socially well connected, and contained a number of Catholic activists. The lawyer Arden Waferer operated at least on the fringes of Catholic oppositional politics, being suspected of (though never charged with) involvement in both the Throckmorton and Babington plots. Around the same time in the mid-1580s a grocer, James Taylor, was transporting

Catholic books and letters from the French embassy. In 1620 it was a physician, John Moore, who was in trouble for collecting for the imperial cause in Bohemia, before he was rescued by the intervention of Gondomar, the Spanish Ambassador. There was a small group of tradesmen, headed by long-time recusant Drew Lovett, a goldsmith, who were active Catholics but appear to have operated within their own community of tradesmen. Lovett was described as 'a common Bayle for priests and entertainer of priests'. It appears that one of the vital roles undertaken by this group was to put up bonds and stand surety both for priests and for fellow tradesmen in trouble with the authorities (McClain, 2004: 159–60; Sheils, 2009: 74–6; Dures, forthcoming).

The importance of women in the Catholic community has long been recognised; various explanations have been offered for this. John Bossy suggested that Catholic nonconformity 'appealed especially to English gentlewomen who felt deprived of their functions by the reformation in which literacy was a significant element'. Bossy also stressed the significance of the wife's role in religion, as Catholicism moved from the parish church to the gentry household (Bossy, 1975: 149–68). Keith Thomas, writing more generally of women, suggested that 'women had more time for piety', and women figure prominently in nonconformist groups in the later seventeenth century, not just in Catholicism. Catholic women seemed more willing than men to express the importance of the spiritual over the material and the practical. The most convincing recent explanation is Walsham's stress on church papistry in which the wife was recusant while the husband conformed, a practice that was widely adopted as women were less exposed to heavy financial penalties for recusancy (Rowlands, 1985: 149–66; Rowlands, 2009: 200–8).

The Elizabethan government was well aware of the problem of recusant women, but the issue presented something of a dilemma. To focus exclusively on punishing recusant women appeared to undermine the existing patriarchy, as the male heads of household were responsible for all women under their protection, and married women theoretically owned no property of their own. Nevertheless, by the 1590s the authorities were increasingly concerned about recusant women; in 1590 Robert Cecil, Lord Burghley, on becoming Secretary of State, listed the issue among his major priorities. Richard Topcliffe, the arch-persecutor of Catholics, saw the problem in terms of the character of women: 'whether she be wife, widow or maid or whatever ... far greater is the fever of a woman once resolved to evil than the rage of a man' (Binczewski, 2020: 1). The legislation that eventually had most impact on recusant women was the 1610 'Act for the Administration of the Oath of Allegiance and the Reformation of Married Women Recusants'. A recusant wife who refused the oath was to be jailed, released only on the husband's payment of £10 a month. The issue of illegal baptisms and burials was also raised, and again it was the husband who was fined £100 for each offence, even though, with baptisms in particular, women were likely to be the offenders (Lux-Sterritt, 2011: 537–50).

Women were influential beyond their own household and could have a major impact in their neighbourhood. One obvious role was assisting in childbirth.

The wife of Dr Thomas Vavasour ran a Catholic clinic in York, and Dorothy Lawson also acted as a midwife in her locality. In addition to traditional medicines, Lawson also used relics to comfort the parturient woman and she was always ready to baptise in an emergency. She catechised her neighbours, male as well as female. Her clerical biographer William Palmes noted that 'when any was to be reconcil'd there-about, shee played the catechist, so as I had no other share in the work but to take their confessions'. In effect Lawson was engaged in the kind of missionary work carried out by the seminarists and she was credited with numerous conversions (Lux-Sterritt, 2011: 541).

Widows played a particularly significant role in the Catholic community. This partly stemmed from their economic autonomy, as it appears that widows generally inherited more than the third of their husband's estate required by ecclesiastical law. This was the case with Jane Shelley, widow of William Shelley of Michelgrove, Sussex; the value of her land was estimated at £2,000 a year, and she was one of the very few recusants to pay the full £260-a-year fine. On her death she left a 'large amount' of money for the Jesuit colleges. Widows were important not just for their economic independence; they appear to have been more willing than recusant wives to involve themselves in dangerous activities. However, we have seen that exceptional individuals such as Dorothy Lawson operated well outside the usual confines of the household and the traditional role of the recusant wife. Ann Douce (or Dowse), a widow of gentry status, was listed by the anti-Catholic writer John Gee as a 'famous book seller' and reported by the spy William Uvendale for selling popish books in High Holborn. Despite such close attendance from the authorities, she continued in the trade for some years. Katherine Cash, the widow of a London glazier, was active in helping seminarists and in 1621 was presented 'for labouring [to] seduce others to popish superstition'. Cash, however, was immediately punished for this activity and forced into full conformity, including taking the Protestant communion (Dures, forthcoming).

Widows figure prominently in the dangerous role of harbouring priests. However, they rarely paid the full legal penalties for this offence, with only three women executed against 27 men for harbouring priests (Rowlands, 1985: 158). The feature that characterised women such as the widow Elizabeth Vaux, and the sisters Eleanor Brookesby, widow, and Ann Vaux, spinster, was their total dedication to the Jesuit cause and their close working relationship with the Jesuit clergy, especially John Gerard and Henry Garnet. Gerard appears to have been involved in Elizabeth's search for a suitable residence in Northamptonshire; Gerard wrote 'we searched everywhere for the perfect house but they all had some feature that made them not quite suitable for our purpose' (Binczewski, 2020: 9). Once she acquired a property, Elizabeth Vaux spent some £1,500 on Kirkby Hatton to make it better suited to the harbouring of priests, including the building of a priest hole.

Eleanor Brookesby and Ann Vaux, daughter of the 3rd Baron Vaux, enjoyed the independence and freedom that could be enjoyed not only by a wealthy widow, but also a single woman as long as she had the support of another woman of independent means. Eleanor was active in the earliest days of the

Jesuit mission. Even before her husband's death she entertained Persons and Campion in the Brooksby house at Green Street, East Ham. Once she was widowed in 1581, she moved to the manor house of Great Ashby in Leicestershire and, although she also acquired a Warwickshire home, it was to Great Ashby that Garnet came in 1586. So too did Ann Vaux and 'the widow and the virgin' worked together to establish Great Ashby as a priestly refuge for the next 30 years. In addition, Eleanor gave financial support to Garnet to acquire a variety of temporary residences in London and the country (Connelly, 1997: 160–7).

We owe our knowledge of the Vaux women to accounts by John Gerard and Henry Garnet (Gerard, 2006. Both dwell on the way that women used the accepted view of feminine weakness or modesty to advantage in difficult situations. Because of her closeness to Garnet, Elizabeth was questioned over the Gunpowder Plot, but appealed to Robert Cecil on the grounds that no serious plotter would entrust their secrets to a woman. Garnet relates how Ann Vaux kept early-morning pursuivants at bay by using the received standards of womanly modesty that searchers should not enter the house until women were fit to receive them, thus giving the priests time to hide and the servants the chance to hide their tools of the trade (Lux-Sterritt, 2011: 545).

The crucial role of women in the Catholic community was recognised not only by their clerical supporters but also by their Protestant retractors. The relationship of these Catholic women to the clergy also throws a light on the nature of the community. The Vaux women, for example, showed their independence and freedom in aiding and protecting the Jesuits, but they also received a good deal of clerical guidance, and the clergy had a creative role in the relationship. It has recently been shown that in the case of Ann Vaux ('the virgin'), Garnet carefully crafted a new image of the saintly female; not in the traditional or Tridentine model of enclosed contemplation, but a model of holiness that suited the conditions and needs of the English mission, inspired, of course, by deep faith – yet practical, outward looking, and courageous in the face of adversity. When faced by her adversaries Ann Vaux always conducted 'arguments with such skill and discretion that she certainly counteracts their persistence ... For though she has all a maiden's modesty and even shyness, yet in God's cause and in protection of His servants virgo becomes virago' (Lux-Sterritt, 2011: 546). Garnet's final correspondence with Ann after the Gunpowder Plot shows a genuine bond of mutual trust and affection, but also his determination to direct her vocation to continue her existing work, rather than following her preferred path of becoming a nun: 'I do wish that, if it may be, you and your sister live as before in a house of common repair of the Society, or where the Superiors of the mission shall ordinarily remain' (Lux-Sterritt, 2011: 547).

It is only recently that there has been much focus on the role of youth in the English Catholic community, although as early as 1982 Susan Brigden suggested that by the mid-Elizabethan period Catholicism might have had 'the appeal of an exotic and forbidden fruit' (Brigden, 1982: 67). For some youngsters, the position of Catholicism as enticing and different carried an appeal. Of greater importance, however, was the recognition by parents, priests, and tutors that the vibrancy of the Catholic community depended on the next generation showing a continued commitment to Catholicism. As Elizabeth's reign advanced, educators focused especially on the young and 'a significant level of enthusiasm for Catholicism among children and young people was thereby aroused and maintained' (Shell, 2005: 190; Underwood, 2014: 160–1).

Catholic youths might receive an education through a variety of channels, most of which carried risk or disadvantages. The most complete Catholic education was to be found abroad, with boys attending schools at Douai or St Omer or elsewhere, while girls attended schools attached to English convents. These schools might see the completion of a youngster's education, or act as a preparation for the priesthood or becoming a nun. Travelling abroad was hazardous, but having a Catholic tutor at home or attending an illicit Catholic school in England also carried obvious dangers. The safest option, attending the local grammar school, exposed Catholic youths to heretical teachings and practices. George and Edward Jerningham, from a strongly Catholic East Anglian family, were regularly beaten at school for their refusal to attend Protestant services or to 'eat flesh on Fridays and fasting days' (Underwood, 2013: 515).

There appears to have been a strong emphasis on the religious upbringing of young children. The degree of recusancy among the children is striking, even though the minimum legal age for recusancy was 16. In 1569 a northern report on recusants included the children of Edward Probin, 'Majorie about six and Mary about 14 years old'. Some youths appear to have had an early awareness of early recusancy. In 1593 Robert Lincoln, then aged 24, and Edward Chester (also in his twenties) both told the Protestant authorities that they had not attended Anglican church since they were eight years old. For a number of young people recusancy was the default position, based on parental authority. In 1598, when the daughters of John Fortescue were examined, the girls argued that they 'never came to church neither intendeth to come' as they had been otherwise brought up. This could also be the case with the children of church papists; Thomas Lane of Fishbourne, Sussex, was presented in 1626 because 'he cometh to church himself but suffereth not his son John Lane and Ann Lane his daughter to come to divine service' (Underwood, 2013: 512–15).

For some young people, however, childhood recusancy was not the norm as their Catholic identity came through conversion. In the early seventeenth century a significant number of those entering the seminaries in Rome and Valladolid described themselves as converts. This included some whose parents were conformist Catholics but who considered that the process of moving from such a background to a supplicant for admission to seminary involved conversion. This was the case with three Fisher brothers, who entered the English College in Rome between 1598 and 1601. As with other youths, George Fisher appears to have been inspired by the Wisbech priests. His conversion involved some rejection of parental guidance and his social circle as 'by the inspiration of the holy spirit [he] left father mother and all his friends' to enter the seminary at Douai. The Wisbech priests not only inculcated a commitment to Catholicism in Robert Colton, 'a poor lad', but also instruction in answering his Protestant interrogators. Colton justified his recusancy by arguing that 'England hath been a Catholic Christian country a thousand years afore this queen's reign and her fathers' (Underwood, 2013: 457).

Devotion and ritual

The mass was the central act of Catholic worship and its centrality continued to be stressed by Elizabethan writers. The mass was a means of attaining God's saving grace, as well as bringing believers attending mass to an identification with Christ. Laurence Vaux in his *Catechism* wrote that 'the effect of this sacrament is to knit, join and incorporate the worthily receivers therefore unto Christ'. Robert Southwell, recognising in the late 1580s that access to mass was very limited for Catholics, worried over their 'sacred hunger' (McClain, 2004: 113–15).

In the 1560s, however, some Catholics were able to maintain the central ritual of their faith within the parish church. Conformist Marian priests contrived to ensure that this parish communion resembled the mass, despite the use of Cranmer's rubric (Walsham, 2011: 104), and it was even alleged that in some northern parishes the priest would say mass for the Catholic parishioners after performing the Protestant rite. By the 1570s, however, mass was only available in households or other places such as prisons, barns, or inns. In certain households, mass could be celebrated in a traditional manner and on a lavish scale. In Lady Magdalen Montague's chapel at Battle in Sussex, 'on solemn feasts the sacrifice of the mass was celebrated with singing and musical instruments, and sometimes also with deacon and subdeacon. And such was the concourse and resort of Catholics, that sometimes there were 120 together' (Questier, 2006: 215).

Dorothy Lawson hosted the mass and celebrated all manner of Catholic feasts in her Northumberland household, as well as providing hospitality for all those attending. In July 1586 William Weston described a flourishing Catholic community in which not only mass but the sacraments were available at the house of the Lancashire Catholic Richard Bold. '[T]he place was most suited to our work ... not merely for the reason that it was remote ... but also because it possessed a chapel, set aside for the celebration of the church's offices ... Mr Byrd, the very famous musician and organist was among the company ... Father Gerard sometimes sang mass, and we took it in turns to preach and hear confessions, which were numerous' (Weston, 1955: 7).

It seems unlikely there were many Catholic households where traditional worship centred on the mass and sacraments was regularly available. However, in the 1630s some Catholics in London had access to worship and ritual in conditions similar to Counter-Reformation Europe. Catholics could attend mass in the baroque splendour of Queen Henrietta Maria's chapel at Somerset House, or the scarcely less grand chapels of the Spanish embassy or the papal agent. The sacraments, too, were available, including marriage (perhaps only for the particularly favoured) and regular baptisms at the queen's chapel. For the most part the mass and the sacraments were administered in more humble locations. The Benedictine priest Ambrose Barlow used a barn and cottages to say mass in the 1620s and 1630s in Lancashire. In the Welsh Marches mass was said at secret locations at night, the equipment brought in 'mail and cloak' bags.

It was prisons, however, which became some of the most important centres for Catholic worship and devotion. Thomas Bell, the seminary priest, broke into York Castle prison in 1582 and remained there for two weeks. During this time the priest offered mass daily, heard confessions, preached sermons, and even sang full high mass with deacon, subdeacon, and music (Lake and Questier, 1998: 201). London prisons were probably even more significant as devotional centres given the large number of priests in prison there, joined at times by a number of important Catholic gentlemen as fellow inmates. For example, there were between 25 and 30 priests in the Marshalsea at any one time, and at different times Newgate had 55 and the Clink 51 (Lake and Questier, 1998: 200).

Catholic devotions were not just attended by priest and gentry prisoners but Catholics from outside the prisons. In 1583 the complaint is about the 'youth of London' going to the Marshalsea; in 1606 it is 'diverse of all sorts' in Newgate; while in 1625 it is 'vulgar papists' who attend mass in New Prison. New Prison appears to have been the focus of particular attention in 1625. There was a spy report complaining of 31 daily masses 'in 14 several chambers', said 'for the prosperity of the emperor and the confusion of Bohemia'. It appears that on at least one occasion full traditional Catholic vestments were worn and ritualistic objects used; in New Prison in 1625 the priest was accompanied by a tailor 'with a censer perfuming the roome and sensing the same (as they use in popish masses)'. Not surprisingly, in a submission to Parliament of the same year, New Prison was described as 'not any other thinge then a mere collage and nursery to encourage and cherish popery' (British Museum MS Lansdown, 38 no 87, SP 16/22/11). London prisons were 'centres of ritual and community'.

Despite the separation of Catholics from the parish church and their limited access to priests, works of devotion continued to focus on the centrality of the mass and Eucharist. Vaux's *Catechism*, printed eight times between 1568 and 1620, instructed Catholics to attend mass every Sunday and holy day to help assure their salvation. The Eucharist, of all sacraments, was particularly efficacious: 'this blessed sacrament is a pledge to bring us everlasting life'. This was conventional teaching on the Eucharist, reinforced by Trent and the Jesuit stress on its more frequent reception; but it was increasingly difficult for Catholics to practice this ideal in Elizabethan England.

By the early seventeenth century seminary priests tried to offer spiritual guidance for the many without regular access to the mass and the sacraments. In 1605 John Radford, a seminary priest from Derbyshire, argued that it was possible to receive the mass and the Eucharist spiritually rather than corporally, that is without the recipient being physically present at mass. Radford stressed that all men share in the sin of Adam so all, through belief, could share in the benefits of the mass. The Jesuit William Stanney, in his 1617 *A Treatise on Penance*, also confronts the issue of Catholics lacking access to a priest; such Catholics should examine their consciences thoroughly and their deep belief would instil 'a fervent desire to receive spiritually their Sweet Saviour in the Holy sacrament of the Altar' (McClain, 2004: 118–20).

Rites of passage presented difficulties for Catholics once they were separated from their parishes. It is difficult to know how many Catholics settled for a christening in the parish church, especially as the validity of Protestant christening was recognised by the Catholic authorities; for some Catholics, however, the prospect of a Protestant christening was troublesome. Giles Nanfan, a Worcestershire Catholic, confided to a friend 'I am in great distresse for Christning my Children I haue sent Divers wayes & can light of none if you can helpe me I shall be much bounde to you' (Underwood, 2014: 15). One mother, Elizabeth Fairhair, solved the problem by christening her children herself, but ended up in prison. A more high-profile case was that of the 2nd Viscount Montague who christened his daughter, provoking the wrath of the Elizabethan authorities and his father-in-law, Lord Buckhurst. The ideal was baptism by a Catholic priest, but this carried obvious difficulties, including a possible wait for an itinerant priest, especially dangerous in an age of such high infant mortality. One Welsh mother in 1591 took the initiative by carrying her newly born to a disused chapel of the Cistercian monastery at Margam where a seminarist, Morgan Clynnog, performed the Catholic ritual (Walsham, 2009: 112). In the same year the Jesuit Robert Southwell stressed how precarious it could be to ensure a Catholic christening, reporting that 'when their [Catholic] wives are great [with child] they are forced to shift them from place to place to conceale their lying in, lest their children be christened heretically'. In York there were better arrangements to avoid 'hieratical christenings'. At the home of Dorothy Vavasour, wife of the recusant prisoner Dr Thomas Vavasour, mother and infant were well looked after 'both for the time of delivery, the christening of their children, and recovery of their health again' (Underwood, 2014: 15).

The issue of burial was equally important – but different, as Catholics strove to be buried in the local churchyard. As Christopher Haigh notes, 'at the very end everyone wanted a Christian burial – and the Church of England had all the graveyards' (Haigh, 2007: 6). For most of Elizabeth's reign attempts to exclude Catholics from churchyards appear to have been minimal. However, in 1606 new legislation laid down that all convicted recusants should be 'reputed to all intents and purposes as duly excommunicated' and there was a drive to excommunicate non-communicants among church papists. Up to this point many Catholics, certainly in the northwest, carried out traditional customs at home, pausing at wayside crosses, before a burial in the local churchyard without, it was hoped, the rites of the established church being performed. Night-time burials had obvious advantages; in Hathersage in Derbyshire there were 13 night-time burials of excommunicated Catholics between 1629 and 1631.

It is difficult to know how far the Protestant clergy were tacitly involved in Catholics being buried without the Protestant rites. Alice Wellington from Allensore in Herefordshire was buried before sunrise in Whitsun week 1605, and although the vicar saw the procession of some 40 or 50 persons from his bedroom, he was too late to intervene. In 1603 Thomas Cletheray was buried at Drypool in the East Riding 'by meanes of Henry Garrat without the minister and without the order of burial by lawe' (Marshall, 2012: 61). At Christchurch in Hampshire in 1604 it was simply recorded that 'Christian Stevens, wife of Thomas was buried in childbirth and buried by women, for she was a papiste'. However, in some places the vicar and Protestant neighbours were involved in Catholic burials. At Childwall in Lancashire in 1611 the vicar conceded 'that all neighbours go one with another to their burials'. This was certainly the case with the funeral of Dorothy Lawson. The day was marked by the lavish entertainment of neighbours, both Catholic and Protestant, before a flotilla of more than 20 boats accompanied the corpse upriver to Newcastle. The local Protestant dignitaries went as far as the door of the church where 'they delivered it [the corpse] to Catholicks only' to place in the grave (Palmes, 1851: 58–61; Marshall, 2012: 58–61; Walsham, 2009: 111–12; McClain, 2004: 205).

Many seminary priests in fact provided guidance on adapting Catholic devotion and ritual to post-Reformation conditions. Robert Southwell in his *A Shorte Rule of Good Lyfe* suggested that Catholics could create sacred spaces out of their ordinary surroundings. Dorothy Lawson, even with her model Catholic household, extended her sacred spaces by dedicating all her rooms save the chapel to particular saints. Southwell stressed that almost any physical space could be made sacred including woods, fields, and gardens so that walks were 'short pilgrimages to visit such saints as are patrons of the place'. Other Catholics covertly continued to visit more traditional sites of pilgrimage. For northern Catholics, the Holy Island of Lindisfarne was a favourite, while in the south the dissolved Benedictine abbey at Glastonbury attracted visitors. The sites of ruined monasteries (including lady chapels) were popular, and in 1614 the High Commission prosecuted 30 recusants from Yorkshire who were praying on the eve of the Nativity of the Virgin Mary at the remains of the Lady Chapel of the former Carthusian priory of Mount Grace. Some poorer papists imaginatively reconstructed the most ordinary of spaces and objects to perform a traditional ritual. In Golborne, Lancashire, during Holy Week 1604, a group met in the house of Peter Croncke. With the use of a basin topped by a broken cross, the company 'did creep' across the floor emulating the Good Friday ritual of creeping to the cross (McClain, 2004: 55–60; Walsham, 2009: 113–14; Walsham, 2011: 189–217).

One traditional devotion which received renewed focus was the rosary, and in both Britain and Holland it became a marker of Catholic identity. The rosary had considerable practical advantages; the 'beads' could easily be concealed about the person. Some, such as Lady Magdalen Montague, had the luxury of being able to proclaim their Catholic identity without suffering the consequences, and could wear them round their neck. Rosary saying could be an act of individual devotion and spiritual reflection, but a range of Catholic writers, including William Allen and Henry Garnet, stressed the advantages of communal rosary devotion in the formation of confraternities. Such rosary confraternities had the advantage of having a papal indulgence attached to membership, with Henry Garnet presenting them as 'a most holesome medicine and comfortable sanctuary' (Walsham, 2009: 106). Furthermore, the rosary was seen as a means of invoking the aid of the Virgin Mary now that the Protestant

Reformation had gradually eliminated all forms of Marian devotion. Henry Garnet sent detailed instructions to sodalities reinforcing traditional Catholic teaching on Mary as a powerful intercessor with God; Garnet also saw the sodalities as a means of invoking the aid of the Virgin Mary for 'rooting out heresie ... the beades must be to our afflicted brethren, in steed of all manner of armour or weapons' (Walsham, 2009: 106).

The sodalities went beyond the recitation of the rosary. Under Jesuit guidance, laymen and -women met together to follow a programme of prayer and conduct charitable works, inspired by their joint devotion to the rosary. This devotion is found in the English Catholic community and among the English nuns in Europe, and more generally among European Catholics. A wide variety of texts supporting the rosary emanated from the major European printing presses. In 1598 *A methode to meditate upon the psalter, or the great rosarie of our blessed Ladie*, printed in Antwerp, combined a text for the literate with pictures for those who could not read. In around 1609 John Fenn, chaplain to the English nuns in Louvain, translated the Italian Jesuit Gaspar Loarte's *How to Meditate the Mysteries of the Rosarie of the Most Holy Virgin Mary*, adding to the growing number of texts which aided rosary devotion. These texts, directed at communities or sodalities, brought a medieval practice into line with the ideal of the Counter-Reformation (Walker, 2009: 149–50).

The *Agnus Dei* was another important sacramental and one that carried more political connotations than the rosary. The *Agnus Dei* had been a popular devotional aid in England and Europe since the eleventh century. It was a precious devotional object, often kept by religious houses as well as families and was thought to ward off many dangers of everyday life. *Agni Dei* were made by the papal apothecary and consecrated by a new pope or every seven years during Holy Week and then distributed as gifts. Although in the reign of Henry VIII there had been polemical attacks on the *Agnus Dei* as 'trash' and 'trumpery', it was only in 1571 that there was a ban on the *Agnus Dei* in England and their continued use was declared treasonous. This was in response to the excommunication of Elizabeth by Pope Pius V; the possession of an *Agnus Dei*, consecrated by the pope, suggested that the recipient of such an object acknowledged the supremacy of Rome and its implications for the English queen. The response to the 1571 ban on the *Agnus Dei* appears to have been an increase in attempts to smuggle it into England, possibly due to production of a new batch with the installation of Pope Gregory XIII in 1572. Initially the Jesuits were forbidden by order of their superior from bringing into England any devotional objects such as the *Agnus Dei*, which were proscribed by the English government. This prohibition was soon relaxed and the Jesuits became major promoters of the *Agnus Dei*, which were also common on their missions in the Upper Palatine and France.

The *Agnus Dei* was a mark of Catholic identity. However, both Rome and the seminary priests were generally keen to play down the 'miraculous' powers of sacramentals; the aim of the *Agnus Dei* was spiritual efficacy through contemplation and was dependent on the disposition of the recipient. The *Agnus Dei* also acquired political significance, and in 1591 the Privy Council noted that wearers of the *Agnus Dei* must have been reconciled to the Catholic church. The miraculous qualities of the *Agnus Dei* were established through narratives such as that of Nicholas Sander in 1572, who recounted how, at a trial in Oxford of recusants prosecuted for possession of crucifixes and *Agni Dei*, a mysterious illness struck down the judge along with some 300 others, many of them Puritans (Muller, 2018: 1–28; McClain, 2004: 106–7).

The removal of images and the visual from churches after 1558 and the gradual separation of Catholics from their parish church meant that some of the greatest aids to Catholic devotion were lost. Religious paintings and images had to be adapted and changed to meet the needs of households and other locations including prisons. As these were objects of suspicion to Protestant authorities, this adaptation tended to include flexibility and moveability. In households, images could still be on an elaborate scale, such as the large painted plaster relief of the crucifixion set high in the closet of Rushton Hall, the home of Sir Thomas Tresham. It seems likely that the sculpture served as a reredos for the celebration of mass. Tresham spent much of his life in the 1580s and 1590s in various prisons where he continued to show a devotion to the crucifixion, but also a certain flexibility; when the guards in the bishop's palace at Ely in 1597 washed out the wall paintings of the crucifixion, Tresham decided to paint elaborate symbolic paintings on cloth so they could easily be removed from the wall (Young, 2014: 207). Tresham derived much of this symbolism from the Christian Cabala, demonstrating the extent to which some English Catholics were prepared to venture well beyond traditional medieval piety into more esoteric strands of Catholic thought (Young, 2020: 145–68).

Although some families treasured medieval relics, most Catholic images originated in Europe and many were brought to England by the seminary priests. One of the most common images was the printed devotional picture. The Jesuit William Weston was possibly referring to such a print when he described how 'pictures of Saints' were attached to the wall of his cell in the Clink prison; they could act as a reredos with a table as an altar (Williams, 2009: 235). What gave these pictures and other objects particular value to the Catholics was that most had been consecrated by the pope or senior clergy (Williams, 2009: 237). Woodcuts and engraved pictures in books were mainly printed in Antwerp, Louvain, and Rouen, and many focused on the mass. Thomas Heskins' *The Parliament of Christ* (1566) depicted scenes of the mass, its inauguration at the Last Supper with the veneration of the host at its centre, and there were more illustrations particularly of the life and death of Christ on the cross. The illiterate, too, were catered for in John Fowler's *Godly Contemplation for the Unlearned* with its 62 woodcuts.

From the mid-1570s books of a devotional rather than polemical character began to dominate the English market. The most popular of these was *The Manual of Prayer*. Printed in Rouen in 1583, it went through 28 editions by 1642. It provided a comprehensive list of prayers for daily devotion, prayers for the dead and the dying, prayers to the saints and for the intercession of the church. Compiled by an English merchant, George Flinton, it drew heavily on the work of Simon Vereept, a Brabantine schoolmaster, but also included early Tudor writers with prayers by Thomas More, Cuthbert Tunstall, and Richard Whitford (Duffy, 2016: 206–25). However, the 'superstitious books' confiscated from Elizabeth and Bridget in 1586 suggests that English Catholics had access to a wide range of devotional and spiritual works, including major authors of Counter-Reformation Europe. The sisters had English translations of the Italian Jesuit Gaspar Loarte's *Exercise of a Christian Life* and the Spanish Dominican Luis de Granada's *Memorial of a Christian Life*. The works of Luis de Granada had a significant impact on the Catholic reform movement across Europe, and were translated into Italian, French, German, and Greek. In England his books were 'nothing less than bestsellers', as popular with Protestants as Catholics (Walsham, 2016: 129–54; Duffy, 2016: 207).

The popularity of John Foxe's *Acts and Monuments*, celebrating the Protestant martyrs of Mary's reign, already ensured that martyrdom was part of confessional identity in Elizabethan England. For Catholics, soon after the execution of Cuthbert Mayne in 1577, the discovery in Rome of the catacomb cemeteries of Via Salaria Nuova in 1578 marked a new chapter in the history of martyrdom. The catacomb findings confirmed the importance of martyrdom as part of an unbroken succession of saints stretching back to antiquity. The renewed focus on martyrdom is particularly apparent in the Jesuit colleges, especially those preparing priests for dangerous locations such as England, parts of Germany, and Hungary. The English College in Rome produced a cycle of martyrs painted in the 1580s by Niccolo Circignani, which included not only Christian martyrs but also British saints beginning with St Alban (d. 305 CE) through to Thomas Becket (d. 1170) and ending in Edmund Campion (Graffius, 2019: 113–14).

English Catholics were ready to embrace medieval saints and martyrs, and Becket in particular. Becket's death at the instigation of King Henry II in 1170, and the desecration of Becket's shrine in Canterbury on the order of Henry VIII in 1538, made the cult of St Thomas particularly appropriate. John Gerard commented on the status of relics of Becket in Catholic households, while fellow Jesuit Henry Garnet felt he was under the protection of St Thomas on arrival in England. William Allen saw Becket as an exemplary defender of the rights of the church against the state. Allen also placed Thomas More, John Fisher, and Edmund Campion alongside St Thomas Becket, since they had all sacrificed their lives for their faith against a hostile state. This association of the early sixteenth-century Catholic martyrs with the officially recognised Becket made it easier to accept as martyrs those executed for their faith in the 1580s and 1590s (Gibbons, 2009: 315–24). Similarly, some Catholics identified with the martyr king and traditional patron saint of England, St Edmund, and both St Thomas and St Edmund appeared in a painting above the main altar in the English College, Rome (Young, 2018: 126–32).

A common theme in martyrologies is the *imitatio Christi* (imitation of Christ), walking in the footsteps of Christ who through his shedding of blood saved sinful man. In the poem 'Why do I use my paper, ink and pen' the author writes that 'the seede will take which in such blood is sowne'. The priest John Cecil, present at the execution of the priest John Boste in York in 1594, reported that when the 300 women who were following the condemned priest were asked by the authorities why they were present, they answered: 'to accompany that gentleman, that servant of God, to his death as the Maries did Christ'. 'The Maries' refers to Jesus's mother Mary and Mary Magdalen (McClain, 2004: 74). John Mush in his *Life of Margaret Clitheroe* draws on the similarities between the death of the martyr and that of Jesus. Clitheroe spent three days alone kneeling in prayer in preparation for her execution, as Jesus knelt in the garden of Gethsemane. Both walked through crowded streets towards their death, in Clitheroe's case, 'a street that was so full of people that she could scarce pass by them' (McClain, 2004: 129–30).

The sites of Catholic executions, the relics of martyrs and the miracles associated with them, as well as the texts and communications circulating on the martyrs, were all crucial in forming the religious identity of the Catholic community. Tyburn became a pilgrimage site for Londoners; in Holy Week of 1626, Henrietta Maria made an ostentatious pilgrimage to Tyburn, and miraculous powers were associated with relics and eagerly sought by Catholics. The portrait of Henry Garnet, executed after the Gunpowder Plot, was said to have appeared on a bloodstained ear of corn obtained from the gallows. The relic was subsequently placed in a reliquary and produced a number of miraculous cures for illnesses and was used as an aid to childbirth.

All executions attracted relic-hunters or even those who created relics such as the men and women who dipped their handkerchiefs in the blood of Robert Southwell's disembowelled body. Protestants dismissed all relics as 'fopperies and fooleries', but William Allen saw such relic-hunting as 'the godly greedy appetite'. Such an appetite was on display at the execution of the seminary priest Thomas Maxwell at Tyburn on 1 July 1616. The London sheriff, learning from the experience of previous Catholic executions, banned the followers of the martyr from taking anything from the gallows under pain of imprisonment. Despite such a warning, Maxwell's faithful followers returned at night and dug up his body from underneath two rotting corpses and rescued his head and body parts 'to carrie them away to be kept with honour and veneration' (Walsham, 2018: 83). In a clear indication that the cult of martyrdom had a European dimension, Maxwell's body was embalmed by the Spanish ambassador, who in 1618 took the head and the bones to the Spanish Franciscan Convent of St Simon on the Island of Redondela. As was common, the relic appears to have been broken up; Maxwell's right hand found its way to the church of St Lorenzo in Santiago, while Count Gondamar, the Spanish Ambassador, acquired some of the remains (Walsham, 2018: 84).

The devotional life of the post-Reformation English Catholic community was in many ways an adaptation of medieval practices, operating outside the structure of the national church, and under considerable restrictions. In other ways it brought in practices previously unknown in the English church, like theatrical exorcisms performed by priests to display the power of the Catholic church (Young, 2013: 203–9) [*Doc. 15*, p. 131]. Some practices, such as fasting, fitted readily into this new world. John Bossy stressed the central role of fasting for the English Catholic community, and despite criticism from some Jesuits of the dangers of the excessive focus on fasting, it remained important in many gentry households. Richard Smith, confessor to Lady Montague, observed that even in her sixties (beyond the age for fasting) she observed 'all the fasts of Lent, the Ember days and whatsoever others were either commanded by pious custom of the country' (Bossy, 1975: 48). Lord Philip Howard continued his regular fasting in the Tower, probably one of the few Catholic rituals possible in the only secure prison in the county [*Doc. 16*, p. 131–2]. However, it seems unlikely that fasting extended down the social scale beyond the gentry, and even when the children of the gentry left the familial household, the observance of fast days could be problematic.

There was a creative response of practising Catholicism in a Protestant country. Without access to traditional shrines, medieval holy sites were sought out and new sacred spaces created. With devotion to the Virgin officially banned, Catholics focused their Marian devotion on an increased use of the rosary. Even where mass was possible, the full visual support in terms of reredos and altarpieces was often difficult, but prints and pasteboard pictures were used instead. Except in the large gentry households, priests were not readily available to provide spiritual guidance, but a plethora of texts, including some illustrations for the poor, acted as 'dumb preachers' for the faithful. In this process of adaptation certain features stand out. Operating outside a formerly structured church and subject to a host of limiting laws, Catholics had to practise their faith according to personal circumstances and to develop a more personal piety and spirituality.

However, this shift towards more personal devotional practices was strongly guided and directed by the seminary priests. It was Robert Southwell and Henry Garnet, among others, who encouraged the formation of confraternities for rosary saying, so turning an individual act of devotion into a communal one. The seminarists provided supporting texts for the rosary and other devotions, so providing a common spiritual programme. Sacramentals and visual material were more valued when they came with a papal or clerical blessing, so the role of the seminary priest was vital. Given that the seminarists emanated from a variety of European colleges, this alone would have ensured English Catholicism was very much part of the wider European Catholic Reformation. The integration of English and European devotional practices was widespread. Recent work has shown that there were networks through which English relics were transported and exchanged throughout Europe. We have noted that the most popular English prayer book, *Manual of Prayers*, was a product of Brabantine and English sources, while the books of Luis de Granada were best sellers in England and Europe. In their own distinctive ways, English devotional practices developed within the context of Counter-Reformation Europe.

The Catholic community and English society

John Bossy's model of the Catholic community posited the idea of a new creative force in the 1570s, fashioned by Douai and its seminary priests and further refined by the Jesuit mission after 1580. Christopher Haigh immediately made a number of critical points in response; one of the strongest was his argument that the 1570s did not represent a sharp break in English Catholicism; there was in fact a strong continuity between pre-Elizabethan Catholicism and its patterns of development up to the Civil War (Dures, 1983: 25–6). Some of Bossy's other ideas about the nature of the Catholic community were equally significant to his emphasis on its novel character. Bossy argued that recusancy gradually emerged as the core characteristic of their community and consequently Catholics were increasingly separated from English society and political life. By the seventeenth century this Catholic body was essentially inward looking, a branch of nonconformity and also political quietist. The most important recent scholarship, however, especially the work of Questier, Sheils, and Walsham, has challenged the idea that the Catholic community was essentially inward looking and separated from English social and political life (Questier, 2006; Questier, 1996; Sheils, 2009: 67–83; Walsham, 1999; Walsham, 2012: 29–55).

As we have seen, there was an increase in recusancy from the 1570s, and over time recusants were less likely than their Protestant neighbours to hold local office or to be involved in national politics. However, it was somewhat different for church papists, and Walsham in particular has given a new emphasis to church papists, who are now seen as a large and vital element in the Catholic community. As William Sheils has noted, 'Recent scholarship has suggested that three quarters of all Catholics in England and Wales between 1570–1640 adopted a church papist position, making it the most common experience of Catholics in this period' (Sheils, forthcoming). Church papists in particular continued to interact with their Protestant neighbours, and it needs to be stressed that recusants and church papists were not totally distinct, unchanging groups; consequently, the boundaries between confessional communities were blurred rather than sharply defined.

This point is reinforced by Questier's emphasis on the importance of conversions across both confessions. While those moving to the Protestant faith might expect to benefit materially, this was by no means the only motivation. Antony Tyrrell, probably best known as an apostate priest, experienced a good deal of mental turmoil in his frequent conversions, as he changed religion in 1584, 1587 (twice), 1588 (twice), and 1605. When he decided to reject Catholicism in 1588, his recantation sermon focused on the expulsion of unclean spirts, influenced no doubt by his experience of assisting the Jesuit William Weston in his exorcism (Questier, 1996: 56, 175–6). By contrast, Sir Henry James converted as a reaction to the Gunpowder Plot, but five years later he was a recusant again. Toby Matthew junior, son of the archbishop of York, appears to have had a steady untroubled conversion. He experienced a number of influences on his path to Rome, but the final stage was his attendance at the Lenten sermon in Florence where 'it pleases his Divine Majesty to alter the object of [his] eyes, which till then had wandered through the corners of the world' (Questier, 1996: 181).

It is church papists, however, who are now recognised as the most important group in the Catholic community. They were frequently decried by contemporaries on both sides of the confessional divide: by Protestants as 'dissimulators' and therefore perhaps to be more mistrusted than recusants, while to some Catholic clergy they were lukewarm Catholics unwilling to follow proper spiritual guidance and at risk of embracing heresy. In reality most church papists were thoroughly Catholic but took up the position as a means of social and economic survival. Church papists were as likely as recusants to send their children to the Continent for a Catholic education. Protestants, in their drive against Catholics, seldom drew a distinction between church papists and recusants. For example, the authorities in the diocese of Hereford admitted that the lawyer Ambrose Griffith was a conformist, 'an half Recusant' but 'a dangerous man' because 'though he goeth to the church yet he runeth the Jesuites' courses most violently' (Walsham, 1999: 81).

The most likely church papist was the male head of household with a recusant wife, recusant children, and recusant servants, as these would not incur anything like the financial penalties of the head of household. Other means than church papistry could be used to avoid the financial penalties of recusancy, but they carried risks. The lands and goods of a recusant could be placed in trust of a third party, but this could lead to a dispute over possession, and the practice was outlawed in 1610. Some Catholics, such as Nicholas Timperley of Hintlesham in Suffolk, obtained a false certificate of conformity to present to the bishop. However, after a prolonged case in Star Chamber, it appears that Timperley conformed, but he managed to avoid a public affirmation of his church papistry. John Grove, a clerk at the Exchequer, ran a small business for a time producing fraudulent certificates of conformity for presentation to the bishop of London. Such practices appear to be very limited, but along with Timperley's pleading in Star Chamber, they do suggest that some Catholics were reluctant to become church papists.

For many, church papistry was not entered into lightly but out of necessity. This judgement is reinforced by the fact that a number of Catholics escaped the harshest penalties by occasional conformity, and some showed scant respect for divine service when they attended. Sir Thomas Cornwallis sat reading a Lady Psalter while others were on their knees in prayer at Brome in Suffolk, while Sir Nicholas Gerard loudly chanted Latin psalms during the service at Etwall, Derbyshire. Conformity could be very occasional. In East Anglia Mr George Dimley and his servants never came to church 'but at Christmas', according to 1595 episcopal recusancy returns. In the same year, a Lancashire Protestant was warning of gentlemen papists who never attended divine service except 'for one Sundaye or two before the assizes' (Walsham, 1999: 75, 90).

There was an acceptance of occasional conformity, even among the Catholic clergy. John Gerard admitted that many practised their religion 'precisely' only when 'circumstances permitted'. When a period of greater persecution arrived then church papistry increased (Walsham, 1999: 76). However, the fact that church papists often figure strongly among non-communicants suggests that the flexibility of their Catholic consciences had strict limitations and, in Walsham's words, the participation in the Protestant communion was equivalent to 'crossing a spiritual Rubicon' (Walsham, 2012: 33). Some church papists, such as William Lenthall of North Leigh in Oxfordshire, explained that though he had 'reformed' himself on church attendance, he was not yet satisfied in conscience about communion. Thomas Wintringham of Skeffling in Yorkshire went further; he not only declined the communion at Christmas 1595 but 'did mocke and floute at them that did receive' (Walsham, 2012: 35).

Church papistry was an essential element within the Catholic community; indeed, in many ways it was at its heart, ensuring the survival of aristocratic and gentry recusancy. Families such as the Meymelles of North Kilvington in Yorkshire survived the period with their Catholicism and estates intact through well-timed outward conformity to the established church. This would also appear to have been the case for yeomen and artisans. Owen Wilbram, a smith by trade from Malpas in Cheshire, attended his parish church while his wife and two daughters and their housemaid were recusants. It has been argued that such arrangements might even have been more important for the 'middling sort' than for the Catholic gentry, as their economic position and social standing were more vulnerable to the penalties of recusancy than their social superiors (Walsham, 1999: 78).

The active involvement of Catholics with their Protestant neighbours is further evidence of a Catholic community that was far from inward looking or separated from wider society. In some circumstances church papistry was important as it enabled Catholics to maintain more easily their influence in the parish, especially in areas of religious conservatism such as Yorkshire. As Sarah Bastow has argued, with the parish as the focal point of the local community, a gentleman's presence at church was important as part of his controlling role in the community. Catholic families, especially those with elements of church papistry, were able to maintain ownership of church property and even advowsons (the right to present a new incumbent); in such parishes even known recusants were less likely to be prosecuted (Bastow, 2002: 204–17). In some cases, known recusancy did not mean exclusion from parish affairs. Richard Cholmley, a North Yorkshire recusant, continued to use his parish church (or at least the church porch) to conduct his business. Another confirmed recusant, Richard Shanne of Methley, West Yorkshire, continued to participate in communal customs such as the perambulation and rush bearing round the parish in the early seventeenth century. During the festivities he distributed cakes, beer, and ale to the Protestant clergy, choristers, and people who stopped by his residence (Walsham, 2012: 51).

Socialising across the confessional divide appears to have been common, at least in certain areas, as Catholics strove to maintain the traditional standards of hospitality expected of the gentry. William Middleton of Stockeld in Yorkshire was esteemed as 'a man who kept a good house' and he continued to entertain his neighbours despite heavy recusancy fines. The same was true of John Vavasour of Hazlewood Castle, who was described by one visitor as 'the only great and bountiful housekeeper in the north' (Cliffe, 1969: 224). The practice of hospitality was sufficiently widespread to draw comment and theological guidance from both Protestant and Catholic clerics. The Puritan William Perkins emphasised the risk of becoming intimate with 'the limbs of the Antichrist', but he recognised that mixing with the 'profane and unregenerate' in worldly matters was almost unavoidable. On the Catholic side there was guidance for the gentry which formed part of the training for priests at English seminaries. This focused on precise issues such as whether it was acceptable for Catholics to remove their hats as a sign of reverence at schismatic prayer or whether they needed to leave. The answer to this and suchlike queries was that good manners should generally triumph, though this had to be balanced against seeming to condone heresy. Such clerical endorsement can also be found in Henry Garnet's *Apologie against the Defence of Schism* (1593), which recognised that social interaction was an important factor in helping to maintain a Catholic presence in the social life of the local community (Walsham, 2012: 46–7).

Bill Sheils has provided a distinctive insight into this interaction between Catholics and their Protestant neighbours. He has shown that in communities such as the North Riding parish of Egton, where, in the early seventeenth century, almost a third of the adult population (including substantial farmers and tradesmen) were Catholic, both Protestants and Catholics recognised the need to maintain communal harmony. It was essential for the functioning of the community that Catholics undertook their share of parochial responsibilities such as involvement in poor relief and law enforcement. Thus in Egton, with its large Catholic minority and no strong Protestant leadership, pragmatism prevailed: Protestants had to 'get along' with their Catholic neighbours. The pragmatism appears to have been at work in the churchwardens' return of Catholics in response to the episcopal visitation of 1615. A number of Catholics were reported in line with the parish's reputation. However, the return included a high proportion of the elderly, women, and single men, but few heads of household who were more likely to suffer fines and other penalties.

The social composition of these returns seems unlikely to be a true reflection of the recusant community, and more reflective of a willingness to protect those Catholics who played a crucial part in the parish community. Catholics also showed pragmatism in the way they engaged with their Protestant neighbours, including ties of kinship and economic activities. Sheils notes that kinship ties between Protestants and Catholics proved 'just as effective in breaking down confessional barriers within generations as [they were] in sustaining them between generations' (Sheils, 1999: 129). Bastow makes a similar point about the Yorkshire Catholic gentry; Catholic marriage sustained the Catholic community, but ties of kinship with their Protestant gentry neighbours ensured social status and economic stability (Bastow, 2002: 372–84).

Despite this continuing Catholic involvement in local affairs, it is still true that from the 1570s Catholics were less integrated than others in wider English society. The Catholic gentry were increasingly forced to withdraw from office: from the bench of magistrates, from the lieutenancy, and from attending Parliament. Here again, church papistry was crucial; church papists were much more likely than committed recusants to retain office. For example, Sir Thomas Tresham of Rushton, Northamptonshire, one of the most prominent recusants in the country, was excluded from office despite his economic and social standing in the local community. There were considerable differences between areas of England and Wales with regard to Catholic office holding. For example, in areas such as Suffolk, Kent, and Gloucestershire, where Protestant preachers gained an early strong following, Catholics were often removed early from office. In the less Protestant areas of Lancashire, Yorkshire, Monmouthshire, and West Sussex, it proved impossible to govern effectively without the local Catholic gentry, so Catholic officeholding continued across the period (Sheils, forthcoming).

Nowhere was the need to accept Catholic power more apparent than in the northern shires where the number and social standing of Catholics remained high. John Bossy estimated that by the mid-seventeenth century more than 20 per cent of households in Durham and Lancashire and between 11 per cent and 20 per cent of those in Yorkshire and Northumberland were recusant households. In 1587 the governor of Berwick complained to Lord Burghley that 'from Yorkshire hither, the most part of Richmondshire, the bishopric [of Durham] the Middle and East March are almost all become papists'. In the border regions of the northern shires the greatest magnate was the staunch Catholic Lord William Howard, controlling lands in Westmorland, Cumberland, Northumberland, and Durham. Howard had to practise occasional conformity under Elizabeth, albeit with a very ill grace [*Doc. 14*, p. 130–1]. He endorsed the Oath of Allegiance, but under the Stuarts (with close relatives at court and protected from prosecution) he was thoroughly recusant (Questier, 2019: 364).

James I, in particular, recognised the vulnerability of the border territory, which, despite the elimination of the formal border, remained unstable and lawless. Lord Howard was essential for keeping the peace in the area; when some Protestants protested against his blatant Catholicism, English commissioners wrote that Howard was 'a great furtherer of justice and a persecutor of the wicked cankers of our country' (McClain, 2004: 206). Howard was the focal point of border Catholicism by the early seventeenth century; he received all the chief recusants at his residence at Naworth Castle and organised secret meetings of powerful Catholics in the area. Local Protestant clergy were still dependent on him and as a result he was able to protect traditional ceremonies such as the 'Christenmass Lord of misrule' in Bampton parish church, Westmorland (McClain, 2004: 203). Elsewhere, in parts of the North officeholding among Catholics, especially church papists, persisted into the seventeenth century. Several members of the Council of the North had close Catholic connections. Sir Thomas Fairfax of Gilling in Yorkshire was made a vice president of the Council in 1606. Fairfax attended the established church, but his Catholic credentials were strong, with a recusant wife and sons educated abroad. He received a dispensation from the Privy Council order forbidding anyone with a recusant wife to hold office. Similarly, Lord Eure of Malton, Yorkshire, was a JP from the early seventeenth century until the Civil War despite being presented as a recusant in 1618 (Sheils, forthcoming).

Just as in the North, some continued Catholic officeholding was essential to effective government in Sussex, the most Catholic of the southern counties, at the beginning of Elizabeth's reign. In the 1560s three of the five leading families were Catholic, and the fourth, Lord Buckhurst, had close Catholic connections;

his daughter would eventually marry the recusant 2nd Viscount Montague. Consequently, two leading Catholics, the earl of Arundel and his son-in-law Lord Lumley, held the lieutenancy jointly until 1569, when their support for the proposed marriage of the duke of Norfolk to Mary, Queen of Scots, led to their swift removal. They were replaced by the 1st Viscount Montague, head of the largest Catholic social circle in the county, and Lord Buckhurst. Their joint lieutenancy lasted until 1586 when Montague lost the office. But Montague was still a person of standing both locally and nationally. In 1586 he was appointed a commissioner in the trial of Mary, Queen of Scots, while in 1591 Elizabeth showed her favour to the Montague household by visiting Cowdray as part of her summer progress.

Montague's conformist Catholicism doubtlessly helped him maintain his local and national influence. His daughter, lamenting the recusancy of her son, claimed that had he remained at Cowdray he would have 'come to it [common prayer] as my father and his doth' (Questier, 2006: 162). In 1592 Montague boasted that he put no pressure on his servants to be Catholic. Although he had a significant number of chaplains attached to his household, they were old Marian priests, not seminarists. Montague's church papistry was supported by his long-serving chaplain, Alban Langdale, the former archdeacon of Chichester, who wrote a manuscript treatise defending occasional conformity, in direct contradiction to the stance taken by the likes of Persons (Younger, 2018: 1069–71; Manning, 1969: 221–2; Questier, 2006: 59–60, 144–66).

The 2nd Viscount Montague, who succeeded to his grandfather's title in 1592, turned out to be a different kind of Catholic, and consequently he never achieved the same local and national standing of his grandfather. However, in 1592 he appeared to be a conformist, ready to follow the path that would keep the family firmly linked to the Elizabethan regime. This was apparent on the birth of Montague's first child, a son, born in 1592. The baptism was to be an event of great social importance, with the Queen, Lord Burghley, and the earl of Sussex acting as godparents. Tragically the child died just before the baptism, which Montague took as a sign of God's disapproval for the proposed Protestant christening. When his second child, a girl, was born, he baptised her himself. This action resulted in temporary house arrest, although he was soon back in favour, receiving minor office from Elizabeth and joining the outer circle of Essex's followers. These events, however, seem to have had a radicalising impact on the 2nd viscount, not so much in a political sense, but in a commitment to recusancy and a determination to have a leadership role in the Catholic community. This, allied to some poor judgement (and perhaps some bad luck), meant that relations with the Jacobean regime were seldom harmonious. In the 1604 Parliament his speech against the recusancy bill was so forthright that Montague briefly ended in the Fleet prison, while in 1605 his links with Gunpowder plotters Catesby and Fawkes led to a year's imprisonment (see Chapter 3).

In 1609 and 1610 there were raids on Montague's house in Southwark, suggesting that the viscount had little court protection following the death of his father-in-law, the earl of Dorset (formerly Lord Buckhurst) in 1608. This seems to be confirmed by his brother-in-law Thomas Sackville, who reported in 1609 that 'the king every daie spake against him [Montague] for maintaining soe many Catholiks, for sending to Rome about bishops and the like' (Questier, 2006: 357). In 1610 Montague sought the help of the earl of Salisbury but to little avail. The Oath of Allegiance was tendered to Montague in 1612 and his refusal to swear to it resulted in a heavy fine. As we have seen, the Oath of Allegiance was viewed as something of a 'quasi conformity test', so there was more at stake than the heavy fine (Croft, 2000: 266). In a bid to impress James with his loyalty, Montague lavishly celebrated the marriage of the king's daughter, Princess Elizabeth, with Frederick of the Palatinate, a union the viscount could scarcely have welcomed (see Chapter 3).

Montague's loss of local power – he was merely a commissioner for sewers – was evident in 1615 when the deputy lieutenant of Sussex threatened the viscount's household 'where wee heare are very manie recusantes' (Questier, 2006: 386). The contrast between the conforming 1st viscount and his recusant and more prominently Catholic grandson could scarcely be clearer. The 1st viscount was a leading office holder in the country for much of Elizabeth's reign, and maintained strong links with the court throughout. The 2nd viscount, though still a member of the House of Lords and a nobleman of social standing in the county, lacked a local power base and struggled to maintain effective links with the Stuart regime.

There were some similarities – but also differences – between the Brownes and the Petres, whose lands were principally in Essex, one of the more Protestant counties in England. Despite the county's Protestant character, the Catholic Petres had little problem in maintaining power within and sometimes beyond the county. John Petre, whose vast estates were centred on Ingatestone Hall, was a significant local figure. He was high sheriff of Essex in 1575–6 and knighted at the end of his tenure. Between 1588 and 1603 he was deputy lord lieutenant of Essex, while in 1588 he commanded 600 local men to oppose the Armada. From 1573 he was a magistrate, and in 1603 James I made him a peer. Throughout this time he appears to have been a church papist, while his wife was a recusant. Significantly, Petre had links to the early seminary priests and the 1580 Jesuit mission.

William, 2nd Baron Petre, did not conform to the established church. Despite this and a Catholic marriage to Katherine, daughter of Edward Somerset, 4th earl of Worcester in 1596, he was politically active long before succeeding his father in 1613. William was MP for Essex in 1597 and was often at the Elizabethan court. His links to the court continued under James, and he attended a number of court masques. After succeeding to the barony in 1613 he was active locally, especially as a JP between 1617 and 1623. He helped to raise a loan to support the Palatinate in 1620, but on the accession of Charles he was disarmed along with other Catholic peers and probably disqualified from Parliament. However, in 1627 he was involved in collecting the forced loan, as were a number of Catholics (see Chapter 3). He persisted in his recusancy but was saved from the usual consequences by the personal intervention of Charles I. William was central to the Catholic community, related to five other Catholic peers including the 2nd Viscount Montague. In 1633 William funded the foundation of the Jesuit College of the Holy Apostles to serve East Anglia with one of the largest benefactions of the period. William's commitment to Catholicism could scarcely have been greater, but he retained the favour of three monarchs, unlike the 2nd Viscount Montague (Kelly, 2018a: 23–6).

In the 1560s Catholics exercised considerable political power, but it has been argued that such power declined throughout the Elizabethan period, and that by the seventeenth century the Catholic community was politically quietist. Certainly, the fall and execution of the duke of Norfolk in 1572 marked a shift of religious power, although the Anjou marriage negotiations of the late 1570s brought a number Catholics to court, and England came close to witnessing a Catholic return to national politics. Thereafter, with the collapse of the marriage, the impact of the Jesuit mission, Catholic plots and deteriorating relations with Spain, Elizabethan politics was very different – as was the Catholic response. Robert Persons took up a position of political resistance and a willingness to back foreign powers to achieve a Catholic England. Sir Thomas Tresham expressed his loyalty to Elizabeth, although on close inspection this loyalty appears to be somewhat conditional. Towards the end of the reign the Appellants showed themselves as more thoroughly loyalist and enjoyed the patronage of Bishop Bancroft, a key figure in the Elizabethan regime.

By the seventeenth century, particularly after 1605, many in the Catholic community accepted that England was not about to reconvert to Catholicism and the community had to accept its minority status, although many seminarists continued to seek converts. Progress was now defined in terms of greater toleration and more freedom to practise Catholicism in England, albeit with limitations. Only the monarchy could deliver such a freedom, so loyalty to the crown was central to the Catholic programme. But this was not quietism: to achieve its goal, the Catholic community had to be part of political debate and use all the levers of political influence at its disposal. For example, in 1609 the secular clergy, using similar anti-Jesuit rhetoric to the Appellants, were trying to persuade Rome to sanction the appointment of a bishop in England and Scotland. This also carried an implicit message to the Jacobean regime; by supporting such an appointment, alongside a more tolerant attitude towards Catholics, monarchical authority would be enhanced through the loyal support of the majority (non-Jesuit) part of the Catholic community. Yet the fact that the Jesuits, along with the Puritans, were projected as agitators undermining the authority of the monarchy does point to the limitations of this approach as a manifestation of the loyalty of the Catholic community.

By the time that a Catholic bishop was appointed in 1624, the Catholic community was already more involved in the public sphere. The Spanish match had generated widespread public debate; for Catholics it opened up the possibility of a new relationship with the Jacobean regime, which they were keen to exploit. In 1621 John Bennet, a leading Catholic secular cleric, was in Rome acting almost as a royal agent, pleading for the necessary papal support for the Spanish marriage. A memorandum sent to Rome stressed the likely benefits that would follow the marriage, including a shift of power within government, with a decline of Puritan influence and the promotion of moderate men. Political developments at home were closely followed. Edward Bennet wrote to his brother John in Rome when the 1621 Parliament ended acrimoniously, expressing his delight in what he believed was the Puritans' overstepping the mark and outraging the king (Questier, 2019: 401, 407).

Although the collapse of the Spanish marriage was soon replaced by Charles's marriage to Henrietta Maria, the swift reneging of promises of toleration appeared to end Catholic hopes of greater political influence. However, Charles's decision in 1627 to resort to the forced loan gave some Catholics the opportunity to find new favour with the regime. A number of Catholics were involved in the collection of the loan. William, 2nd Baron Petre, was involved in Essex, the earl of Derby and Viscount Savage in Cheshire, with Savage also operating in Suffolk. Complaints about Catholic participation were voiced strongly in the Commons in 1628, with one speaker complaining that the MPs who had expressed their opposition to prerogative taxation in the 1626 Parliament had been 'thrust out of all commissions and authority in their country' whereas 'others, some papists, some ... men of a more pliable disposition' were 'ready (by an implicit faith) to act whatsoever shall be commanded them' (Questier, 2019: 436n269).

The Catholic case that they were loyal subjects of the Stuart monarchy was being made for them. Other prominent supporters of the forced loan were some of the avant-garde clerics of the established church with whom the pro-episcopal Catholic clergy felt a certain affinity; and soon bishops Laud and Neile were made privy councillors. However, such changes, along with other grievances against royal government, prompted the Petition of Right in 1628. Central to the parliamentary grievances was a denunciation of popery and accusations of a popish plot which had engulfed a corrupt court. So Catholics were becoming an even greater focus of public debate and central to an emerging ideology of anti-popery within the parliamentary opposition. Peter Lake summed up the situation at the end of the 1620s in terms of two similar but mutually exclusive conspiracy theories, 'the one centred on a populist Puritan plot to undermine monarchy, the other on a popish plot to overthrow English religion and law' (Lake, 1989: 91).

In the 1630s, with the development of court Catholicism and in the absence of Parliament, Catholics appear to have moved close to the centre of national politics. However, with its dependence on Henrietta Maria and papal emissaries, court Catholicism brought effective power and political influence for only a very limited range of Catholics. Nevertheless, beyond the inner court circle there was an intense political interest and constant lobbying. The most active group was the pro-episcopal group who, with renewed vigour, was seeking the appointment of a bishop in England, which, it claimed, would clearly draw the Catholic community close to the Caroline regime. A letter of 1634 which aimed to convince Rome that a Catholic bishop would not be 'offensive to the king and State' stressed that the appointed bishop 'would be a man of a temperat disposition in respect of State matters and zealously affected to his prince and countrey'. Moreover, he would 'take an o[a]th of fidelity and obedience to the king' (Questier, 2005: 236). In a blatant appeal to the crown, the letter promises that such a Catholic bishop 'by his gravity and authority may persuade Catholickses more forcibly than any other can, to graunt extraordinary contributions or benevolence when they shalbe required for supply of his Majest[i]es ... occasions' (Questier, 2005: 239).

In the end, however, it was not the arguments of the seculars that brought about a significant repositioning of the Catholic community in national politics but the Scottish crisis that emerged in 1638. As the crisis moved into rebellion, the papal emissary George Con offered to prompt Catholics to offer financial and military support for the monarch; Catholics would show themselves as loyal subjects in contrast to the traitorous Calvinist Scots, some of whom had close contact with disloyal English Puritans. There appears to have been a degree of unity in the Catholic response. The strongest public advocate of the financial contribution was Anthony Champney, dean of the secular clergy's episcopal chapter, while the main organisers of the Catholic contribution were Wat Montagu and Sir Kenelm Digby, both supporters of the seculars. However, there were also Jesuit contributions; in fact, the Jesuits claimed that whatever success the contribution had enjoyed was down to them. Indeed, the most significant military contribution, the 'Welsh popish army', was commissioned by Henry Somerset, earl of Worcester, a strong supporter of the Jesuits. However, it is not clear how far the whole Catholic community backed the scheme, especially given the hostile publicity the contribution generated. For some, such a public platform represented an opportunity to establish a permanent position in national politics, while for others such a public platform represented a dangerous exposure to attack from the many anti-Catholic elements in English society.

5 James I and the Catholics, 1603–1625

By the time of Queen Elizabeth's death on the morning of 24 March 1603, the succession of James VI of Scotland to the English throne seemed assured. The Catholic European monarchies were prepared to accept James without challenge, while the majority in England, Catholic as well as Protestant, appeared to give enthusiastic backing to the Scottish king. Sir Thomas Tresham was the first to proclaim the new king in Northampton on the morning of Elizabeth's death, where he contrasted his unconditional loyalty with a conditional Protestant response (Kaushik, 1996: 60–1). In 1606 Baron Arundell of Wardour reminded Sir Robert Cecil that he had 'caused King James to be proclaimed in Shaftesbury on a market day, eight days before any neighbour town durst do the like'. John Gerard claimed that on James's accession 'Catholic noblemen at London cast store of money about the streets in sign of their universal joy' (Questier, 2006: 266n105).

The Jesuit response was particularly significant, given their general opposition to James prior to 1603. As early as 28 March 1603 Henry Garnet petitioned the new king while pledging that the English Jesuits would be entirely loyal to him, reassuring James that the Jesuits 'never held that it was lawful to kill a prince or virtually never – certainly not one who was "a true prince" and not a usurper' (Questier, 2019: 274). In June the Jesuit-run English College in Rome was celebrating James's accession with a solemn mass wishing the king 'long life and happiness'. Robert Persons, in a letter to James in October, claimed that the principal Catholics abroad all supported the new king, a point shown by the number of Catholic clergy returning to England. Behind the solid show of support and protestations of loyalty was the hope – perhaps even the assumption – of some form of toleration for Catholics. In July 1603 the ex-Jesuit Thomas Wright, noting that the new queen (Anne of Denmark) was a Catholic, expressed his confidence that England would have toleration similar to that of the Huguenots in France. Persons, too, was confident of a good outcome on religion. Following an unnamed Italian source, he argued that as James had acceded to the English throne without help from any particular power, 'he will hold this indifference towards all, and a moderate course in matters of religion' (Willson, 1966: x; Questier, 2019: 270–4).

It would soon become apparent to James that the path to the English throne was not entirely smooth, and the religious situation was challenging. Just days after he crossed the border in late April 1603, the king received a petition for toleration by

DOI: 10.4324/9781003130376-6

Catholics, but before he had reached the capital another petition pleaded 'Good kynge, let there be a uniformity in true Religion without disturbance of papistes or puritanes' (Newton, 2005: 32). Tresham might have declared his unconditional loyalty to James, but most Catholics, including Tresham, believed that greater toleration than they had enjoyed under Elizabeth would be forthcoming. A number of Catholics had been in touch with James prior to Elizabeth's death, and all seemed agreed that the Scottish king was sympathetic to English Catholics. James appeared to concur with one of those leading Catholic negotiators, the earl of Northumberland, that 'it weare a pittie to losse so good a kingdome for the not tollerating a messe in a cornere' (Newton, 2005: 18). James himself, in reply to the Catholic petition discussed above, said that 'he would not use extremity if they [Catholics] continued in duty like subjects' (Newton, 2005: 32). But what did such promises, if indeed they amounted to promises, mean in terms of the application of the penal laws in England? According to William Watson, a leading Appellant, James offered immediate but blunt clarification on his arrival in England. Once the new king had been assured of Protestant backing he supposedly said: 'Na, na, good faith, wee's not need the papists now'. The response of Watson was equally immediate; he planned the Bye Plot.

The plot that was headed by William Watson, the Bye Plot, was one of a series of three, along with the Main and Grey Plots. The Bye Plot was distinctively Catholic. James was to be kidnapped and held hostage as a guarantee of religious toleration. Leading councillors such as Howard and Cecil were to be replaced, which accounts for the support of the Protestant George Brooke. Brooke was the younger brother of Lord Cobham who, along with Ralegh, were the leaders of the Main Plot. If the wheel of fortune had turned differently, Cobham and Ralegh might well have been lead councillors of James, but in their disaffection they planned to replace the Scottish king with his cousin Arbella Stuart, supposedly with the support of the archduke's ambassador Count Aremberg. Initially, Lord Grey was part of the Bye Plot, recruited to bring in much needed military support. However, he soon went his own way, leading Watson to declare that one of the aims of the Bye Plot was to protect James from a coup by Grey and the Puritans. It is difficult to know what to make of the plots, especially the Bye Plot, except to note the irony that it was led by Watson who, as an Appellant, had argued passionately for loyalty to the English state. Perhaps the conspiracy was a reflection of the emotional investment Watson had made in the belief that toleration would immediately follow the death of Queen Elizabeth, an investment that included many months lobbying in Edinburgh to ensure such an outcome. The wider Catholic community was not impressed by Watson's actions and could not wait to condemn the plot and stress their loyalty to James; indeed, Archpriest Blackwell was probably the initial source of government information about the Bye Plot (Nicholls, 1995: 821–42; Questier, 2006: 268; Newton, 2005: 40).

In February 1604, when James issued his proclamation against Jesuits, seminary priests, and recusants, it was clear that there was a difference of interpretation between the royal and Catholic view of what the king had promised Catholics prior to his accession to the English throne. Cecil had tried to clarify the issue at the time of the Bye Plot, insisting that James always meant 'moderation', not 'toleration'. Given the Protestant character of James's new kingdom, it does seem inevitable that concessions to Catholics would have been limited. As early as 1600 James had given assurances that he would 'not only maintain and continue the profession of the Gospel there but withal not suffer or permit any [other] religion to be professed and avowed within the bounds of that kingdom [England]' (Questier, 2019: 241). It might have been an example of special pleading, but Cecil, in his negotiations for the Anglo-Spanish Peace of 1604, claimed that the king was not able to grant Catholic toleration. This was not due to 'ill will' but because 'the Puritans are so powerful that they would not allow him [a change] or he would have to fear rebellion in the kingdom' (Loomie, 1973: 20). In addition, a factor that appeared to weigh heavily with the government was the great increase in the number of recusants reported across the country since the death of Elizabeth, especially in the North (Haigh, 1975: 276–7). According to Archbishop Hutton of York, this was due to the harshness against the Puritans and favour towards Catholics. As a result, papists 'have grown mightily in number, courage and influence … Some have come down to this country in great jollity almost triumphantly'. Consequently, many who had previously attended their parish church 'are of late become recusants' (Lockyer, 1998: 127).

The February proclamation signalled the end of Catholic hopes for toleration, and by November 1604 recusancy fines were again collected. In the course of 1604 and 1605 the government clampdown went beyond the re-imposition of recusancy fines, and the religious situation grew more tense and troublesome. On 22 March 1604 James's speech to Parliament made a blunt denunciation of Catholicism, describing it as a 'great sect not worthy of the name of religion' in contrast to the true religion of the established church (Questier, 2019: 287). As the bill based on the February proclamation was going through the House of Lords it was subjected to a stinging attack by the 2nd Viscount Montague, a leading Catholic peer. Montague's speech caused outrage in the Lords and in government circles, but it encouraged numerous supporting Catholic petitions against the bill. One such petition, from Thomas Pounde, a kinsman of Montague and long-time religious prisoner under Elizabeth, lamented the cruelties inflicted on Catholics. He was tried in the Star Chamber and forced to make a public submission at York and Lancaster Assizes (Questier, 2006: 272–9). The situation did not improve in 1605. In March the Venetian ambassador was reporting that Catholic houses were being searched and Archbishop Bancroft was ordering bishops in the Province of Canterbury to take a tougher line with recusants. Life was probably worse for Catholics in the North; between the autumns of 1604 and 1605 five Catholics were executed (Questier, 2019: 287, 295).

From the government's perspective the main problem was a Catholic threat, especially in the Welsh borders; the bishop of Hereford, Robert Bennet, was convinced that disturbances in the area in May 1605 were the beginnings of a Catholic rebellion. The Catholic earl of Worcester who, as lord lieutenant of Monmouthshire, was sent to quell the disturbances, thought they were riots. The king appears to have thought them more serious and in a speech to the judges in Star Chamber allegedly told them that the trouble in Herefordshire was 'rebellious' and it was 'needless any longer to spare their blood'. The wiser counsel of Worcester appears to have prevailed and little more is heard of the troubles. However, in the years 1604–5 England seemed a long way from James's oft-stated ideal of 'a general Christian union in religion'. November 1605 would prove that point to a striking degree.

The Gunpowder Plot

The Gunpowder Plot was directly linked to James's failure to grant some form of toleration to Catholics. The five earliest plotters swore an oath of conspiracy after the proclamation of February 1604, and the digging of the tunnel under the Palace of Westminster began after the collection of recusancy fines in November 1604. The origins of the plot, however, go back beyond the issues of 1604. Bossy saw the plot 'as the last fling of the Elizabethan tradition of a politically engaged Catholicism'. He argued that 'one must surely recognize in the mind of Robert Catesby, its moving spirit, a garbled version of political themes which had been enunciated by pro-Spanish Catholics in the reign of Elizabeth' (Bossy, 1973: 95). Although we have stressed the widespread support both in Europe and among English Catholics for the accession of James, there were individuals who opposed him, and not just those in the Bye, Main, and Grey plots. In June 1603 both Guy Fawkes and John Wright, Robert Catesby's agent, were still lobbying the Spanish, despite the fact that in February the Spanish Council had advised Philip III not to back a Spanish succession to England. Guy Fawkes tried to convince the Spaniards that revolt was simmering among English Catholics, and that hostility between the English and Scots would produce trouble regardless of religion [*Doc. 10*, p. 126–7]. But Philip III's ambassador in London warned his king not to trust the analysis of Fawkes and his supporters: 'In matters of importance that hold so many risks, I assure your Majesty that I would not dare to trust these people in question, although I believe them to be very sincere Catholics' (Loomie, 1971: 132). As the constable of Castile warned, '[English Catholics] do not want foreigners, especially the Spanish, to come in here, out of fear for their own power' [*Doc. 11*, p. 127].

The Anglo-Spanish peace of 1604 finally signalled the end of Spanish support for armed English Catholic opposition to the English state, but it did not end all Catholic scheming in Europe. Under the 1604 peace treaty James had been compelled to permit the Spanish to recruit an English regiment in Flanders. By 1605 the English ambassador to Flanders, Sir Thomas Edmondes, was convinced that trouble was developing in the region. Hugh Owen, the pro-Jesuit intelligencer, was at the centre of a web of plotting. Robert Catesby had tried to gain control over the English regiment along with Sir Charles Percy, but the king had vetoed Percy's appointment. Edmondes arrested Owen and his servant Bailly, and unsuccessfully applied for their extradition. The government in London did not act directly on Edmondes's report, but it kept a close watch on events in Flanders and especially the English regiment. Not surprisingly, therefore, James and Cecil were furious to learn that in August 1605 the prominent Catholic Baron Arundell had gone to Flanders to become colonel of the English regiment without the king's permission. He had then compounded his offence by appointing the Bye plotter Sir Gavin Markham as his lieutenant. Such was the outrage at court that the earl of Northampton felt obliged to put in a plea for Arundell: 'I am sorry for the folly of my cosin, the lord Arundell' and in particular the appointment of Markham which 'hath more vexed the king than his [Arundell's] former presumption in embarkinge [to Flanders] expressly against the kings commandment' (Questier, 2006: 89; Nicholls, 1991: 7–8, 42).

Given the connections to Spain and the Spanish Netherlands, it is not surprising that the plotters were linked to the Jesuits in England – or at least to Henry Garnet, the Jesuit superior who was later executed for his prior knowledge of the plot. There were other significant points about the conspirators. They were from, or closely related to, wealthy and prominent Catholic families, and a number had been involved in the Essex rebellion of 1601. Thomas Winter, his brother-in-law John Grant, the Wright brothers, and Robert Catesby, had all been involved in the Essex rebellion of 1601, when the earl of Essex attempted unsuccessfully to seize power from Elizabeth I. At the time, some saw the Essex revolt as a 'popish conspiracy', although others likened Essex more to the Puritans. For William Watson, Robert Persons had conspired to 'stir up earl Robert to Rebellion' (Lake and Questier, 2019: 97).

Those at the heart of the plot had thus been alienated from the English government for a number of years before 1605, and several were the sons of men who suffered long years of imprisonment and house arrest in Elizabeth's reign (Young, 2014: 195–218). Perhaps an unequivocal declaration of toleration by James in 1603 might have changed their thinking, but their grievances were deeply rooted. After the arrest of the plotters, suspicion also fell on a number of Catholic peers. Lord Stourton, a close friend of Catesby, had decided not to attend Parliament on 6 November; Lord Mordaunt, brother-in-law to the plotter Francis Tresham, likewise was not planning to attend Parliament's opening. Viscount Montague was another close friend of Catesby, while Henry Percy, 9th earl of Northumberland, was suspected of having a detailed knowledge of the plot through his cousin Thomas Percy. Montague never came to trial but the other three suffered fines and imprisonment, which in Northumberland's case amounted to 16 years in the Tower (Nicholls, 1991: 81–210; Questier, 2019: 269–333).

Reactions to the Gunpowder Plot

The Gunpowder Plot made a profound impression on James and caused huge political turmoil. 'The king is in terror' wrote the Venetian ambassador, 'he does not appear nor does he take his meals in public as usual' (Willson, 1966: 227). On 21 November the same ambassador reported that London was in a state of panic, while a month later the situation was worse: 'Every day something new about the plot comes to light, and produces great wrath and suspicion … everyone is armed and ready for any event' (Okines, 2004: 276). Meanwhile, James's first political reaction was to seek the help of the papacy, and the new relationship between England and Spain enabled the king to use Spanish influence. In a letter dated 10 November 1605 Cecil told the Spanish ambassador that

> if his Holiness would be pleased to write a very moderate letter ... pledging that all Catholics of this kingdom would be good, loyal subjects and that he will require this of them under excommunication, and even to take up arms in the King's defence against those who might want to agitate and wage wars against this crown, then the King will remit the fines and penalties and allow them to have clergy within their residences so that they might live as they please.
>
> (Loomie, 1973: 71)

Rome, of course, could not make such a commitment, and Anglo-papal relations deteriorated in January 1606, when Pope Paul V succeeded Clement VIII, with whom James had been on good terms ever since his accession. According to the Venetian ambassador, in early 1606 James made a speech violently denouncing Rome and Catholicism:

> I have dispatches from Rome informing me that the Pope intends to excommunicate me; the Catholics threaten to dethrone me and to take my life unless I grant them liberty of conscience. I shall most certainly be obliged to stain my hands with their blood, though sorely against my will ... I do not know upon what they found this cursed doctrine that they are permitted to plot against the lives of princes.
>
> (Willson, 1966: 227)

Even before James's attack on the papacy Catholics were suffering the consequences of the plot. A letter from London in November 1605 states 'that the persecution of Catholics has never been as severe as at the moment. Prisons are full and many have left for Flanders' (Loomie, 1973: 71). Recusancy fines rose significantly between 1605 and 1606, and in that one year convictions for recusancy in London and Middlesex rose threefold. A new session of parliament in 1606 saw harsher anti-Catholic legislation. 'An act for the better discovering and repressing of Popish Recusants' covered a wide range of issues, but made two changes of particular importance. There was an attempt to tackle the old problem of church papists by fining those who refused Anglican communion, though thanks to pressure from the Lords, non-communicants were fined only £20 per year. Another change under the statute was the right given to the crown to take two-thirds of recusants' lands instead of £260. Previously land could only be sequestrated if the recusant defaulted on the fine. An accompanying statute of 1606, 'An Act to prevent and avoid dangers which may grow by Popish Recusants', stipulated that no convicted recusant could come to court without licence, nor practice medicine. Indeed, no recusant or anyone with a recusant wife, could 'excersise any public office in the commonwealth'. The most important and troublesome measure for Catholics to emerge from 'An Act for the better discovering and repressing of Popish Recusants' was an Oath of Allegiance to be administered to Catholics (La Rocca, 1987: 251–62).

Apart from the Oath of Allegiance (discussed further below) few of these new measures proved particularly burdensome to Catholics, although they had some significance. A number of officials continued in public office despite their recusant wives, including Henry Spiller, who was in charge of recusant revenue at the Exchequer. Only a small minority of recusants ever paid the £260 recusant levy, though one wealthy widow, Jane Shelley, conformed after the new legislation when the Exchequer demanded the sequestration of two-thirds of her land instead of £260 per year. Fines for not taking communion were low, at £20 per year, and with enforcement left to informers, the impact was limited (though there is some evidence of enforcement [Questier, 1996: 144–5]). Perhaps more importantly, the act on communion opened up an area of potential trouble and harassment for the church papists. Moreover, Walsham has pointed out the innovative nature of the communion clause. The Elizabethan government had never entered into this area so it represented 'a significant encroachment by the state' and 'it asked deeply committed Catholics to cross a spiritual rubicon: to participate in a rite they regarded as a sacrilegious parody of the miraculous living sacrifice of the mass' (Walsham, 2006: 60).

Overall, the government's response to the Gunpowder Plot was measured and nuanced. There was an understandable element of desperation in the immediate aftermath; Cecil's promise that recusancy fines could be remitted and Catholic gentry permitted to maintain their priests if the pope would back James was greeted somewhat sceptically by the Spanish. James's tirade against the papacy when it failed to support him was hardly diplomatic. Nevertheless, even as the prisons were filling with Catholics, the king was keen to show a different side to his response. As early as 9 November James addressed Parliament with a cautious but powerful speech. The reason for the plot was 'meerly and only Religion' but it did 'not follow That all proffesing that Romish religion were guiltie of the same [treason]'. He insisted that Catholics 'may yet remaine good and faithful subjects' (Okines, 2004: 276). James also asked Parliament for calm and to give the government time to separate the guilty from the innocent. The king returned on a number of occasions to the distinction between the wicked few and the majority of Catholics: 'no sect of the heathen, though they worshipped the very Devil, preached the overthrow of governments as did some Catholics, yet many Catholics were good men and loyal subjects' (Willson, 1966: 226). The other point that the king was keen to stress was the absence of foreign powers in the plot as 'none would abuse himself so much'. With the Habsburg powers more likely than France to have supported the plotters, on 6 November 1605 Cecil wrote to Thomas Parry, the English ambassador in France, that as both the Spanish and Flemish ambassadors had planned to attend the opening of Parliament, their innocence could be assured (Nicholls, 1991: 62).

These two ideas, the concept of the loyal Catholic and continued good relations with Europe, were guiding principles of James's response to the plot over the next few years. In stressing the existence of loyal Catholics the king was readily acknowledging the importance of the Catholic body in English social and political life; elimination of Catholicism was not possible, and maybe not even desirable. Therefore, James chose to continue on the path started in 1604, with the addition of the Oath of Allegiance. In his mind this policy represented a balance between controlling the numbers and activities of Catholics, particularly recusants, and their priests, and keeping the Catholic community loyal and supportive of monarchy through relative moderation. The European dimension was equally important. Good relations with Europe were essential for the king's idea of universal peace, as well as his dynastic ambitions for marriage alliances with the major European powers, most of which were Catholic.

It was also recognised, especially by Robert Cecil, who had negotiated the Anglo-Spanish peace of 1604, that good relations with the Habsburgs were hugely helpful for religious stability in England. As we have seen, the English government was concerned about activities in Flanders on the eve of the Gunpowder Plot, and in particular the potential role of the English Regiment. That continued and Spain was aware of English concern. In December 1605 the Spanish ambassador commented that many Catholics had left for Flanders: 'In London they have become watchful and wish to close the door so that more do not leave'. The source goes on to suggest that 'if this goes on for a year, they will number eight or ten thousand men and set up a force to enable them to live as Catholics' (Loomie, 1973: 71). The English government was aware that the English Regiment was a potential problem. Significantly, James made a crucial amendment to the Anglo-Spanish treaty that enabled him to stem the flow of English volunteers to Flanders (Okines, 2004: 286). The issue, however, remained; even in 1615 the government was attempting to get a number of prominent Catholics to return from Flanders, including Sir Edward Parham, who had been involved in the Bye Plot.

The Oath of Allegiance

The most important section of the 1606 statute 'An act for the better discovering and repressing of Popish Recusants' was the clause that introduced the Oath of Allegiance [Doc. 12, p. 127–8]. The oath could be tendered to all recusants by a bishop or two justices of the peace. In addition to recusants, those who had not taken communion in the established church at least twice in the previous year could be made to swear to the oath. People who went abroad to serve a foreign government would be deemed felons if they did not first take the oath. The penalties for refusing the oath were clearly laid down. A first refusal resulted in imprisonment until the next assizes or quarter sessions when the oath was again tendered. A second refusal meant the punishment of praemunire, which entailed loss of goods and imprisonment at the king's pleasure.

The centrepiece of the oath was an uncompromising condemnation of the pope's claim to have the right to depose princes. James argued that all he intended was to ensure the loyalty of his subjects, and that the oath was more moderate than the Commons had wanted. Initially the oath had included a clause asserting that 'the Pope had no power to excommunicate', but James managed its removal. Historians have disagreed on the exact purpose behind the oath. For Sommerville the oath was about political obedience and was an understandable response to the Gunpowder Plot. The oath 'was intended to target those who, like the plotters, believed that heretical rulers could (at least in certain circumstances) be deposed or killed by their subjects' (Sommerville, 2005: 166). For Questier the oath was no mere loyalty test, and its purpose was to split the Catholic community. There were certainly some significant reasons for even loyal Catholics to refuse the oath; indeed, James himself probably realised that many Catholics, not just extremists and Jesuits, would find the oath difficult. Most leading Catholic theologians such as Bellarmine and Suárez immediately pronounced the pope's deposing power certain and a matter of faith: denial was close to heresy. Persons took a similar line.

The Oath of Allegiance was tendered much more widely after 1610, the year of the assassination of the French King Henry IV, and this suggests that, for James, protecting himself against disloyal Catholic subjects was a major aim of the oath. In practice, however, the oath was not just an intolerable burden on Catholics, but it also failed to achieve James's goal of clearly identifying Catholic loyalists and their opposite. Instead, it identified those whose Catholic faith meant total obedience to papal directives against those who could combine a commitment to Catholicism with occasional defiance of Rome (Sommerville, 2005: 163–77; Questier, 1997: 318–20; Okines, 2004: 278–81).

So some Catholics took the oath but others refused, feeling obliged to 'submit themselves to the ruling of the Pope who had declared the oath unlawful'. Typical of the Catholic stance was the statement that 'the faithful do not want to be lacking in due allegiance to the king yet are troubled in conscience' [*Doc. 13*, p. 128–9]. The oath proved particularly troublesome to Archpriest Blackwell. Blackwell initially accepted the oath, was promptly reproved by Rome into denouncing it, only to be pressurised again into acceptance by the English government. This prompted Pope Paul V to remove Blackwell and appoint George Birkhead as archpriest with instructions to order Catholics not to swear the oath or to attend Protestant churches. The Venetian ambassador described the pope's actions as 'fiery and hotheaded' and it certainly added to Catholic troubles.

It is difficult to express precisely the experiences of Catholics in the wake of the Gunpowder Plot, as within James's broadly moderate and cautious response there was the novel burden of the oath and the king's response to particular events at home and abroad. It needs to be stressed that initially the oath was not administered as widely as it would be after 1610. This is apparent in James's instruction to the judges in 1608 that the oath be tendered 'but to apostates and practizers' (i.e. recently converted and activist Catholics) while 'mild inclination was shown to the rest'. While in reality such a distinction might not be particularly meaningful, it signalled to the judges that they administer the oath with discretion. But 1608 was the same year that the pope issued a bull deposing Blackwell, which was expected 'to breed much wrath in the King and the Council against recusants'.

Shortly afterwards, at St Paul's Cross, Robert Tynley, archdeacon of Ely, attacked Catholicism as a religion which 'utterly perverteth the lawful subjection of people to their Sovereignes'. In October 1608, however, the Privy Council had written to the bishop of Chester instructing him to proceed against recusants 'moderately' and 'only against obstinate persons' (Okines, 2004: 287–9). At times royal policy appeared to be nuanced to the point of contradiction. Towards the end of 1609, however, royal policy was going in a clearer direction, one that meant that a 'milder course' would be 'held with Catholics'. This was probably in response to closer relations with the Catholic archduke of Flanders, and the fact that the archduke had expelled Hugh Owen and two Jesuits from his dominions, which England had been seeking since 1605 (Questier, 2019: 324). Overall though, it is fair to say that James refused to follow the policy demanded by some of his Protestant subjects after the Gunpowder Plot. Thomas Elliot called for the 'devilish, arrogant, perverse and damned traitors, seminary priests' to be encased in lead and 'set upon the highest pinnicale in every city and port' and there to starve to death (Questier, 2019: 305). James's response was far from this.

Increased persecution

By 1610, however, a number of factors were combining to persuade James towards greater persecution of Catholics. The fourth session of the 1604 Parliament which met in February 1610 called for a stricter application of the penal laws and in particular the more stringent administration of the Oath of Allegiance. The need for such a policy was alarmingly reinforced with the news of the assassination of Henry IV of France on 4 May 1610. The assassin, Ravaillac, said he was inspired by the Jesuit writer Juan de Mariana and the preaching of other Jesuits. The House of Commons responded accordingly, demanding the expulsion from England of all Jesuits, and a 'revival of severities against recusants'. James admitted that the penal laws could be enforced more strictly, but somewhat disingenuously blamed the judges for the lack of strict enforcement. The oath was immediately administered more widely and a new anti-Catholic severity was imposed. In mid-1610 the archpriest George Birkhead reported to Richard Smith that 'the prisons are filled againe' and 'the oath is more exacted than ever' (Questier, 1996: 144).

Writing in 1611, a Catholic priest lamented that he 'left in England a great persecution of the Catholic laity over the oath. Except for my Lord [probably Viscount Montague] and his people I hear that few have refused it'. But not all recusants submitted, and by 1613 there were some 40 recusants and 11 priests in London prisons, while reports suggested that some 60 poor recusants were imprisoned in York for refusing the oath. The financial costs of refusal could be severe, with Viscount Montague paying a staggering £6,000. Yorkshire recusant gentry such as William Vavasour and William Middleton offered more modest sums of £700 and £400 respectively. The oath was administered most intensely in late 1612 and 1613; by 1615 the Jesuits claimed that Lord Chief Justice Coke had summoned 1,600 Catholics to take the oath (Cliffe, 1969: 177–8; Questier, 1996: 144–5).

A change in ecclesiastical leadership contributed further to the suffering of Catholics. The appointment of George Abbot as archbishop of Canterbury in 1611 drew a sharp reaction from Catholics, one of whom described the new archbishop as 'a brutal and fierce man and a sworn enemy of the very name of catholic'. A priest writing in 1611 saw the appointment as a sure sign that the king 'meditates the extermination of all catholics'. The same writer contended, with reference to the persecution in 1611, that 'the times of Elizabeth, although most cruel, were the mildest and happiest in comparison with those of James' (Longueville, 1894: 50). Abbot, in a letter to Archbishop Matthew of York (probably of 1612), says that the king had instructed the Council and the judges to 'rid his kingdom of popish recusants'. The Lord Mayor of London responded to Abbot in November 1612 stressing how he was going to enforce the penal laws more strictly 'out of zeal for religion and the better safety of the king'.

In the years 1610 to 1613 foreign affairs were important in shaping James's religious policy. In 1610 England drew close to the anti-Habsburg powers led by France over the Jülich-Cleves crisis (a war fought between Catholic and Protestant claimants over the succession to the united duchies of Jülich-Cleves-Berg). The proposed anti-Habsburg coalition, however, collapsed with the death of Henry IV of France. Moreover, France and Spain drew closer together and there was a proposed double dynastic marriage to cement that unity. Though James continued to look for a Catholic marriage for his son Henry – and then after Henry's death in 1612 for Charles – England felt the need to avoid diplomatic isolation in the short term by looking to Protestant Europe. In 1612 James's daughter Elizabeth married the Calvinist Frederick of the Palatinate; by 1613 England had a defensive alliance with the German Protestant princes.

In the course of 1613 changes of foreign policy (at least in emphasis), the shifting fortunes of factions at court, and finally the arrival of the influential Gondomar as Spanish ambassador, all had an impact on royal thinking and tended towards a lessening of severity against Catholics. There were fewer complaints from Catholics about their treatment. In May 1613, however, England appeared to be remaining within the European Protestant camp as James brokered a deal between the German Protestant Union and the Dutch. But in the same month contrary factors were at work. James experienced Catholic opposition in the Irish Parliament and there were rumours of an Irish papist plot. Gondomar, among others, soon persuaded the king that Abbot was to blame for a royal policy that had pushed the Protestant agenda in Ireland too hard. The king immediately turned on Abbot, complaining it was 'by his means ... that he [James] was accounted cruel and barbarous in Catholic countries contrary to his own disposition' (Questier, 2019: 351). Abbot's power within the Privy Council was now waning, undermined by reports of problems in Elizabeth's marriage to Frederick, which Abbot had vigorously promoted. By November 1613, with reports that the Habsburgs were contemplating aid to Irish Catholics, James was sensing his diplomatic vulnerability in a Europe still dominated by the Catholic powers.

Even in these years of increased Catholic persecution between 1610 and 1613, James never abandoned his belief that within the Catholic community there was a loyal core of 'ancient papists ... so honest and fair conditioned'. In 1611–12 the king decided to invite Catholics to participate in a scheme to purchase the new title of baronet. This idea, promoted by the earl of Salisbury, was primarily to raise much needed money for the Crown, with each new title costing £1,095; but the high percentage of Catholics involved also suggests that James wished to bind leading Catholic gentry families to the regime with 'an expensive public affirmation of loyalty' (Croft, 2000: 281). The immediate response of Catholics shows their willingness to participate. Five of the first 18 baronets, and over a quarter of all initial creations, were non-recusant Catholics (conformists with strong Catholic connections, church papists, and crypto-Catholics), but there were also a number of long-term recusants, including some with close connections to the Gunpowder Plot. Thomas Brudenell of Deene in Northamptonshire was a convicted recusant, and his wife Mary was the sister of the Gunpowder plotter Francis Tresham. Brudenell's sisters-in-law, Elizabeth and Frances Tresham, were married to the Catholic peers Lord Monteagle and Lord Stourton respectively, both on the fringes of the plot. Another new baronet was Sir Thomas Gerard, brother of the Jesuit John Gerard, who was a close friend of Robert Catesby, and who, according to Guy Fawkes, administered the oath of secrecy to the plotters. According to the Venetian ambassador, the money raised from the sale was to finance the plantation of Ulster – indicated by the red hand placed as a mark of difference on the coat of arms of a baronet – so the new Catholic baronets were contributing to the Protestantisation of Ireland.

Recusancy fines, as we discussed earlier, had become a source of steady if unspectacular income rather than the prime weapon of persecution. That is not to underestimate the ongoing financial burden on recusants, but the operation of recusancy fines now responded more to the government's financial needs than to the general level of persecution at any particular time. As the Crown strove to increase its revenue from all sources after 1610, there was a close scrutiny of the operation of recusancy fines. Two commissions, appointed in 1612 and 1615 respectively, called for a tougher administration of the fiscal laws and condemned the practice of recusants receiving the leases of their sequestrated lands (which allowed Catholics to move back onto their confiscated estates as tenants). But a minority view also emerged from these commissions, which urged a more moderate policy of greater realism. If the government insisted on its every due, then 'the recusants simply flee their homes and lurk in secret places'. If the administration of recusancy fines was too severe, the richer Catholics would conform so that 'no benefit will accrue to the king'. This, in fact, appears to have happened in 1615 when a drive to exact more money resulted in a higher number of Catholics conforming. The operation of recusancy fines and sequestrated land became a source of patronage as well as income for the Crown, particularly for members of the royal household.

Hopes for toleration

Hopes for greater toleration were linked to the prospect of a Catholic and (more especially) Spanish marriage for Charles; after 1614 such a match became a more serious prospect. The failure of the 1614 Parliament to provide much needed finance for the Crown due, according to James, to the presence of 'unquiet spirits' in the Commons, meant that there was little prospect of Parliament's recall in the near future. A Spanish match became more attractive; such a union would not only enhance England's status in Europe, but the accompanying dowry would alleviate the Crown's financial problems. Progress on the marriage turned out to be slow, even though in March 1615 Sir John Digby, the king's ambassador in Madrid, received a concrete proposal for a marriage treaty. By early 1618, however, Digby was able to report that the treaty was progressing well, but there were domestic implications for the king. The Spaniards had made their demands concerning religion explicit and although they were resolved to 'satisfye him in temporall regards and poynt of portion [dowry], he [Digby] was of the opinion that the calling of a parliament wilbe of no kynde usefull' (Questier, 2009: 3; Redworth, 2003: 15–16). Any marriage treaty with Spain would involve considerable concessions to English Catholics, and such a policy would not be tolerated by Parliament.

By 1618 the Spanish match was already becoming the defining political issue within government circles, and there were strong opponents as well as supporters. Secretary Winwood, who died in October 1617, was described as showing 'great malice' towards the Spanish, and his successor Sir Robert Naughton, a godly Protestant, was similarly anti-Spanish. Archbishop Abbot was always an opponent of the marriage, and in the years 1618–22 some of the fieriest criticism of royal policy was voiced from the pulpit. However, Catholic and pro-Spanish influences were on the increase, with the Spanish faction dominant. This faction not only included the Howards and traditional Catholic sympathisers, but also the likes of Lord Chancellor Bacon and Sir John Digby, whose support for Spain stemmed from political considerations. The Spanish also gained more influence. It was pressure from the Spanish embassy that led to the removal of Lord Sheffield as President of the Council of the North after he insisted that the priest William Southerne be hanged in April 1618. The new president was Lord Scrope, a crypto-Catholic.

In May 1618, however, a revolt in Bohemia would lead to the European conflict generally known as the Thirty Years' War, a conflict which would make the Spanish match simultaneously more important and hugely more problematic for James. The Bohemian revolt represented a serious challenge to Habsburg domination in central Europe, but when in 1619 James's son-in-law, the Protestant Frederick of the Palatinate, decided to accept the offer of the Bohemian crown, the Stuart government was faced with enormous problems. There was immediate and widespread support for Frederick in England, although it was widely accepted that his action would provoke Habsburg retaliation. Moreover, with the truce between Spain and the Dutch ending in 1621, Dutch support was unlikely, leaving Frederick diplomatically isolated; Protestants in both Europe and the whole of Britain looked to James to champion the European Protestant cause. This was a role that James was unwilling to embrace, lacking both the inclination and resources. By late 1620, however, the crisis had become more acute as Frederick's territories of the Upper and Lower Palatinate were occupied by Imperial and Spanish troops respectively.

The king recognised that to ignore the fate of the Palatinate altogether was politically too dangerous; he had to negotiate the withdrawal of Habsburg troops from the Palatinate, but the approach had to include at least the threat of military action. In turn this required a level of finance that only Parliament could provide.

The Parliament that met in January 1621 dealt with a range of issues, but religion and foreign policy dominated. The king refused to allow Parliament's demands for tougher laws against recusants, though in March a number of Catholic priests were expelled and all Catholics were ordered to leave London for the duration of the Parliament. James insisted that marriage negotiations should continue in tandem with military preparations, even after the pro-Spanish Sir John Digby argued on his return from Madrid that only military action would free the Palatinate. The Spanish, for their part, demanded that legal penalties for English Catholics be removed. The gulf between the king and Parliament became bitterly apparent by December 1621. Parliament launched an attack on all aspects of Stuart foreign and religious policy. The pope and the Habsburgs were responsible for all the problems in Europe, while papists were behaving outrageously at home. James, sword in hand, should be leading Protestant Europe and Charles should marry a Protestant. The king's response was to dissolve Parliament on 6 January 1622 (Questier, 2019: 372–410: Redworth, 2003: 19–38).

The dissolution of Parliament effectively removed the option of military action to aid the Palatine, so the marriage negotiations acquired a greater urgency. As a sign of his good faith, in August 1622 James ordered the release of recusants from prison, even if their offence included refusing the Oath of Allegiance or distributing Catholic books. By December 1622 important secret articles had been agreed in Madrid. By early 1623 Catholics were optimistic that all persecution would soon cease; by August 1623 James appeared to have conceded Spanish demands for complete toleration. The Spanish wanted toleration to be achieved by a proclamation, but James was aware that this could provoke a domestic crisis. Instead, a royal pardon was to be granted to Catholics and this was drawn up by September 1623. It seems unlikely that the pardon was ever published, but Catholics were jubilant; the Puritans were furious. By the end of October 1623, however, following the bizarre visit of Buckingham and Prince Charles to Madrid, the marriage was off. The Madrid visit might have been undertaken for the legitimate purpose of pressurising the Spanish to finalise the treaty, but the method chosen and its abject failure meant humiliation for Prince Charles and indeed the English Crown at the hands of Spain (Questier, 2009: 37–54; Redworth, 2003: 174–83; Patterson, 1997: 329–30).

Yet there was no hint of humiliation as Charles returned to England to widespread popular acclaim and celebrations. Bells were rung and bonfires lit in London and Coventry, with great festivities in Oxford. Two chapels, in Kent and Exeter College, Oxford, were dedicated to Charles's return (Pursell, 2002: 720). At least some of those joining the celebrations would have agreed with Sir Benjamin Rudyard that the return of the prince was 'the turn of Christendom'. The end of the Anglo-Spanish alliance would lead to a diplomatic revolution, war with Spain, and the kingdoms of Great Britain as the champion of Protestant Europe. When

Parliament assembled on 19 February 1624, such a revolution appeared possible. Buckingham led the attack on Spain and popery. The Spaniards had been part of a popish plot including the attempted conversion of Charles. However, at the same time as Buckingham's anti-popish tirade, Lord Kensington was in Paris to negotiate a new dynastic union with France. James was determined not to accept the mantle of the leadership of European Protestantism; if England was heading towards war with Spain, then an alliance with France was a political necessity. The consequences for toleration for Catholics were, of course, similar to the Spanish match, and in August 1624 the king instructed the judges not to convict any recusants. The negotiations with the French were less fraught, and although they appeared to demand concessions for English Catholics, such concessions were not as evident in the public domain. The French did not insist on James issuing a proclamation to announce toleration, nor even to grant a pardon to Catholics; they would be satisfied as long as no new convictions were made. Yet even this was sufficient for some Catholic celebrations and Protestant denunciations.

By the time of James's death in March 1625, Catholics enjoyed a fair degree of toleration, but it is difficult to generalise about their treatment over the reign. However, certain points are clear. Except from late 1603 to late 1604, the fiscal penalties for recusancy were enforced up to 1623. Other factors such as the tendering of the Oath of Allegiance, the severity of episcopal action against recusancy, and the ruthlessness or otherwise of key officials such as the Lord President of the Council of the North, all tended to fluctuate. According to Catholic sources the years between 1610 and 1613/14 stand out as the period of greatest severity, as the Oath of Allegiance was widely administered and Archbishop Abbot, from 1611, appeared to enjoy a good deal of power in government. Ultimately, of course, religious policy depended on the king, and James was not always clear or consistent. But a major factor in shaping the king's attitude towards Catholics was foreign policy. As England drew closer to Spain after 1614, English Catholics could hope for more sympathetic treatment. This was reinforced by the fact that the possibility of a Spanish marriage meant the king could rule without resorting to Parliament.

The issues of persecution or toleration were not the sole criteria of Catholic positioning in the English nation; there were other factors of significance. There were more Catholic influences in the Stuart court than in the last decades of Elizabeth. James had a Catholic wife, Anne of Denmark, and though she exercised her religion with discretion, her open disapproval of the Protestant Palatine marriage showed her true sympathies. There were a number of crypto-Catholics at court; at the beginning of the reign the most prominent was the earl of Northampton, while at the end there were a number of prominent Catholic converts in the Buckingham circle. A royal chaplain, Benjamin Carier, converted to Catholicism in 1613, while Lord Wotton, employed on embassies to Spain and France and after 1612 a member of the Treasury Commission, was a secret Catholic.

More significantly the Catholic body was more politically involved, and in some parts of the regime, though not others, more politically acceptable than at the end of Elizabeth's reign. The Gunpowder Plot might have been a disaster for the whole

Catholic community, but James's insistence that most Catholics were still loyal enabled an appropriate Catholic response, despite the complication of the Oath of Allegiance. From 1608 onwards a section of the secular clergy lobbied Rome to appoint an English bishop. In this lobbying there was also a signal to James, namely that a more disciplined, well-ordered Catholic body would draw closer to, and be more supportive of, the established church and the English state. Catholic letters, especially from 1609 onwards, show a close interest in the affairs of the Jacobean court, and in particular issues such as royal marriages which they rightly perceived as impacting on their own position. Catholic commentators also noted with particular delight when James turned on his parliamentary critics for denouncing his pro-Spanish policy and alleged sympathy to Catholics as happened in 1614 and 1621. In 1614 the Welsh Catholic priest Edward Bennet judged that 'no doubt the Lower House was too bold to look into her Majesty's actions'. As Questier writes: 'On this basis some Catholics might well have looked a good deal more loyal than some MPs' (Questier, 2019: 357; Questier, 1998: 15–34; Loomie, 1996: xii–xiii).

6 The Catholics in Caroline England, 1625–1642

The reign of Charles I was a mixed blessing for English Catholics, who benefitted from the protection of a Catholic queen (Henrietta Maria) and from potential patronage emanating from an increasingly Catholic court culture. England enjoyed active diplomatic relations with Rome, but on the other hand, the popularity of Catholicism at court had little impact on ordinary Catholics. Always short of money in the years of his personal rule, Charles had little incentive to ease penal laws that benefitted the Exchequer. A still greater problem for Catholics, however, was the intense popular animosity towards Catholicism and everything it represented generated by Charles's style of government. In the 1630s anti-Catholicism and anti-popery rose to fever pitch, forming a key component of the grievances that exploded into Civil War in the 1640s.

Charles I and the Catholics

The new reign of Charles I opened promisingly for Catholics. Observing the agreement of his marriage treaty with France, Charles wrote to the Lord Keeper in May 1625 instructing him to suspend all proceedings against recusants. Similar letters were also sent to the ecclesiastical authorities. The Catholic body had done its best to persuade the king to grant toleration by pleading its loyalty in the strongest possible terms: 'We believe also and sincerely protest before God and men without any equivocation or mentall reservation that we owe obedience and Allegiance to our Soveraigne Lord King Charles, his heires and successors, and will perform it faithfully to him and them, notwithstanding any Absolution or dispensation to the contrary' (Butler, 1821: 150).

In August 1625, however, under pressure from both Parliament and the Privy Council, Charles issued a proclamation ordering the enforcement of all penal laws. The 1625 Parliament passed a new statute increasing penalties for sending children to Catholic schools abroad, while recusants were to be double taxed, with poorer recusants subject to a poll tax. In November Charles not only levied the recusancy fines due under the penal statutes, but also ordered the Oath of Allegiance to be widely administered. In October 1625 a proclamation ordered the disarming of leading Catholics, while another proclamation of January 1626 resulted in a mass indictment of Catholics (Questier, 2009: 123–7).

The king's swift reneging on the terms of his marriage treaty and his ruthless enforcement of the laws against Catholics sit somewhat uneasily with the general (though by no means universal) judgement of historians that Charles's policy toward Catholics was one of relative toleration. One explanation for the shift is that, under pressure from parliaments in the years 1625–9, Charles was harsher on Catholics in these early years than in the 1630s. We shall argue that there is strong evidence to support this, but other factors also need to be taken into account. Charles's natural inclination was to see Puritans rather than Catholics as the major enemy. Although Charles derived his views on Puritanism from his father and from the experience of popular agitation against the Spanish match, it was only after 1629 that anti-Puritanism became central to his religious policy. This gave Catholics the opportunity to project themselves as loyalists, deserving of lenient treatment. The king was open to such arguments, but Catholic recusants remained nonconformists, and Charles disliked all forms of nonconformity. Therefore, recusants had to be made to pay for their refusal to conform to the established church. The king was also desperately short of money throughout his reign, so collectively recusants needed to pay heavily.

It appears that from the beginning of his reign Charles wanted to frame his punishment of Catholics in terms of equivalence, as a compensation to society for the trouble caused by Catholic nonconformity. This meant that in the war years 1625–9 recusant fines and arms taken from Catholics were intended to contribute directly to the war effort. Sir John Eliot and Christopher Sherland first suggested in Parliament that forfeited recusant property might go directly to pay for a fleet against Spain. Likewise, when Catholics were disarmed in October 1625, 'there was supposed to be some kind of equivalence in the public mind between the sequestration of arms and armour from recusants' households and the provision of military equipment for the war with Spain' (Questier, 2009: 127). In 1626, when Charles established a separate recusant account of receipt in the Exchequer, he explained that this was done so that the 'said Revenue of the Recusants may be clearly receaved and it used without the mixture of other monyes and by that means bee more readie for service and maintenance of our Navy' (Dures, 1983: 71–2).

The regime continued in its tough line against Catholics. Indeed, at the opening of the 1628 Parliament the government appeared to be promoting its anti-Catholic credentials in order to urge parliament to grant supply. Sir John Coke, the Secretary of State, decided to close down the Jesuit community in Clerkenwell, living in the London home of the Catholic earl of Shrewsbury. Coke not only denounced the Jesuits but also attacked the secular clergy with their close connection to Rome and European Catholic monarchs. Jesuit treachery was further publicised by the circulation of a false letter which purported to reveal a Jesuit conspiracy to undermine the state resulting in the restoration of Catholicism in England by the Spanish king (Questier, 2006: 440–1). Charles even responded by issuing a proclamation which ordered the detention of all Jesuits and the strict punishment of those who received them (Sharpe, 1992: 301). Coke's attempt to play the anti-popery card was totally unsuccessful. Articles drawn up by Eliot, Pym, Sir Thomas Wentworth, and John Selden decried the alarming increase in recusants, condemned the practice of allowing Catholics to compound for their estates, and accused bishops Neile and Laud of preaching popery. By the time Parliament was dissolved in March 1629, and following more criticism about 'innovation in religion', Charles had promised to maintain 'the true religion and doctrine established in the Church of England' (Smith, 1993: 119).

Parliament saw royal policy towards Catholics as lenient, where in reality the financial burdens were heavy and continued to be so throughout the 1630s. A new policy of compounding was introduced in the North in 1627 and extended thereafter; not all recusants compounded, but the system was widely applied. It fitted Charles's idea of equivalence; to compensate for their troublesome non-conformity recusants should co-operate fully with the authorities and in return favours would be granted. Composition involved a recusant making an agreement with commissioners to pay a fixed sum in fines, sometimes over an agreed period of time. This removed an administrative burden from officials executing the penal laws; the existing system, essentially the one established by the 1587 statute, was open to obstruction, delay, and legal challenges. In return, the Catholic compounder enjoyed a number of concessions as a State Paper of the 1630s makes clear. He was not liable for his wife's recusancy, nor could she be imprisoned on this account. No informer was permitted to sue a recusant, and this was understood to curb the activities of the hated pursuivants. Recusants were not to be punished in ecclesiastical courts. Crucially, those who compounded were not subject to any further inquisition into their lands, which meant that composition payments could not increase. Previously some recusants were subjected to a second or even third inquisition into the value of their land, always resulting in a higher valuation and an increased payment to the Exchequer (Cliffe, 1969: 218–19).

The operation of compounding varied from place to place. In London its main apparent impact was that a number of landless recusants paid money to the Exchequer for the first time. For example, Ferdinand Emerson, a cutler, was first convicted in 1602 when he was charged to lose his goods to the value of £5. In fact, he paid nothing to the Exchequer until 1628, when he began to pay a composition of £2 a year. In Yorkshire, by contrast, recusants generally paid more in composition than they had previously paid into the Exchequer – at least this was the case after 1629 when Thomas Wentworth became president of the Council of the North.

Wentworth was determined to maximise revenue from recusants. At his trial he claimed that such revenue increased within four years from £2,300 to £11,000 per annum, 'more than ever was raised formerly in so short a time' (Lindley, 1971: 212). This did not prevent Puritans from criticising his policy of compounding as being too lenient, though more thought Wentworth was harsh on northern Catholics. The Lord Treasurer, Sir Richard Weston, was critical: 'You proceed with extreme Rigour, valuing the Goods and Land of the poorest at the highest Rates, or rather above the value [previously made] without which you are not content to make any Composition'. Those less sympathetic to the Catholic cause, such as Christopher Wandesford, an officer of the Exchequer, praised Wentworth as a 'light and comfort to the whole country ... for Papists already hand down their Heads like Bulrushes and think themselves like Water spilt on the Ground' (Havran, 1962: 95).

The late 1620s and 1630s saw increasing revenue from recusants. Recusant revenue in Suffolk rose from £103 4s 0d in 1627/8 to £728 in 1633/4, although after that date there was a small decline (Lindley, 1971: 214). F. C. Dietz argued that recusant revenue over the whole country rose from £6,396 in 1631 to £32,000 in 1640 (Dietz, 1943: 268; Havran, 1973: 91–2). Such figures need to be treated with caution, but the upward trend in clear. Clarendon was certain of Charles's stringent policy: 'The penal laws (those only being excepted which were sanguinary, and even those sometimes let loose) were never more rigidly executed, nor had the crown ever so great a revenue from them, as in his time; nor did they ever pay so dear for the favours and indulgences of his office towards them' (Lindley, 1971: 212).

Despite the heavy financial burdens, Catholics enjoyed greater freedoms in the 1630s. The widespread use of composition itself reduced the burdens on recusants. Crucially, royal policy shifted; the king increasingly identified Puritans not Catholics as the major enemy, whereas in the years 1625–9 he was more ambivalent. In 1628, as we have seen, Charles was prepared to project an anti-Catholic image in the hope of achieving generous financial support from Parliament. According to Richard Cust, the king came close to committing himself to a more throughgoing anti-Catholic policy in 1628–9: 'For a few weeks in late 1628 and early 1629 it looked as if the patriots might persuade him [the king] to re-commit to war against Spain and pro-Calvinist/pro parliamentary policies at home' (Cust, 2007: 130). Instead, the experience reinforced Charles's more natural religious inclinations, especially his deep suspicion of Puritans whom he saw as a popular, seditious sect. The breakdown in 1629 led Charles to see a close identity between Puritans and the parliamentary opposition. Addressing the Lords in March 1629, Charles blamed the breakdown on a minority in the Commons, 'some few vipers that did cast the mist of undutifulness over most of their eyes' (Cust, 2007: 119). Later he described Parliament as 'that Hidra ... as well cunning as malicious' (Cust, 2007: 132). The language is similar to that used by Charles about the Puritans. In 1640, in a preface to the Canons issued to the Church of England, the king accused Puritans of operating under 'the mask of zeal and counterfeit holiness' so that they can spread 'poisoned conceits among the weaker sort who are prone to be misled by crafty seducers' (Cust, 2002: 247).

The decision to rule without Parliament had important implications for foreign policy, which in turn was closely linked to religion. In the confusing four years 1625–9, England had been at war with Spain, then France, but with an underlying objective of contributing to the restoration of the Palatinate to Charles's sister and brother-in-law, Elizabeth and Frederick. The absence of Parliament after 1629 meant the absence of funds for waging war, and inevitably pushed England back towards a peace policy similar to that of the early 1620s; the Palatinate could be restored through the good offices of Spain without England's direct involvement in the Thirty Years' War.

Peace with Spain also suited Charles's personal sentiment as 'he had enormous respect for the Spanish with their *gravitas* and instinctive sense of honour and hierarchy' (Cust, 2007: 124). The close alliance was maintained throughout the 1630s except for a brief period in 1635–6 when there was a shift towards the French who had just entered the Thirty Years' War on the anti-Habsburg side. However, the pro-Spanish (and indeed crypto-Catholic) party had been dominant at court since the early 1630s. With Sir Francis Cottington and Sir Richard Weston already influential, their power was consolidated in 1632 when Sir Francis Windebank was appointed Secretary of State ahead of the 'Protestant causer' Sir Thomas Roe (Cust, 2007: 125).

The 1630s thus saw a significant shift of religious focus. Puritans were clearly identified as the monarchy's major enemy, while the dominance of ceremonially inclined Laudianism within the Church of England, and the close alliance with Spain, encouraged Catholics to stake a better claim to be part of the religious and political establishment. But with the financial burdens on recusants as onerous as ever, was there toleration for Catholics? In 1971 Keith Lindley was clear that 'Roman Catholics in the reign of Charles I did not experience a period of exceptional leniency and general calm' (Lindley, 1971: 220), and more recently Kevin Sharpe has reached a similar conclusion. Both put great emphasis on the financial burdens, although Sharpe also argues that the fines were meant as a punishment not merely as a source of revenue; Charles was not prepared to treat recusancy lightly. Sharpe stresses the proclamation against the Jesuits in 1628 and the report of the Venetian envoy, Contarini, that Catholics feared that their children would be taken away from them to be raised in Protestant households. Much of Sharpe's evidence of harshness against Catholics appears to come from before 1630, although he points to Bishop Wren presenting more recusants than theretofore to the Norwich sessions in 1636 (Sharpe, 1992: 301–3). All historians accept the fact that financial exactions in the 1630s remained high, but the examination of a range of evidence, including the views of Catholics themselves, suggests that Catholics enjoyed more freedoms than in any previous period apart from 1603–4 and the early 1620s.

Hugh Aveling, whose extensive work on northern Catholicism has never been seriously challenged, judged the period from 1627 to 1639 to be one of 'extraordinary relative peace for Catholics' in the North Riding of Yorkshire (Aveling, 1976: 96). There were few impositions beyond the financial, mainly due to compounding. Crucially, the Oath of Allegiance was rarely imposed, though Charles was prepared to use it against Puritans (Fincham, 1993: 49). Given that under James I the oath had been such a source of anguish and financial burden for the Catholic community, its sparing use was significant. Conditions in the North owed much to the work of Thomas Wentworth as Lord President of the North from 1628–40, although his predecessor, Lord Scrope, was more sympathetic to Catholicism. Wentworth, like his master the king, believed that Catholics should pay for their nonconformity, and he was determined to maximise revenue from recusants; but equally he was scrupulous in adhering to the agreement on composition. So there were no prosecutions for harbouring recusant servants, and he endeavoured to prevent ecclesiastical authorities from harassing recusants. Under Wentworth there was an increase in licences for Catholics to be buried in the parish churchyard, yet another good indicator of 'relative peace'. Wentworth clashed with Bishop Morton of Durham on this and wider issues, complaining that the bishop 'perpetually vexes compounders for recusancy for their Clandestine Marriadges, Christenings, baryalls and such like' (Marshall, 2016: 64; Cliffe, 1969: 218–22; Havran, 1962: 95–6).

Michael Questier has argued that the 1630s was a decade in which 'de facto toleration was being established' and one where 'many contemporaries (and not just Catholics) believed ... that in this period the English Catholic Community was edging towards the enjoyment of some kind of official tolerance' (Questier, 2006: 486; Questier, 2005: 28). Questier's evidence comes particularly from newsletters written from London by the pro-episcopal party of secular clergy to likeminded clerics, including Bishop Richard Smith. By November 1632 Smith was reporting that the pursuivants were at last being controlled. In October 1633 Smith believed that fewer Catholic priests were in prison; Newgate Prison was in fact quite emptied. Again in 1633, John Southcote, Smith's leading supporter, wrote that the pursuivants had done little recently either in Norfolk or London, 'and it is generally confessed that we never had a greater calm since the queene came in than now' (Questier, 2005: 192), while another letter stresses that 'All publick chapels are mightily frequented without disturbance' and that the superior of the Dominicans is allowed to go freely 'where he will' (Questier, 2005: 182). The newsletter in 1635 conceded that recusant payments were 'commonly racked very high' but generally struck an optimistic note. Pursuivants still had their commissions 'yet Catholiques are not generally so much molested by them either in city or countrey as they have beene'.

The letters, written by the pro-episcopal lobby, had an interest in projecting an optimistic view of Catholic conditions. A letter written in 1636, however, does offer a convincing explanation for the calm of the 1630s: church and state were in the hands of 'moderate men'. The king himself, despite his dislike of recusant nonconformity, was generally sympathetic to Catholicism. Henrietta Maria played a crucial role in helping Catholics, especially in the later 1630s. Wentworth played by the rules of composition. Furthermore, Archbishop Laud, though not a great saviour of 'papists', was not a severe persecutor, unlike his predecessor, the Calvinist Archbishop Abbot. In judging the Catholic experience under Charles I, it is important to remember one basic point: only three Catholics were executed during his reign up to 1642, compared with 183 between 1577 and 1603, and 28 (excluding the Gunpowder plotters) between 1607 and 1618 (Havran, 1962: 113–14).

Court Catholicism

There had been Catholic influences at the court of James I, but the court Catholicism of Charles was altogether more significant. There were a number of reasons for this. The most important was the king himself, as it was the monarch who formed the character of and set the tone for the royal court.

Charles was no Catholic, crypto- or otherwise, but he was comfortable in a cultural ambience that owed much to Catholic Europe. The king, confident that the Church of England was the true church, was nevertheless sympathetic to aspects of Catholicism and opposed to traditional anti-popish rhetoric. Charles was reported as saying that in religious discussions 'too much time is spent on controversies which displease me, I would rather study were devoted to reunion' (Milton, 1995: 62). The Anglicanism in which the king had such faith was, by the 1630s, distinctly Laudian. The rise of Laudianism had seen more censorship of anti-popish publications, but with its stress on the sacraments, its clericalism, and its acceptance that Catholicism could be part of the true church (albeit a somewhat corrupted part), Laudians had shown that Catholic and Protestant churches could have much in common (Milton, 1995: 372–3).

The individual who gave the 1630s court Catholicism its particular form and vitality was, of course, Henrietta Maria, Charles's queen. Writing in 1643 and drawing on the deeply entrenched 'popish plot' idea, William Prynne wrote of 'a most strong ... desperate confederacie prosecuted (wherein the queen Majestic hath been chiefe) to set up Popery in perfection' (Freist, 2011: 34). The queen's position as a supporter of English Catholics came with the marriage. The papal dispensation for the 'mixed marriage' had been granted in return for far-reaching rights for Catholics. There were also expectations on the young queen, with the Pope indicating in a letter of 26 March 1625 that her mission in England was not so much to reign as to bring about a Catholic restoration. These expectations were reinforced in 1626 when a book by Nicolas Caussin, a leading Jesuit at the court of Louis XIII (Henrietta Maria's brother), was dedicated in its English version to Edward Sackville, earl of Dorset, lord chamberlain to the queen; the subject of the book was a heroine who used both piety and sexuality to achieve the conversion of her heretical husband (Freist, 2011: 40).

In fact, Henrietta Maria could initially do little for English Catholics, although she soon made her own faith clear. After the marriage, the queen still played a secondary role to the duke of Buckingham in the exercise of political influence, and possibly in the affections of the king. England's new queen refused to witness either the coronation or the opening of Parliament in 1625, after which Charles and his queen 'spoke not a word for three days' (Albion, 1935: 85). The king's failure to grant the religious toleration agreed under the marriage treaty, together with the queen's ostentatious practice of her religion, kept tensions high between them. During Holy Week 1626, Henrietta Maria and her ladies lived like cloistered nuns in Somerset House, where a gallery had been divided into cells for them. The queen caused a scandal by visiting Tyburn, the place of numerous executions since the 1570s and something of a pilgrimage for London Catholics; she knelt and prayed before the gallows. The London gossip John Pory wrote that the French priests had made 'the pore queen to walk a foot (some add barefoot) to Tyburn to honour Martyrs who had shed their blood in defence of the Catholic cause' (Havran, 1962: 44). The French Oratorian priests were in fact a major issue between Charles and his queen. In August 1626, the king decided to show his displeasure by expelling the Oratorians and most of Henrietta Maria's French household.

From 1630, however, Henrietta Maria's influence and the strength of court Catholicism increased. The assassination of Buckingham in 1628 led to a closer relationship between Charles and his queen, and by 1630 her Catholic household was restored. The most significant arrivals were 12 Capuchin friars who turned the queen's faith into a public affair once again. The friars settled at Somerset House and were permitted to wear the religious habit. The circle surrounding the queen included many Catholics and Catholic sympathisers. Thomas Savage, the queen's chancellor, was a Catholic, as was his wife who befriended Henrietta Maria. The groom of the bedchamber, Endymion Porter, was a crypto-Catholic, while his wife was converted to Catholicism by the papal agent George Con; thereafter the Porter household was a hotbed of Catholic activity (Freist, 2011: 42–3; Hibbard, 1983: 40–1; Huxley, 1959: 176).

It is worth noting, however, that Henrietta Maria's circle of courtiers were not exclusively Catholic. One of her court favourites was the earl of Holland, who was distinctly Puritan. Holland also provided a link to the court for a wider group of Puritans such as the earls of Bedford and Warwick. The religious pluralism of the queen's patronage drew sharp criticism from the Jesuits. In 1632 the seculars reported that the Jesuits 'affect not the person of our most religious and Catholicke queen as appeareth by the perpetual muttering against her of their chief adherents; and calling her the head of the puritan faction'. The seculars sprang to the queen's defence, quoting her chaplain Robert Phillip that 'she never missed a daye to heare masse since she came to England, but the twoe days of her deliverie of child' (Questier, 2005: 24). This exchange, however, probably tells us more about the bitter dispute between Jesuits and seculars than the piety of Henrietta Maria.

Notwithstanding the queen's wider contacts, both royal households and the court had strong Catholic influences in the 1630s. A number of the king's leading ministers, such as Sir Richard Weston, earl of Portland, Sir Francis Cottington, and Sir Francis Windebank, were crypto-Catholics according to Du Perron, the queen's almoner. Cottington was probably the most Catholic, converting to Catholicism in Spain in 1628. On his return to England he conformed, but in 1636 he again declared himself a Catholic. He died in exile at a Jesuit College in Valladolid. Weston, too, died a Catholic and had a Catholic wife, but according to the gossip writer Edward Rossingham, 'he never had reputation and credit with that party [Catholics] who were the only people of the kingdom who did not believe him to be of their profession' (Sharpe, 1992: 148). In similar fashion, Windebank converted to Catholicism just before his death in exile in France in 1646. Even in 1641, already safely in exile, he was still professing commitment to Anglicanism and also protesting that 'he never did anything concerning papists that he had no immediate order from the king' (Sharpe, 1992: 158).

Windebank certainly worked closely with George Con and Henrietta Maria, and in his role as Secretary of State he granted pardons to individual Catholics. William Prynne in *The Popish Royall Favourite* (1643) accused Windebank of consorting with priests and Jesuits including 'Francis Smith alias Francis Ryvers ... a grande Jesuite, a great secular and chief agent in the great and damnable plot of Gunpowder treason'. Of course, by 1643 Prynne and others were drawing up a charge sheet against the whole court of the 1630s. In some respects the labels given to Cottington, Weston, and Windebank are not really significant. All three – and indeed others at court – had Catholic sympathies and contacts. Ultimately, the king controlled religious policy, even if he was often greatly influenced by Henrietta Maria; so Windebank's protestation that in helping Catholics he was carrying out royal policy is probably true.

The court had an impact on London Catholicism. In the area surrounding the court there was an increase in the number of Catholics, spearheaded by the men and women from the queen's household. Somerset House became a focal point for Catholic activities, especially after the opening of the new chapel designed by Inigo Jones in December 1635. The chapel was splendidly baroque, with the reserved sacrament on permanent display on the high altar, angels, and 100 candles. The opening was celebrated by an audience of 2,000 people, and bonfires in the gardens of Catholic embassies. Children were brought to the chapel for baptism, and a tailor was a go-between for the queen and the London Catholic community.

The papal agents, too, had their chapels, and Con's was particularly striking. The Pope's Chapel, as it was known, displayed the Barberini arms, reminding visitors that Con had been secretary to the pope's nephew, Cardinal Francesco Barberini. Con boasted that nine masses a day were said in the chapel on feast days; the chapel also became fashionable for weddings and memorial services (Hibbard, 1983: 57). Embassy chapels had long been centres for London Catholics, but the tolerant altitude engendered by court Catholics led to more services, especially at the Spanish Embassy. Between 1631 and 1637 the ambassador, Juan de Necolalde, recorded frequent masses with English sermons, a choir for sung masses, and chaplains for christenings and marriages. He even created a separate door for courtiers. By the late 1630s, an Irish Dominican, Terrence O'Connell, suggested that there had been such an increase in services in London chapels that many wealthy Catholics no longer felt the need to maintain a priest in their private household (Loomie, 1987: 406–8).

The arrival of the papal agents Gregorio Panzani in December 1634 and – even more – George Con in July 1636 had a significance beyond the availability of their chapels. Both were soon involved in court politics. Panzani worked closely with Cottington and Windebank towards a reunion between Rome and the English church. He promised that if the English government would 'show itself good humoured to the Roman Catholics then Rome would respond'. There was some response in certain quarters. Laud's ally, Richard Montagu, pointed out that over the last few years people's language and inclinations towards Catholicism had changed so much that it might appear that reunion was near at hand (Milton, 1995: 62). Such hopes, although they were shared by Panzani, were excessively optimistic; Panzani, never a successful diplomat, was soon replaced by Con.

Con had an immediate impact on all aspects of court Catholicism. According to Hibbard, 'Con aimed to form a "dévot" party at the English court that would advance English Catholicism' (Hibbard, 1983: 51). In so doing, he particularly influenced the queen, who began to play a more aggressive role in promoting Catholicism. In a letter to Cardinal Barberini in 1637, the queen stated that her 'strongest passion [was] the advancement of the Catholic religion in this country' (Freist, 2011: 43). His diplomatic skills and sociability enabled Con to mix easily with a range of people at court, including the king, and he was liked by both Catholics and Protestants. Over private dinners the king and queen, along with Fr Robert Philip, the queen's trusted chaplain, talked openly with Con about the advantages and disadvantages of reunion with Rome (Hibbard, 1983: 49). Con reported back to Rome that Charles could be interested in reunion along the lines of a 'Gallican' type of settlement in which England, while retaining its ecclesiastical independence, would be Catholic enough for acceptance among the European Catholic monarchies. Con realised, unlike Panzani, that Rome would never accept such conditions.

Con was scarcely more successful over the Oath of Allegiance. The Benedictine monk Leander Jones had unsuccessfully tried to achieve a compromise between Charles and Rome in 1634, and of course the issue between the monarchy and English Catholics had been unresolved since 1606. Con tried again and sent a modified version to Rome in December 1636. In this version the Catholic subject vowed unconditional fealty to the king and promised to defend him against 'all invasions, depositions, rebellion by any prince, priest or people'. But Rome objected to the inclusion of the words 'priest' and 'deposition' as they implied a denial of the Pope's deposing powers. Thereafter, little or no progress was made on the oath (Albion, 1935: 315).

The failures over reunion and the oath stand in contrast to Con's success in proselytising and strengthening the Catholic presence at court. Conversions had occurred earlier in the 1630s, but in 1637 there was a spectacular new wave linked to Henrietta Maria and in particular the Porter household. Olive Porter, wife of Endymion Porter and one of Buckingham's nieces, was at the heart of these conversions. In the spring of 1637 she was instrumental in the deathbed conversion of her father, Lord Boteler, an event that led to an open quarrel with her Protestant sister Lady Newport. In similar fashion, Tom Porter, Olive's brother, became a Catholic just before his death in the summer of 1637.

Most spectacularly, Lady Newport converted to Catholicism, and this caused something of a sensation at court. There were a number of other high-profile conversions, especially women, which led to the lament 'our great women fall away every day' (Hibbard, 1983: 55). In the same year, 1637, a number of prominent Catholics returned from exile to the English court. Wat Montagu, a courtier in the early 1630s but forced into exile on his conversion in 1635, returned from the Roman court. At the same time, Sir Kenelm Digby (son of the Gunpowder plotter Sir Everard) was welcomed back; he had spent his exile in Paris where he converted a number of English Protestants to popery.

Such events and Con's high profile at court inevitably provoked opposition, and a major opponent was Archbishop Laud. Always aware of his vulnerability to the charge that there was a close identity between Laudianism and popery, Laud was an early critic of crypto-Catholic ministers, accusing Weston and Cottington of being too lax on Catholics: 'the wisest physicians [Weston and

Cottington] do not always hit upon the malady and the malignancy of the disease ... For now [the recusants] ... think themselves freed from all command' (Havran, 1973: 121). Laud's rivalry was personal as well as political with Con; were Con to receive a cardinal's hat, an honour he was desperately seeking, then Laud could find himself ecclesiastically outflanked at the English court.

The major clash over policy came in late 1637 when Laud pressed the king to issue a proclamation against proselytising and the open access to London chapels enjoyed by English Catholics. Charles was ready to act, angry over the number of recent conversions and showing his periodic suspicion of embassy chapels, particularly the Spanish. Resenting the apparent influence of the Spanish ambassador over London Catholics, Charles exclaimed 'what I desire to do for the Catholics must come from me alone. I do not wish them to depend on anyone but the Pope and myself' (Loomie, 1987: 407). So the proclamation was duly published in December 1637, with the king stating that 'I want to show that I am of that religion that I profess'. All chapels were subject to more scrutiny, but the queen's chapel was exempt, and the king promised further that individuals named by the queen would not be affected by the proclamation. In the end Con reported with some satisfaction that the proclamation was little more than a threat (Hibbard, 1983: 62).

Although much has been written on the subject in the last 40 years, Aveling's judgement that court Catholicism 'combined menace and fragility in so confusing a way that the soberest observers found it difficult to gauge its real strength' (Aveling, 1976: 132) still carries conviction. To its opponents, court Catholicism was certainly menacing. From the 1620s many inside and outside Parliament linked the protection of fundamental English liberties with the defeat of popery. This was not just a domestic issue, as popery needed to be defeated in the apocalyptic struggle of the Thirty Years' War. The monarchy was the ultimate safeguard against the ever-present threat from Rome and English Catholicism. Yet in the 1630s the king appeared to be promoting Catholicism at home while, in close alliance for most of the decade with Catholic Spain, he remained neutral in the war. What could be more menacing than the threat that the Antichrist would triumph? High-profile demonstrations of the Catholic faith could leave the whole English Catholic community exposed to a backlash if the radical Puritans emerged as the dominant political group in the conflicts of the late 1630s and early 1640s – which indeed materialised by 1641.

The feature of court Catholicism that heightened its menace and increased the venom of the eventual attacks was the role of Henrietta Maria. The queen, according to her critics, epitomised the dangers of Catholicism in her actions and personality; she was theatrical, seductive, and idolatrous. At court, the queen was indeed engaged in theatrical performances, taking speaking parts, perhaps even dressing as a man. Such performances reinforced the association of women, theatricality, the foreign, and the Catholic (Dolan, 1999: 99). Henrietta Maria was firmly in William Prynne's sights in his *Histriomastrix* published in December 1632, with his reference to 'women actors notorious whores'. Prynne went on menacingly to draw an analogy between the Caroline court and that of the Roman emperor Nero who died a violent death 'to vindicate the honour of the Roman Empire', which was 'basely prostituted by his viciousness' (Sharpe, 1992: 648).

In the attacks on Henrietta Maria and court Catholicism there was a strong theme of seduction. The queen had seduced the king, while in a wider sense the baroque culture of the court was seducing the aristocracy. Henrietta Maria was not only a seducer but was associated with the idolatrous cult of the Virgin Mary, with 'Queen Mary herself [being] in the King's own bed' (Dolan, 1999: 120). A later source would make even more of the queen's name, suggesting that 'some kind of fatality, too, the English imagined to be in her name Marie', linking Henrietta Maria not only to the Virgin Mary but also to Mary Tudor and Mary Stuart (Dolan, 1999: 101). Although overall there was little public criticism of the queen and the court in the 1630s owing to tight censorship and the brutal punishment of the likes of Prynne, many criticisms of the queen were duly noted and appeared in a devastating attack in the Grand Remonstrance of 1641. Even the wedding contract was published in full, trying to prove that the match was fundamentally wrong from its inception.

By late 1637, however, it was the strengths of court Catholicism that were apparent. It is true that, despite the best efforts of the queen and the papal agents, only limited benefits had accrued to Catholics. Reunion between the churches of Rome and England had not been achieved, nor any breakthrough on the Oath of Allegiance. Catholics at court enjoyed extensive freedoms, but those outside London benefited a great deal less from court Catholicism. On the other hand, the presence of the papal agents and the active role of the queen meant that there was a stronger Catholic voice in government than at any time since the days of Gondomar in the early 1620s. The papal agent Con, in particular, had achieved a position of sufficient power at court that, as the Scottish crisis unfolded in the course of 1638, he was able to exert pressure on royal policy, urging the king to confront rather than appease the rebellious covenanters. In that confrontation Con argued that the king needed to avail himself fully of Catholic support. In Con's mind, this should have led to a re-alignment of Catholic and royal interests and a significant shift in the position of Catholics within the English state.

Anti-Catholicism

As England became a Protestant nation in the course of Elizabeth's reign, anti-Catholicism became an essential element in English culture as Protestantism identified itself in opposition to Rome and popery: 'The contrast between Catholics and Protestants was central to the definition of identity and difference' (Dolan, 1999: 1). It went further than contrast, insofar as hatred of popery was seen as a positive manifestation of true religion. This hatred of popery was seen most clearly in the identification of the pope as the Antichrist; indeed, it has been argued that this was unchallenged orthodoxy in the Elizabethan church. The late Elizabethan and early Stuart period saw a significant increase of sermons and treaties on the theme of the Antichrist: 'It has been estimated that between 1555 and 1628 over 100 systematic expositions of the Romish Antichrist were published in England or by British authors' (Milton, 1995: 93). Strictly speaking, anti-Catholicism was distinct from anti-popery; while anti-Catholicism was hatred and opposition to Catholics and to the church of Rome, anti-popery extended much further to hatred or opposition to anything deemed redolent of Catholicism, including Laudian ritualism and theological Arminianism (the anti-Calvinist position that emphasised free will in an individual's salvation).

Apocalyptic expectations, a preoccupation with the end of the world and the arrival of the thousand-year kingdom of Christ, were clearly linked to anti-Catholicism. Based on a reading of the Book of Revelation, editions of which flooded Europe after the Lutheran Reformation, the arrival of the Antichrist heralded the imminent apocalypse. Moreover, in 1522 Lucas Cranach, in his illustrations to Luther's New Testament, equates the papacy with the whore of Babylon, 'the mother of prostitutes and abominations of the earth' of Revelation 17 (Cunningham and Grell, 2000: 30). The identification was readily taken up in England, as shown by William Perkins in 1601: 'by the Whore of Babylon is meant the present of Rome: & this whore is said to be drunk with the blood of the Saints ... they of the Romane Church have long thirsted with the bloode of prince and people in this land' (Streete, 2017: 4).

In England, as elsewhere, the identity of the pope and Catholic church with the Antichrist and whore of Babylon led to a denunciation of Catholic beliefs and practices. At the heart of these was a simple but fundamental belief: that popery was an anti-religion, the opposite of true religion. Catholicism was carnal, Protestantism was spiritual; one was inward, the other outward. The pope was the cause of this anti-religion. He was also a tyrant who usurped the rights of princes, while on a spiritual level his tyranny led the Catholic church into darkness as against the light of the Protestant gospel. It was papal tyranny that led to idolatry; instead of the worship of the one true God, papists worshipped the saints and the Virgin Mary. The centrepiece of the Catholic mass, transubstantiation, was 'bread worship'. Papists were hypocrites, with their insistence on good works rather than having faith that Christ's sacrifice on the cross would save them. Yet a recurring theme of anti-Catholic sermons and treatises was the seductive quality of popery; the glitter of the popish imagery would appeal to 'the heart of carnal man, bewitching it with great glistering of the painted harlot' (Lake, 1989: 75, 72–8).

In addition to this literal demonisation of Catholicism which occurred across Europe, domestic anti-popery was shaped by treatises directed to an English audience. No publication was more significant in this respect than John Foxe's *Acts and Monuments*, first published in 1563 but with numerous later editions. In England it was the most read book after the Bible: Ignatius Jordan, mayor of and MP for Exeter in the 1620s, was said to have read the Bible 'above 20 times over' and *Acts and Monuments* some 17 times. According to Foxe, Britain had converted to true Christianity in early apostolic times, and not five centuries later at the instigation of the pope as claimed by Catholic histories. Under

Henry VIII England was the first country in Europe to throw off entirely the popish tyranny. The true church survived fierce persecution under Mary, its survival always guaranteed by God because the English church was destined to play a leading role in the final downfall of Rome as foretold in the Revelation of St John. Some historians have downplayed the significance of nationalism in Foxe, rightly arguing that Foxe was focused on the English church rather than the nation. However, others have pointed out that by the seventeenth century, commentaries on Foxe suggested that England was indeed the Elect Nation (Milton, 1995: 409). But even in the original 1563 publication Foxe compared Elizabeth to Constantine: 'yet wherein is your noble grace to him inferiour?' With its echoes of Henry VIII's claims of 'imperial kingship' in the 1530s, this certainly has strong overtones of nationalism (Álvarez-Recio, 2018: 76).

Foxe's *Acts and Monuments* aimed to establish England's unique role in the preservation of the true church of Christ and in the ultimate defeat of the anti-religion of popery. Starting with the 1569 Northern Rebellion, however, anti-Catholicism was increasingly shaped by the Protestant reaction to major Catholic threats. Such threats proved the tyranny of Rome and the danger of English Catholicism if left unchecked. The immediate Protestant response to the Northern Rebellion was to see the pope as the instigator. Although we have seen in Chapter 1 that the papal bull of 1570, *Regnans in Excelsis*, arrived after the rebellion, commentators were soon asserting that the bull had been in the possession of the rebels: 'it seemeth by all probabilitie ... that the originall of this Bull sealed was among our rebelles and kept close among them ready to be published' (Wiener, 1971: 31).

The memory of the rebellion and the celebration of deliverance became part of popular culture. It was only after 1570, according to the chronicler William Camden, that Elizabeth's accession day of 17 November was celebrated in many towns and parishes across England. The occasion was marked in different ways, with bonfires, bellringing, free food and drink, but also with special prayers and sermons. Edwin Sandys explained that the purpose of the celebrations was 'to give God thanks for that great benefit which were received as this day [17 November], when in his mercy he gave us our gracious elect Elizabeth, whom he used as his mighty arm to work our deliverance, to bring us out of Egypt, the house of Roman servitude'. Thus the memory of the rebellion became part of the Protestant calendar. Almanacs listed the rebellion along with the Armada and the Gunpowder Plot as three of the most important historical events since creation (Kesselring, 2007: 164–6).

The victory over the first Armada in 1588 provoked a similar Protestant reaction. The pope was again seen as central, but with Spain as the actual invading power, the foreign menace of Catholicism was emphasised even more. Some were quick to highlight the idolatrous nature of the popish force the English had just defeated. Dean Nowell of Saint Paul's triumphantly waved captured banners of the Virgin with Christ from his pulpit. In a similar fashion to the aftermath of the 1569 rebellion – but this time more formally – 19 November was decreed as a day of national celebration, with bells and bonfires in parishes and towns. In addition to the pope and Spain, the finger was pointed at English Catholics. In his *Historical Dialogue touching Antichrist and Popery*, the Suffolk minister Thomas Rogers warned that, despite their protestations of loyalty, Catholics could not be trusted: 'papists being the solicitors, papists the prosecutors of this war, papists the soldiers' (Marshall, 2017: 565–6). Many commentators emphasised the theme of deliverance. John Piers, bishop of Salisbury, in his sermon of thanksgiving, reminded his congregation that such deliverance should not be taken for granted. The Armada had been allowed to sail because of the sins of Englishmen, their pride and covetousness. Despite England's failings, God in his mercy had chosen to save the country as the enemy came 'to suppress the Holy Word, and the blessed Gospel of thy dear Son our Saviour Jesus Christ' (McDermott, 2005: 300).

Over the course of the 1580s and the 1590s there was an equally significant development in anti-popery as the Jesuit emerged as a Catholic stereotype. Soon the Jesuits would be established in popular imagination, alongside the pope, as instigators of all plots and schemes that menaced Protestant England. Protestants had good reason to fear the Jesuits. The Jesuits were a major instrument in a militant Counter-Reformation, successful in many parts of Europe, especially across the lands of the Austrian Habsburgs. English Protestants had long-established links with their Continental brethren; the long war against Spain further strengthened the belief that the fate of true religion rested on outcomes in Europe, not just in England. The more immediate problem, however, was the arrival of the first two Jesuits, Campion and Persons, in England in the 1580s, signalling a new dynamism in the Catholic mission. The Jesuits had a fearsome reputation across Europe and were said to possess characteristics that fitted well into the anti-Catholic trope. The Jesuit was a hypocrite, and he was 'Machiavellian', totally lacking scruples: 'The Jesuites will be Spaniards or Frenchmen, or whatsoever else if opportunitie be offered thereunto … The Iesuites change and recharge their own rules and laws at their own good will and pleasure' (Álvarez-Recio, 2018: 116).

According to a French source, the Jesuits promoted rebellion through confession, denying absolution 'unless they [the penitents] would vow and promise to bande themselves against their Soveraigne' (Álvarez-Recio, 2018: 119). They constituted a threat to the patriarchy in the way they usurped the authority of the father or the lord in taking over the household, gaining particular power through their seductive influence over women, especially wives. The Jesuit reputation was not helped by the hostility of other religious orders and, above all, that of the English secular clergy. One of their most virulent critics was Thomas Bell, a secular priest who became a Protestant in 1592 and received a pension from the government to write anti-Catholic works. Thus the reputation of the Jesuits continued to evolve by the time of the Civil War. According to a radical Puritan, they had acquired diabolical powers, with 'a mandrake's voice whose tunes are cries so piercing that the Hearer dies' (Wiener, 1971: 34). The Jesuit became a shorthand for the most wicked form of popery, leading to the term 'a Jesuitical papist'.

We have seen the significance of the Armada as another anti-Catholic marker, but the continued war with Spain and wars with Ireland in the last years of Elizabeth's reign had a further impact on the nature of anti-popery. It became more militarised and, with the accession of James I, more British – a point that would become significant in the late 1630s. In the early seventeenth century, various tracts and treatises linked militant Protestantism and a sense of British identity as well as a commitment to European war. It should be noted that although the Treaty of London 1604 brought peace between England and Spain, the war between Spain and the Dutch continued until 1609, while the Jülich-Cleves Crisis lasted from 1609 to 1614. Many English and Scottish soldiers were involved in these conflicts. For John Russell, King James was placed on earth by God 'not only to unite Britain in true religion but also to purify all Christendom of its idolatry'. Arthur Dent, the militant Essex preacher, hoped that England and Scotland would join other Protestant princes in Europe to lead an army against Rome and 'slay in the field thousands and thousands of her solediers'. Richard Bernard, vicar of Worksop, believed that James should 'wash his feete in the blood of his enemies, namely the servants of the papal Antichrist' (White, 2012: 21). None of these clerics could be described as mainstream clergymen of the established church, but very similar sentiments and language can be found across the Church of England, especially after the outbreak of the Thirty Years' War. They were fairly well thought of among the godly within the church, not just the radicals; Dent was widely read, a bestseller, and Bernard had the support of Archbishop Matthew.

The major fear of good Protestants, though, remained the popish enemy at home. The accession of James I saw a flood of writings on the dangers of the Antichrist, accompanying fears that the king would grant toleration to the Catholics. In 1604, with the re-imposition of recusancy fines, that particular danger passed. In November 1605, an infinitely greater danger confronted the nation in the form of the Gunpowder Plot. The anniversary of deliverance from the plot became a great national holiday, with accompanying services and sermons. According to David Cressy, 'of all historical providences engrained in the memory of English Protestants, the discovery of the Gunpowder Plot on the eve of 5 November, was the most enduring' (Cressy, 1992: 68). The liturgy issued for the celebration attributed the conspiracy to diabolical guile, the nation saved only by the miraculous power of God. This was reinforced in illustrations such as the frontispiece of John Vicars' poem, which shows 'Guy Fawkes and the devil, the Parliament house with barrels of gunpowder underneath, and the eye of heaven sending a beam down to dislodge the treachery' (Marotti, 2005: 145).

The official account of the Gunpowder treason published as *A True and Perfect Relation*, mainly the work of the earl of Northampton and Sir Edward Coke, focused firmly on the role of the Jesuits: Coke called it 'The Jesuit treason'. The publication also emphasised that the Gunpowder Plot was only one of the many assaults on the English monarchy, all masterminded by the Jesuits. The usual menacing traits were attributed to the Jesuits: they were diabolically cunning and subversive in that they were defenders of papal deposing power which sanctioned regicide. They were guilty of the practices of lying and equivocation and aiding the invasion of the country by foreign powers (Marotti, 2005: 133–6). The theatre contributed to the anti-popish assault with plays such as Thomas Dekker's *The Whore of Babylon*, first performed in 1606. As we have seen, Babylon was identified with the pope and the Catholic church. At the start of the play the empress of Babylon is shown exercising supreme temporal as well as spiritual power: 'Empresse of Babylon: her canopie supported by four cardinals: two persons in pontificall roabes on either hand, the one bearing a sword, the other the keises; before her three kings crowned' (Streete, 2017: 48).

In the immediate aftermath of the Gunpower Plot but also well beyond, anti-popish sermons, treatises, and plays continued with no decline in volume or ferocity. When the Catholic priest William Bishop complained about the slanderous attacks on Catholics following the plot, Robert Abbot, later to be bishop of Salisbury, replied that the attacks had not been vehement enough. There was not one minister 'who in his sermons doth so th[o]roughly lay foorth the villanie and wickednesse of your profession as in trueth the cause and matter thereof doth require' (Milton, 1995: 36). In a more general sense, it was not possible for Puritans to have too much anti-popery, as a heightened sense of threat from the papal Antichrist was one of the signs of election to salvation.

No new event brought the issue of anti-popery to political centre stage until the outbreak of the Thirty Years' War in 1618. When James's son-in-law Frederick of the Palatinate, a Protestant, accepted the throne of Bohemia (traditionally held by the Catholic Habsburgs) there was huge optimism in many sectors of English society. This optimism was expressed in the now familiar apocalyptic language. Archbishop Abbot predicted that Catholic princes 'shall leave the whore and leave her desolate'. A Protestant astronomer saw in Halley's Comet astrological proof that 'the House of Austria cannot continue above the year 1623 and Rome 1646' (Cogswell, 1989: 114). This optimism was based on the expectation that England would support Frederick and the Protestant cause; James instead chose peace with Spain and the pursuit of a Spanish marriage for his son Charles. This policy was greeted with predictable horror by many Protestants: 'Have peace from Babylon?' Theophilius Higgons asked; 'you can have no peace *with* her'. Instead, she needed to be destroyed with fire and sword (Cogswell, 1989: 113).

The anti-popish attacks or criticism of the king's policy of the Spanish match became more muted as strict censorship was imposed on press and pulpit. By 1622 Buckingham boasted to Gondomar 'no man can now mutter a word in the pulpit, but he is presently catched and set in straight prison' (Cogswell, 1989: 119). Even in 1621 Samuel Ward, the Puritan preacher at Ipswich, had to print his critical publication in Amsterdam. Seeing the proposed Spanish marriage as again needing God's special deliverance, his broadsheet was entitled *To God in memory of the double deliverance from the invincible Navie and unmatchable powder Treason*. Although the king could silence the pulpits, he could not prevent popular expressions of anti-Catholic and anti-Spanish feelings. In 1623 the Spanish ambassador formally protested that the delegation was besieged in their embassy, attacked by stones thrown whenever they left the building.

However, the worst violence involved the French, not the Spanish embassy. In October 1623, the temporary building of the French embassy collapsed, killing 90 Catholics and injuring hundreds who had gathered to hear a Jesuit preacher. The London crowd set upon the survivors, 'assaulting them with curses as well as rubble and rocks'. A girl was dragged from the wreckage, but the crowd seemed intent on beating her to death. The Venetian ambassador, generally a sober commentator on events in London, described it as 'a general and bloody riot perpetrated by Calvinist fanatics' (Walsham, 2006: 114).

It is difficult at times to gauge the depth of anti-Catholicism in Caroline England. Court Catholicism of the 1630s was certainly more provocative to the sensitivities of good Protestants than any issues since the Spanish match, yet anti-Catholic rhetoric and anti-popish alarms were relatively muted. It is tempting to see the ferocity of anti-popery in the years 1640–2 as a release of pent-up fury against court Catholicism, but we cannot simply read the ideas of the early 1640s back onto the 1630s; a closer analysis is needed. Court Catholicism became more aggressive in 1637, while after the Scottish crisis developed, there was fear of a new popish plot. It was in the early 1640s, however, that anti-popery hit unprecedented levels. The depth of anti-Catholic fears 'are seen most clearly in the years 1640–42, the period when the immediate causes of the civil war were set in train. In three years the number of known panics over Catholic plots was six times that of the preceding four decades' (Clifton, 1973: 158).

For much of the 1630s anti-Catholic rhetoric was less widespread than earlier decades, and this was due to the control that Archbishop Laud and his fellow Arminian bishops exercised over the English church and the wider public. There were more outspoken attacks on anti-papal treatises, and greater censorship of publicised material. The chaplains of both Laud and Bishop Juxon purged anti-papal passages from several books and sermon collections. Purged passages included references to Rome's idolatry, the pope as the Antichrist, and the papacy as 'that drunken woman'. Each purging showed the gulf between Laud's ideas on Rome and the Catholic church and the ideas that were almost orthodoxy in the Elizabethan and Jacobean church. So it is scarcely surprising that anti-Catholic attacks in the 1630s were often made in the context of anti-Laudianism. Laudianism was the immediate enemy, and represented imminent danger. The godly believed that Laudianism was a Trojan Horse 'ready to open the gates to Romish tyranny and Spanish monarchy'. The same point was made less flamboyantly by Richard Sibbes: 'nothing in papery [was] so gross but [it] had small beginnings, which being neglected by those that should have watched over, the church grew at length insufferable' (Clifton, 1971: 36; Walsham, 2006: 204).

The way that anti-popery became encased in anti-Laudianism in the 1630s can be seen from the publications of William Prynne. His *Histriomastix* was one of the major anti-Catholic treatises of the decade, but Prynne expended a good deal of energy attacking Laud and Laudians. Laud himself, who 'will far sooner hug a popish priest in his bosom than take a puritan by the little finger' was a target, but so too were his fellow bishops and Laudian clerics (Milton, 1995: 85). Prynne's pamphlet *Newes from Ipswich* was a scurrilous attack on

Bishop Wren of Norwich and it went through four editions between 1636 and 1641. The pamphlet denounced all the Laudian bishops for 'their Romish innervations, whereat the whole kingdom cries shame, which breed a general fear and sudden alteration of our religion'. These prelates are 'anti-Christian'; they were said to have 'a pope in their belly' (Durston and Eales, 1996: 111). In 1637 Prynne wrote a pamphlet against a Laudian cleric in Colchester, Matthew Newcomen, who would only give communion to those who knelt at the communion rails (Walter, 1999: 179). In the 1640s, of course, Prynne returned to full-scale attacks on aspects of popery. His *Popish Royal Favourite* of 1643 is a recitation of the popish menace over the previous decades, while subsequently he saw the malign presence of papists and Jesuits everywhere: they infiltrated the radical movements such as the Levellers and Ranters, and were even responsible for the 1649 regicide (Walsham, 2006: 204).

But even by the late 1630s there are signs of an increase in anti-Catholicism. By 1638 some of the Gunpower Plot sermons, whose anti-popish invective had been modified by Laud, appeared to be reverting to full-blown anti-Catholicism. Richard Heyricke, dean of Manchester, whose previous November 5 sermons had been critical of court Catholicism, in 1638 emphasised the 'bloodthirstiness' of 'such papists that adhere to the pope of Rome as to their head, Italian, Spanish, Jesuited, Gunpowder papists'. He made the usual call for greater punishment of Catholics: 'cruelty for Christ is godliness'. By the next year, the sermon was more pointedly political. Heyricke blamed the first Bishops' War not on the Scots but on Jesuits and their supporters in a sermon 'laying open the perjuries, treacheries, treasons, the murders, massacres, cruelties of Rome-Christians' (Hibbard, 1983: 145–6). In spite of court Catholicism, there were few popular fears over Catholicism in the 1630s. Northampton and Bristol reported alarms in 1630 and 1636, while in 1633 Buckinghamshire reported fears of a Catholic uprising in the king's absence on his visit to Scotland. But the greatest alarm was raised in 1639 when a Spanish fleet appeared in the Channel heading to the Netherlands: 'It was thought by many that these Wallons and Irishes were intended to be used against us' (Clifton, 1973: 158). The transport of troops must have been a regular occurrence in the 1630s, so perhaps this particular alarm reflected the growing fears of a 'popish plot'.

Popish plots, the fear of popery, and the collapse of the regime

When rioting broke out in St Giles' Church, Edinburgh, in July 1637 against the imposition of the new English Prayer Book, few would have predicted that this event would develop into one of the defining issues, not only in Anglo-Scottish relations, but in the crisis that engulfed Britain up to 1642. Charles's failure either to make concessions or defeat the Covenanters had a significant impact on religious politics. On the one hand, the Covenanters soon found a sympathetic audience with the anti-Laudian Protestants in England, a sympathy which they fully exploited through extensive propaganda. On the other, the papal agent George Con (himself a Scot) argued that only by drawing upon the support of Catholics in his three kingdoms could the king hope to defeat the rebellious Scots. The greater use of Catholics, militarily and financially, in the years 1639–41 engendered the belief that royal policy was harbouring a 'popish plot' whose aim was to make Catholicism the dominant or even the sole religion in England, Scotland, and Ireland.

Con saw the trouble in Scotland as an opportunity to further the interests of Scottish Catholics, which he had promoted since his arrival at the English court in late 1636. Backed by crypto-Catholics such as Cottington and Windebank, Con advocated a hard line against the Covenanters. He portrayed the Scottish troubles as part of a Calvinist conspiracy. At the same time, and somewhat contradictorily, Con cast doubt on the Covenanters' religious sincerity, stressing instead their treasonous political intent. As Charles was already thinking along the same lines and was also ready to blame the French for exploiting the trouble in Scotland, Con's comment struck a chord with the king. The papal agent also contrasted Catholic loyalty with the treachery of the Covenanters.

It is difficult to know how quickly or comprehensively Con's advocacy of a tough stance against the Scots led to a defined policy of greater reliance on Catholics across Britain. In return for this support, Catholics could expect concessions, and the sight of Catholics receiving better treatment would increase the possibility of financial help from Spain and Rome. Con made concrete proposals for the military and political support of Catholics, and in June 1638 he reported that the king seemed willing to rearm the Catholics who had been legally forbidden to bear arms since the reign of Elizabeth, although there were many exemptions from this prohibition. According to Robert Baille, a leading Covenanter, it was indeed in the summer of 1638 that Charles made it clear that he intended to rally British Catholic forces to defeat the Scots. Charles's representative in Scotland, the 6th marquess of Hamilton, warned the Covenanters that if they continued to oppose the king they would be 'threatened with an Irish army on the West, [and] by all the power three marquesses in Scotland and the popish party can make with the help of the north of England' (Hibbard, 1983: 96).

Subsequently the threat included the use of Spanish troops. Baille, of course, was keen to blame the breakdown between the king and the Scots on provocation by Charles. The fact that Hamilton continued to negotiate until late 1638 suggests he was cautious regarding Baille's claims. However, it is clear that even in 1638 Charles saw the use of force at least as an option, as he told Hamilton that he had ordered arms from Holland, while Wentworth was doing the same for his Irish army. Moreover, by the end of 1638, plans were taking shape to bring together a British army in which the Scottish and Irish contingents would be heavily Catholic (Russell, 1990: 76).

Once England decided on military confrontation with the Covenanters in early 1639, Charles hoped that Scottish Catholic forces could defeat their Protestant opponents on home territory. The great lowland Catholic families led by Robert Maxwell, earl of Nithsdale, would provide the main force, supported by English troops from Carlisle. Highland Catholics would be aided by an Irish army led by Randal, 2nd earl of Antrim. The choice of Antrim reinforced the idea that royal policy was a product of court Catholicism. Antrim, a friend of both Charles and Henrietta Maria, was married to Buckingham's widow who was openly Catholic and influential at court. By the spring of 1639, however, it was clear that the royal plans were failing. Salvetti, the Florentine agent, commented on the situation in Scotland: 'Although some Scots, mostly Catholic are with the king ... they are not enough for a party and will be of little help to the king'. Meanwhile Antrim never managed to leave Ireland to link up with the Highland Scots; with no support from Wentworth, Antrim's forces drifted away, with his leading officers joining the Spanish army in Flanders. So Charles's ambitious plans for the Scottish and Irish 'popish armies' came to very little in the end, but their efforts fitted well into the Covenanters' propaganda that behind royal policy lay a threatening 'popish plot' (Hibbard, 1983: 35, 115–17).

It was therefore an English (and Welsh) force that confronted the rebellious Scots in May 1639, not an army from the 'Three Kingdoms'. This English army was also known as 'popish' in some circles, though it hardly deserved this description. The majority of the army was not Catholic, and most of the leading officers were distinctly Protestant. The commander was, however, the earl of Arundel, who was seen as a crypto-Catholic and identified by many foreign ambassadors as a potential head of a Catholic party. For Baille, Arundel was 'a known papist and head of the Spanish and popish faction in England'. Con had in fact complained about how little Arundel had done for English Catholics, but his Catholic reputation was sealed when he travelled to see the king in Con's coach emblazoned with the papal coat of arms. The presence in the army's camp of Endymion Porter, along with a number of Catholic priests, all added to the popular sense of popery within the royal forces (Hibbard, 1983: 100–1).

The 'Catholic Contribution', a plan to raise a separate sum of money from English Catholics and with the expectation that they would be prominent in volunteering for the royal army, seemed to highlight the point that the war against the Scots was driven by a Catholic agenda. The plan, first drawn up in late 1638, soon had strong support among Catholic clerics, the queen, and court Catholics. The 'Contribution' was a concrete expression of Con's general idea that Charles should rely on Catholic support. Cardinal Francesco Barberini backed the plan, informing Con how keen he was to see Catholics enlist and give money. In January 1639 Anthony Champney, now dean of the chapter of the secular clergy (and therefore de facto leader of the secular clergy in the absence of Bishop Richard Smith), wrote a circular letter exhorting Catholics to help Charles. Catholics should be willing to be part of the effort to subdue those unjustly rebelling against their king. Here was the Catholic opportunity to show true loyalty and refute the Puritan portrayal of the traitorous papist. Con added a final but very different argument: if Catholics failed to give money voluntarily, Charles could resort to higher recusancy fines. The sums raised were disappointingly low: £14,000 after a promised £40,000–50,000, and Catholics noticeably volunteered only in the Welsh force. This probably reflects Catholic reluctance outside London and the court; they were rightly sceptical of real benefits and fearful that such public positioning would result in a backlash from any future Parliament and indeed a wider public (Questier, 2006: 499–502).

So with the 'Armies of the three Kingdoms' proving to be something of a mirage and the English army inadequate, Charles was forced into the Truce of Berwick in June 1639. When in turn the truce failed to lead to any lasting settlement with the Scots, Charles's advisors pressed him to summon Parliament (the Short Parliament of April 1640). Many Catholics, including the new papal agent Rossetti, feared a full-scale assault; in fact, the anti-popery was quite restrained, though telling points were made. Harbottle Grimstone argued that although the Scots represented a serious threat, there was 'a case of greater danger at home domestical'. Pym, moderate by later standards, did focus on the presence of 'a plot ... to reduce our land to the pope'. This plot encompassed the promotion of Arminians as well as Catholics, which Pym then linked to a range of secular grievances, including taxation [*Doc. 19*, p. 133–4].

The failure of the Short Parliament, however, was swiftly followed by outbreaks of popular anti-Catholicism as a rumour quickly spread that the dissolution was the result of a 'popish plot' at the Stuart court. Angry mobs rioted in Southwark, then threatened Arundel and Somerset House, before turning on the Spanish embassy, 'threatening to pull down the house and kill the ambassador' (Loomie, 1987: 401). The mayor of Norwich feared an attack on the city by 12,000 papists. John Gell of Hopton in Derbyshire heard that the papists of Lichfield had ordered 200 hatchets to massacre Protestants. In Colchester, Irish arsonists were said to be in the streets; and there were anti-Catholic alarms in dozens of communities including Bristol, Salisbury, York, and Newcastle (Clifton, 1973: 158; Sharpe, 1992: 910).

By the time of the second Bishops' War in August 1640, political tensions had risen and divisions widened. Relations between the Covenanters and the king's political opponents were drawing ever closer, while the revived model of a British force to oppose the Covenanters looked stronger and more Catholic than in the earlier war. In Scotland, the earl of Montrose and 17 other Scottish nobles signed the Cumbernauld Bond against the Covenanters, suggesting increased Catholic strength in Scotland. The Welsh contingent in the English army consisted of 2,000 men, three times the size of the previous year, with the Catholic earl of Worcester prominent in commissioning the troops. Above all, Catholic troops were being raised in Ireland, this time by the earl of Strafford, who undertook to provide 9,000 men.

Despite such promise, the 'Three Armies' failed to deliver, forcing Charles to accept the Treaty of Ripon in October 1640. The political fallout was immense. There was now a rebel army camped in the north of England able to ramp up the 'popish plot' narrative, which was of course a narrative fully endorsed by the likes of Pym and his allies. Significantly, the plot was now said to include not just Catholics but Laud, Strafford, and many at court. Not surprisingly, the papal agent Salvetti declared that the king's only friends were Catholics, while the English Puritans and Covenanters were united in their determination to eliminate Catholicism and change the government of Charles. In fact, the outcome was the calling of the Long Parliament in November 1640 (Hibbard, 1983: 156).

The assault many Catholics had feared from the Short Parliament materialised after November 1640 in the Long Parliament. Although it would transpire that a significant number of MPs and peers feared the disorder of a Puritan upheaval as much as popery, it was the religious radicals who led the agenda. Charges against Strafford were linked to his alleged support of popery and his supposed intention to bring over an Irish Catholic army to England. The attack on Strafford was soon accompanied by details of wider alleged Catholic conspiracy. Sir John Clotworthy stressed the dangers from a well-trained Irish army of 10,000 men, 8,000 of them papist. Pym told the Commons of William O'Connor, an Irish priest who had served in the household of the queen, where 'many thousands in [her] pay [were] ready to cut all Protestants' throats'. In addition, the earl of Worcester was preparing a papist army in South Wales. Alexander Rigby raised the issue of the 'Catholic Contribution' and stressed the link between Henrietta Maria, the papal agent Rossetti, and the Catholics of Lancashire (Lancashire had paid most toward the 'Contribution'). Lancashire papists, he claimed, were fasting weekly for the queen's 'pious intentions'. Lancashire was the most Catholic of counties and a natural landing place for an Irish army. Such reports were therefore alarming (Hibbard, 1983: 173–4; Fletcher, 1981: 4).

Within a few months, however, control of the parliamentary agenda by Pym and his followers was being challenged. Although in December 1640 London had petitioned for the abolition of bishops, by early 1641 the main petitions were for their retention. By May the trial of Strafford had stalled. In the same month Pym revealed the existence of an 'army plot', a plan to bring the English army south in a show of force to intimidate Parliament. The timing of the plot was so favourable to Pym and his followers that doubt has been cast over the plot's existence, but modern historians have judged it authentic (Hibbard, 1983: 194–5; Cust, 2007: 283; Russell, 1990: 281–2). The leaders of the plot, men such as Henry Percy, Henry Wilmot, and George Goring, were not Catholic but were closely connected to Henrietta Maria. Furthermore, one source suggests that a wider group of supporters included the distinctly Catholic Sir Kenelm Digby and Wat Montagu. Rumours that this English army would be joined by the Irish army, backed by the French military, were sufficient to ensure that the plot was seen as another 'popish conspiracy'. 'What a great scorn the papists have made of us', declared Pym, insisting that all papists must be disarmed and punished. On 7 May a search and arrest of priests and Jesuits was carried out in London, while mobs attacked the Spanish and Portuguese embassies on the basis of rumours that armed Catholics were meeting there (Hibbard, 1983: 195). The idea of the 'popish plot' was reinforced in parliamentary circles.

The Irish Rebellion, which broke out in October 1641, stirred up fears beyond the earlier 'popish plots' of 1639–41 [*Doc. 18*, p. 132–3]. Anti-Irish rhetoric had always been closely associated with anti-Catholicism, but with added dimensions. According to Cornelius Bruges in his sermon on Gunpowder Treason Day 1641, the Irish were brutal, violent, and barbaric. Bruges mentions the Irish 'cutthroat' who roams English towns and shires ready to attack Protestants, already a recognisable character from numerous anti-Irish narratives: 'The Irish rebels were not men, but tigers, not beasts but devils'. Bruges saw the Irish Rebellion as a foretaste of what English Catholics would do if powerful enough 'to be able to master the Protestants in England'. The more militant preacher, Stephen Marshall, urged the godly Protestants to wage a holy war in Ireland. And in appropriately apocalyptic language he warned the faint hearted, 'cursed is everyone that withholds his hand from the shedding of blood'. Both language and themes used in demonising the Irish rebels fitted the established 'popish plot' tradition. An important element of the tradition was the emphasis on deliverance and here both authors make a significant political point. The House of Commons, not the monarch, is the true protector of English Protestant identity and national security (Marotti, 2005: 153–4).

The Irish Rebellion had an immediate and widespread effect across England. At Pudsey in Yorkshire a church service was interrupted by someone who called out: 'Friends we are all as good as dead men, for the Irish they are come as far as Rochdale ... and will be at Halifax and Bradford shortly' (Coward and Gaunt, 2017: 217). This prompted one of the congregation from Bradford to call out that on his return home he would meet 'but incarnate devils and death'. In Norwich and Guildford papists allegedly started fires; from London, Colchester, and across to Wales there were reports of Catholics storing arms (Clifton, 1973: 160). However, all of these rumours focused on the threat Catholics posed to their Protestant neighbours; there are few reports of violence against Catholics as occurred later in the summer of 1642 as the country drifted into civil war.

For all the outraged reaction to Catholic atrocities in Ireland, Parliament produced few novel or radical anti-Catholic measures. Henrietta Maria was the major focus of hostility as she was thought to have been involved in earlier negotiations with the rebels. Salvetti reported that the parliamentary leaders 'dare to name her the principal author of that revolt, calling it the queen's rebellion' (Hibbard, 1983: 214). One publication, *The Declaration of Fears and Jealousies*, claimed that the Irish rebels 'call themselves the Queen's Army', and that booty captured from the English was inscribed with Henrietta Maria's mark (Dolan, 1999: 129).

According to Clarendon, one of the most significant consequences of the rebellion was the propaganda weapon it handed to Parliament. Pym exploited the opportunity to the full. According to Pym, the king's refusal to separate himself from the Catholic party was the cause of the present problem in England and Ireland. He concluded that 'there hath been one common council at Rome and in Spain to reduce us to popery' (Hibbard, 1983: 215; Lindley, 1972: 163). The rebellion was part of a European design against Protestantism: the Irish, in league with English and Welsh Catholics, were thought to be planning an invasion of England. So the 'popish plot' scenario was played to the hilt. But some thought that Pym was overplaying the anti-popish card. Thomas Wiseman, Remembrancer of the City of London, writing of this intense anti-popery warned 'but oftentimes wee have much more printed then is true, especially when anything concerns the papists, who, though they are bad enough, our preciser sort strive yet to make them worse' (Russell, 1991: 415). But even according to Wiseman papists were bad, and the legacy of the years 1639–41 was a deep-rooted popular belief in 'popish plots' and widespread anti-Catholicism.

In the summer of 1642 anti-Catholic violence was reported in a number of areas, but particularly in areas of radical Protestantism such as the Essex/

Suffolk border. Individual Catholics were attacked and hounded; Elizabeth Darcy, countess Rivers, was forced to flee her house in St Osyth for Long Melford, where a mob followed her; she was forced to take refuge in Bury St Edmunds, which shut its gates against the rioters, until she escaped to London (Young, 2015: 10–14). These attacks were part of an increasing social conflict as the gentry were the prime targets, and Royalist gentry in particular. If the Catholic gentry were not 'getting along' so well with their neighbours in the course of 1642, it was more likely that those neighbours were their social inferiors or keen Parliamentarians. Recent important work by Eilish Gregory has examined the use of sequestration against Royalists, Catholics, and clergy of the established church accused of 'bringing in popery' as a means of raising revenue for the Parliamentarian regime (Gregory, 2021: 7).

Catholics adopted a variety of positions in the English Civil War, ranging from active Royalism to neutrality and even accommodation with the Parliamentarian cause, and English Catholicism of course survived the Civil War. However, the outbreak of armed hostilities between king and Parliament in 1642 represented the failure of the Elizabethan settlement that had endured, against all odds, since 1559. Although that failure stemmed primarily from unresolvable internal divisions within English Protestantism, the awkward position of Catholics at the court of Charles I was also a contributing factor to the breakdown of the old Elizabethan ecclesiastical polity. Catholics after 1642 – and indeed after the Restoration's new religious settlement in 1661 – faced a new negotiation of their position, and new challenges.

Documents

Document 1

Count Von Helffstein to the Emperor Ferdinand I, 16 March 1559

When Elizabeth ascended the throne she approached the religious question with great caution, as the imperial ambassador noted with approval in March 1559.

From the very beginning of her reign she has treated all religious questions with so much caution and incredible prudence that she seems both to protect the Catholic religion and at the same time not entirely to condemn or outwardly reject the new Reformation … In my opinion, a very prudent action, intended to keep the adherents of both creeds in subjection, for the less she ruffles them at the beginning of her reign the more easily she will enthral them at the end.

Source: Von Klarwill, 1928: 47

Document 2

John Scory, bishop of Hereford, to the Privy Council, 1564

Except for the Catholic bishops and a number of the cathedral clergy, only a small minority of the Marian clergy resigned rather than accept the Elizabethan Religious Settlement. But many who continued in office showed strong Catholic sympathies, as this report by Bishop Scory on Hereford Cathedral indicates.

I. Besides mine own knowledge, Mr John Ellis, dean of the said church, hath certified to me as followeth: that all the canons residentiary (except Jones, qui dicit et non facit [speaks and does not do], which is rash, hasty and indiscreet) are but dissemblers and rank Papists. And these have the rule of the church and of all the ministries and offices of the same and are neither subject to the ordinary jurisdiction, nor of the dean nor of the bishop … So that they may now do as they like without controlment. They neither observe the Queen's Majesty's injunctions given unto them in her Highness's visitation nor the Archbishop of Canterbury's injunctions given them in his visitation nor yet the injunction of the Queen's Majesty's High Commissioners … The Communion was not ministered in the Cathedral Church since Easter (as I am informed). The canons will neither preach, read homilies, nor minister the Holy Communion, nor do anything to commend, beautify or set forward this religion, but mutter against it, receive and maintain the enemies of religion. So that this church, which should be the light of all the diocese, is very darkness and an example of contempt of true religion, whom the city and country about follow apace.

Source: Caraman, 1960: 43

Document 3

Alexander Nowell's sermon to Parliament, 1563

In his opening sermon to the 1563 Parliament, Alexander Nowell protested that Elizabeth's policy towards the Catholics had been too lenient. He argued that clemency should not be shown to supporters of false religion; on the contrary, they should be put to the sword. On more than one occasion Elizabeth showed her open disdain for Nowell and his views.

The Queen's majesty of her own nature is wholly given to clemency and mercy, as full well appeareth hitherto. For in this realm was never seen a change so quiet; or so long reigning without blood (God be praised for it). Howbeit those which hitherto will not be reformed, but obstinate ... ought otherwise to be used. But now will some say, Oh bloody man! that calleth this the house of right, and now would have it made a house of blood. But the Scripture teacheth us that divers faults ought to be punished by death: and therefore following God's precepts it cannot be accounted cruel. And it is not against this house, but the part thereof, to see justice ministered to them who would abuse clemency. Therefore the goodness of the Queen's majesty's clemency may well and ought now therefore to be changed to justice seeing it will not help. But now to explicate myself, I say if any man keeping his opinion, will, and mind close within himself, and so not open the same, then he ought not to be punished. But when he openeth abroad, then it hurteth, and ought to be cut off. And specially if in any thing it touch the Queen's majesty. For such errors of heresy ought not, as well for God's quarrel as the realm's, to be unlooked into. For clemency ought not to be given to the wolves to kill and devour, as they do the lambs. For which cause it ought to be foreseen; for that the prince shall answer for all that so perish, it lying in her power to redress it. For by the scriptures, murderers, breakers of the holy day, and maintainers of false religion ought to die by the sword.

Source: Haugaard, 1968: 330

Document 4

Edmund Campion on the dangers of the mission, 1580

Edmund Campion vividly related details of the persecution of Catholics in this letter, probably written to William Allen in November 1580. The persecution was initiated by the regime in response to the threats in Ireland, but above all to the arrival of Campion and Robert Persons. Campion is perhaps being a little prophetic in suggesting 'innumerable' martyrdoms, as worse was to come in the course of the 1580s, starting with his own cruel martyrdom.

E[dmund] C[ampion] to [Dr Allen?]. Having been here five months, I write to you what has happened since I last wrote from St Omer. I sailed on the day of St John Baptist, my peculiar patron, and my little man [Ralph Emerson?] and I reached Dover early next morning. We were all but taken, for we were brought before the mayor as favourers of the old faith, and dissembling our names; he thought I was Dr Allen, and said he would send us before Council. I prayed to St John, and by his help we escaped, an old man coming forth and telling us we were dismissed; but I believe I shall some day be apprehended.

I came to London to the house where father Robert [Persons] was. Young gentlemen came on every hand and embraced me, giving me apparel and weapons, and conveyed me out of the city.

I ride daily in the country, meditating my sermon on horseback, hear confession, and after mass, preach, being greedily heard, and give the sacraments. The country priests are virtuous and learned; they have raised such an opinion of our society that all Catholics do us exceeding reverence; therefore those who are to be sent should be well trained for the pulpit.

I cannot long escape the heretics, they have so many scouts; I wear ridiculous clothes, often change my name, and so often read newsletters that Campion is taken, that I am without fear. Let those whom you send take into account the solaces that countervail these miseries, and by their sweetness make worldly pains seems nothing, viz., a pure conscience, courage, zeal, a worthy work amongst high and low, in great numbers, even the milder Protestants; it has become a proverb that he must be Catholic who faithfully pays what he owes; and if a Catholic do an injury, it is thought unworthy of his calling. There are no men more corrupt and impure that the ministers, and we may well be indignant that fellows so base and unlearned should overrule the noble wits of the realm.

Threatening edicts come forth against us daily, yet we have escaped thus far; men neglect their own safety to take care of mine. I had set down in writing the causes of my coming; that I was a priest, and wished to teach the gospel and minister the sacraments, asking audience of the Queen and nobility, and professing disputations. I kept one copy in case I fell into the officers' hands, and left the other with a friend, but he did not keep it close; it was greedily read, and my adversaries were mad, answering out of the pulpit that they would dispute, but the Queen would not allow matters already established to be called in question. They call us seditious hypocrites, and even heretics, which is much laughed at. The people are ours, and the spreading this writing has advanced the cause. With a safe conduct, we would go to Court. But they have filled the old prisons with Catholics, make new ones, and affirm that it were better to make a few traitors than that so many souls should be lost.

They brag no more of their martyrs, since now, for a few apostates and cobblers of theirs turned, we have bishops, lords, knights, the old nobility, flower of the youth, noble matrons, and innumerable of the inferior sort either martyred or dying by imprisonment. In the house where I am, there is no talk but of death, flight, prison, or spoil of friends; yet they proceed with courage.

Many new soldiers restored to the church give up their names, whilst the old offer up their blood.

We need much your prayers and sacrifices. There will never want men in England that will take care of their own and others' salvation, nor will this church fail, so long as priests and pastors are found for the sheep. The rumour of present peril causes me to make an end.

Source: Green, 1872: 24–5

Document 5

William Weston on immeasurable suffering, 1585

Persecution in the 1580s was of unprecedented severity, although in 1585 persecution had not yet reached the draconian levels of 1588 and the years immediately following.

The days that followed the Parliament [of 1584–5] were bitter days for Catholics and filled with immeasurable suffering. Earlier, indeed, there had been great cruelty. Many had been broken. But now the fury of the persecution burst upon them more savagely still. It was the power held by the Earl of Leicester that was responsible, combined with Cecil's counsel, for these two men were in control under the Queen. Catholics now saw their own country, the country of their birth, turned into a ruthless and unloving land. All men fastened their hatred on them. They lay in ambush for them, betrayed them, attacked them with violence and without warning. They plundered them at night, confiscated their possessions, drove away their flocks, stole their cattle. Every prison no matter how foul or dark, was made glorious by the noble and great-hearted protestations of saintly confessors, and even martyrs. In the common thoroughfares and crossways watchmen were abruptly pasted, so that no traveller could pass peacefully on his way or escape stringent scrutiny. On the same night and at the same hour, now a single town, now several throughout the kingdom, experienced the sudden incursion of secret spies: inns, taverns, lodging-houses, bedchambers, were searched with extreme rigour, and any suspected person, unable to give a satisfactory account of himself, was put in prison or under guard until morning; or until he could clear himself before the magistrates of the suspicion that he was a Catholic, and, in particular, a Catholic priest. Untrue reports were set in motion that a hostile Armada was being prepared, even approaching England; counterfeit letters were written, purporting to come from Catholics, disclosing plots against the Queen – it was the fashion to believe they planned the Queen's death. Some spies, in fact, went so far as to disguise themselves as Catholics and get themselves arrested and imprisoned in order to confess their guilt and inflame the people's passion against the Catholics, and so have sharp vengeance demanded on them.

In London sometimes – I witnessed this myself and listened to Catholics groaning and grieving over it – a report would go round and be confirmed as certain fact, that the Queen's Council had passed a decree for the massacre of all Catholics in their houses on this or that night. Then many people would abandon their homes and lodgings and pass the night in the fields; others would hire boats and drift up and down the river. And a rumour was afoot, supposed to come from the lips of Cecil himself, that he was going to take steps to reduce Catholics to such destitution that they would be incapable of helping one another and, like swine, would be grateful if they could find a husk on which to appease their hunger. In fact, it appeared to me that the prophecy of our Saviour was then fulfilled, 'They will put you out of the synagogues: and whosoever killeth you will think that he doth a service to God'.

Source: Weston, 1955: 31–2

Document 6

Catholicism: the 'old faith'

The claim that Catholicism was the religion of continuity, while the Elizabethan church was a recent innovation, was the most common defence used by Catholics for their recusancy.

I was born in such a time when holy mass was in great reverence, and brought up in the same faith. In King Edward's time this reverence was neglected and reproved by such as governed. In Queen Mary's time, it was restored with much applause; and now in this time it pleaseth the state to question them, as now they would do me, who continue in this Catholic profession. The state would have these several changes, which I have seen with mine eyes, good and laudable. Whether it can be so, I refer to it your Lordships' consideration. I hold me still to that wherein I was born and bred; and find nothing taught in it but great virtue and sanctity; and so by the grace of God I will live and die in it.

Source: Clifford, 1887: 38–9

Document 7

The continuity of Catholicism, 1586

The document shows the itinerant lifestyle of the schoolmaster and seminary priest Thomas Bramston, according to his deposition of 1586. However, Bramston's account is deliberately vague, and given the draconian statutes of 1581 and 1585, his account appears to be aimed at not implicating Sir Thomas Tresham, or indeed himself, beyond admitting he was a priest.

Thomas Bramston saith he hath taken no degrees in schools. He saith he was brought up in his young years in the grammar school in Canterbury under old

Mr Twine. From Mr Twine he went to Westminster and there continued a year and was a novice in the abbey. From thence he went to Mr Roper of Eltham, where he went to Westminster and there continued a year and was a novice in the abbey. From thence he went to Oxford to St John's College where he continued about three or four years and was fellow of that college. From thence he went to Dr Feckenham who was in the tower, where he continued so about two years. From thence he went to serve Sir Thomas Tresham, to whom he did belong coming and going, about ten years and was schoolmaster to his house until such time as the Act of Parliament was made that none should teach either publicly or privately but such as would conform themselves to the religion now established, which as he thinketh was about the 18th year of the Queen's Majesty's reign [1576]. From Sir Thomas Tresham's service he went over sea, and confessing that he is a priest, he will not answer to any question, neither when he went over, but saith that he was no priest when he was schoolmaster in Sir Thomas Tresham's house, which was ten or eleven years since.

Source: Foley, 1878: 224–5

Document 8

A copy of a letter from Cardinal Allen found in Mr Wiseman's house, 1592

From the 1560s William Allen insisted on recusancy for Catholics, and the same line was taken by the seminary priests. The Jesuit mission made 'reconciliation' their initial prime objective. However, faced with unprecedented penalties for recusancy in the 1580s, many of the Catholic gentry opted for at least some conformity and church papists became an essential element in the English Catholic community. Allen is recognising this reality.

[Cardinal Allen] Requires those that are priests to use great compassion towards such of the laity as, from mere fear, or to save a wife and family from ruin, are so far only fallen as to come sometimes to [Protestant] churches, or be present at their services; for though it be not lawful nor excusable to do so, yet necessity makes the offence less, and more easy to be absolved. They [the priests] are therefore not to be too hard in receiving them again, and absolving them when they confess and are sorry for their infirmity, and yield hope that hereafter they will stand more strongly, or have means to escape, and not be led into the like temptation. They [the priests] must use this mercy, though they fall more than once, and though there is fear that they will fall again, and no more severity is to be used than in any other sins. Such matters cannot be subject to certain rules, they must use wisdom and charity ... Yet they must have great regard not to teach nor defend that it is lawful to communicate with the Protestants in their prayers, services or conventicles; this is contrary to the practice of the Church in all ages, and of the holy doctors, who never communicated, nor allowed any Catholic to pray with Arians, Donatists, or what other soever; neither is it a positive law of the Church, for so it might be dispensed with upon some occasion; but it is denied by God's eternal law, as has been proved in sundry treatises, and practised from the beginning of their missions.

Source: Green, 1867: 292

Document 9

The church papist

Despite the widespread practice of church papistry, the Catholic conformist was the butt of contemporary abuse. Protestants were suspicious of such people, seeing them as the worst type of Catholic because of their deviousness and lack of respect towards the services of the established church. A head of the household would sometimes conform in order to alleviate the pressure of recusancy fines; the reference to the church papist charging his wife 'what she stands him in religion' refers to the husband withholding expenditure on his wife's clothes because her recusancy makes him liable to fines and therefore costs him money.

A [Church] Papist is one that parts religion between his conscience and his purse and comes to church not to serve God but the King. The fear of the law makes him wear the mark of the Gospel which he useth, not as a means to save his soul, but his charges. He loves Popery well, but he is loth to lose by it, and though he is something scared by the Bulls of Rome, yet he is struck with more terror at the apparitor. Once a month he presents himself at the church to keep off the churchwardens ... kneels with the congregation, but prays by himself and asks God's forgiveness for coming thither. If he is forced to stay out a sermon, he puts his hat over his eyes and frowns out the hour; and when he comes home, he thinks to make amends for his fault by abusing the preacher ... He would make a bad martyr, and a good traveller, for his conscience is so large that he could never wander from it, and in Constantinople would be circumcised with a mental reservation. His wife is more zealous in her devotion and therefore more costly, and he bates [charges] her in tires [clothes] what she stands him in religion.

Source: Caraman, 1960: 272–3

Document 10

A memorandum by Guy Fawkes, July 1603

In 1603 Guy Fawkes, hoping to encourage Spain to support a rising against James I, argued that England was ripe for rebellion. Rebellion was due not just because of religious divisions, but also because of the great opposition to the Scots in England.

The peers of England are seen to be unhappy with the Scots mainly for their crudity and particularly for the many quarrels at court. There, a royal page slew a page of the Earl of Northumberland with a dagger. Another Scot struck an Englishman in the Presence Chamber, yet they did not punish him but merely excused him as insane ... Some of the principal gentlemen have not wished to come to the court, although many of their friends have implored them to do so. It is certain if it were not for the fathers of the Society, the schismatics in England would have long since taken up arms ... because of the slight satisfaction offered to the Catholic religion. A thing which they desire as much, or more, than the Catholics, so as to end the war of conscience which kills them by degrees.

There is a natural hostility between the English and the Scots. There has always been one, and at present it keeps increasing through these grievances, so that even were there but one religion in England, nevertheless it will not be possible to reconcile these two nations, as they are, for very long.

Source: Loomie, 1971: 63

Document 11

The constable of Castile on the position of English Catholics, November 1604

The possibility of Spanish intervention to restore Catholicism to England had already greatly receded by 1603, but the peace of 1604 (the Treaty of London) formalised this position. The constable of Castile, Juan Fernández de Velasco, visited London in August 1604 as ambassador extraordinary to sign the peace treaty. After leaving England he wrote this review of the religious situation in England. It is a fairly realistic assessment, but was aimed at any critics of the peace and at a handful of Catholic exiles in Spain who were still advocating military intervention in England.

The temporal resources of the Catholics of this kingdom alone are very weak, and they could not and would not dare to attempt anything. While a foreigner's strength might encourage them, it is much more likely after a landing that the interests of other princes would become apparent. They do not want foreigners, especially the Spanish, to come in here, out of fear for their own power.

Source: Loomie, 1971: 35

Document 12

The Oath of Allegiance, 1606

In the aftermath of the Gunpowder Plot, James I introduced the Oath of Allegiance. Historians have differed on whether its purpose was merely to try to ensure Catholic loyalty to the Crown, or to split the English Catholic community. The oath was enormously troublesome to the Catholic body, as refusing it carried huge penalties, but refusing it in effect meant denying the papal claim to depose princes (clause 3).

The tenor of which oath hereafter followeth:

xv. I A. B. do truly and sincerely acknowledge, profess, testify and declare in my conscience before God and the world, That our sovereign lord King JAMES is lawful and rightful King of the realm, and of all other his Majesty's dominions and countries; and that the Pope neither of himself nor by any authority of the church or of Rome, or by any other means with any other, hath any power to depose the King, or to dispose any of his Majesty's kingdoms or dominions, or to authorize any foreign prince to invade or annoy him or his countries, or to discharge any of his subjects of their allegiance and obedience to his Majesty, or to give licence or leave to any of them to bear arms, raise tumults or to offer any violence or hurt to his Majesty's royal person, state or government, or to any of his Majesty's subjects within his Majesty's dominions.

(2) Also I do swear from my heart, That notwithstanding any declaration or sentence of excommunication, or deprivation made or granted, or to be made or granted, by the Pope or his successors, or by any authority derived or pretended to be derived from him or his see against the said King, his heirs or successors, or any absolution of the said subjects from their obedience: I will bear faith and true allegiance to his Majesty, his heirs and successors, and him and them will defend to the uttermost of my power, against all conspiracies and attempts whatsoever which shall be made against his or their persons, their crown and dignity, by reason or colour of any such sentence or declaration, or otherwise, and will do my best endeavour to disclose and make known unto his Majesty, his heirs and successors, all treasons and traitorous conspiracies which I shall know or hear of to be against him or any of them.

(3) And I do further swear, That I do from my heart abhor, detest and abjure, as impious and heretical, this damnable doctrine and position, That princes which be excommunicated or deprived by the Pope, may be deposed or murdered by the subjects, or any other whatsoever.

(4) And I do believe, and in my conscience am resolved, That neither the Pope nor any other person whatsoever, hath power to absolve me of this oath or any part thereof, which I acknowledge by good and full authority to be lawfully ministered unto me, and do renounce all pardons and dispensations to the contrary.

(5) And all these things I do plainly and sincerely acknowledge and swear, according to the express words by me spoken, and according to the plain and common sense and understanding of the same words, without any equivocation or mental evasion, or secret reservation whatsoever: and I do make this recognition and acknowledgement heartily, willingly and truly, upon the true faith of a Christian.

So help me God.

Source: Statutes of the Realm, 3 James I c. 4

Document 13

Catholic reasons for refusing the Oath of Allegiance, c. 1607

Some Catholics took the Oath of Allegiance, but more appear to have refused. The reasons for refusal ranged from arguing that the oath concerned the nature of the church as well as temporal allegiance, to pleading that the oath was too complicated for simple men to understand. The account below, probably written in about 1607–8, is typical of documents circulating at the time explaining the reasons why Catholics refused to take the Oath.

Reasons of refuzall.

1. Yf the late parliament oathe did conteyne nothing but onely matter of temporal allegeaunce to the Kinge's Majestic, his heires and lawfull successors, no true English subjecte, beinge offred the same, but would take it hartelie and willinglie, But beinge a mixte oathe, partlye acknowledginge temporall allegiance, but cheifelie denyenge the aucthoritie and power of the Churche, which howe farre it reacheth is unknowne (consideringe the ritch endowmentes of power and aucthoritie given thereunto, and to the pastors thereof, by our Savior Christe in holie Scriptures), it is therefore impossible to be trulie lymitted by an othe.

2. Yf anie successor should usurpe the governement of this realme, and should embrace Turkysme or Arranisme, and commaund the same to be professed thoroughe this realme, or should seeke the subvertion of the lawes and State; or yf the two kingdomes of England and Scotland (nowe united) shoulde hereafter discend to diverse heires of bothe nations (which God forbid): that oathe doeth bind us to assiste anie such successor to our uttermost power, and also to the allegeance of suche a successor of Scotland, contrarie to the loyaltie of such a true Englishe subjecte, bycawse theis wordes are wantinge in the second clause of that oath: his heires and lawfull successors kinges and queens of this realme.

3. The Pope, beinge a temporall kinge, hath diverse dukes and princes his subjectes, which hold of him their temporall estate, whome (if they deme him his right) he maie lawfullie commaund to be invaded, deposed and killed either by lawe of armes or course of justice. How then can that oathe be taken without manifest perjurie, comprehendinge the negative universallie in the third clause, videlicet: that princes which be excommunicate etc., without anie excepcion?

4. Diverse partes of that oathe doe conteyne pointes of doctrine and schoole learninge controverted amongst the greatest divines both aunciente and moderne, as appeareth by the late booke set out of Mr Blackwell's examynacion. Howe then maie anie man – especiallye unlearned – safely sweare that thinge to be true which is doubtfull and questionable, or sweare that he is resolved in conscience, when the thinge he doth sweare unto is in question and not defyned? For allbeit, by the cannon lawe and judgement of all schoole dyvines, it be concluded that the Pope, albeit hee bee an absolute kinge and pastor of the universall Churche, yet yf he fall into heresie maie be deposed, or rather, ipso facto is deposed, yet with safty of conscyence yt cannot be sworne unto, mucheles a question of schoole learnynge untermined; for that in an oathe wee, call the sacred majestie of God to witnes, who is truthe it selfe, and therefore ought to sweare nothinge but that wee know assuredlie to be true as that wee lyve.

5. How can a man truelie sweare that he doeth abjure a posicion which he never held, and that the said doctrine is hereticall: yt being never for such condempned either by aucthoritie of the Churche's ancient fathers, generall

counsell or schoole of divines, especiallie seeinge the whole oathe is to be taken accordinge to the expresse wordes and common sence thereof?

6. Finallie, the oathe beinge tendred under great penaltie to the refuser, how can anie man truelie sweare that he doeth take yt hartelie and willinglie?

Source: Petti, 1968: 160–1

Document 14

Complaints against Lord William Howard, 1616

Lord William Howard of Naworth in Cumberland belonged to one of the great northern Catholic families whom the regime had to tolerate because his power was essential to the maintenance of law and order in the border regions. It helped that he was a known loyalist who endorsed the Oath of Allegiance. Note the supposed links with London, possibly with Dr Frier, a prominent London Catholic physician. The writer is obviously not a follower of Lord William.

In Christenmas last at Bampton in Westmorland within the diocese of Carlile, the tenantes and servants of my Lord Wilyam, together with others in the parish, did erect a Christenmas lord, and did most grosselie disturbe the minister in time of Service; the minister himselfe granting toleration because he doth ordinarilie dine and suppe at the Lord Willyam's table, but never prayes with him, and thes Christenmas misrule men some of them drunke to the minister when he was at prayers, others stept into the pulpit and called the parishioners to an offering for maytenance of ther sport, others of the Lord Willyam's servants came into the Church disguised, others shotte gunnes in the Church, and brought in flagges and banners, others sported themselfes with pies and puddings in the Church, using them as bowles in the Church-allies, others played with dogges, and used them as they used to fear sheap, and all these were done in the Church and in time of Divine service, and the said Lord doth bring the ministers about him in comtempt, scorne and derision.

A minister in London hath confidentlie reported that the said Lord Willyam hath 50,000^{li} of the Jesuites' moneyes committed into his handes in trust to be disposed for the benefitte of the Jesuites and mayntenance of others of that profession, and for the confirmation of this report Mrs Paine, dwelling in Iselington, did tell a gentleman living in Saint Martin's that she had seane a letter written to Doctor Frier, a phisition and recusant, from his daughter, now in a monasterie beyond the seas, wherein she did intreat her father to give thanks to the Lord Willyam for her quarteridge, which she receyved from the Lord Willyam, and she sayd Mrs Payne did see the said letter and hard it read by the Doctor.

The Lord Willyam is thought to keep a priest in his howse, which upon examination may more plainelie be knowne.

The Lord Willyam oppresseth and terrifieth all men with suites (against whom he hath anie show of occasion, though never so triviall) that are not wholie his, and of his faction, in all his Juries and other unfitte courses, as Namelie these gentlemen of place and account in the countrie, viz: – Sir James Bellingham, Knight, Sir Henrie Curwen, Knight, Henrie Dacres, Esquire, Richard Rigge, Esquire, Thomas Salkeld, Esquire, in manie severall actions, Hugh Salkeld, gentleman, his owne tenants of Gilesland.

Generallie, if ther be anie suite in the countrie, if he be not a principall mover of it, yet he interposeth and joynes himselfe with the one side though it do nothing at all concerne him, and he so forceth it with his great powre in Court and countrey that all turbulent persons ar by him protected and set on worke.

Source: Ornsby, 1878: 423–5

Document 15

Annual letter of the Durham (Northern) mission, 1638/9

Although the remote moorland areas of the northwest were challenging for the mission, the Jesuits were reaching out to the non-gentry classes in the moorlands of Westmorland in the late 1630s. One of the appeals of Catholicism appears to have been the reputation of Catholic priests for exorcism.

In these years the number of conversions was, respectively, thirty-seven and eighty. The Fathers had entered upon a new mission in the mountains of Westmorland. Several instances of the miraculous powers of the Church's exorcisms are mentioned. One of them was that of a Protestant woman who had suffered much pain and vexation, which was attributed to witchcraft. She had applied for relief to Protestant ministers, but without effect. She now betook herself to one of the Fathers, who, having instructed her and administered the Sacrament of Penance, applied to her the exorcism of the Church, on which she became perfectly freed from her torments. Thinking herself now safe, the inconstant woman returned to her former heresy, but soon relapsed into a state of hopeless bodily disease.

Source: Foley, 1878: 122–3

Document 16

Devotional practices of Philip Howard

The pre-Reformation church put more emphasis on fasting than most of the missionary priests. But the tradition of regular fasting and abstinence from meals continued to be practised by the Catholic gentry well into the seventeenth century. This document describes the strict fasting routine followed by Lord Philip Howard.

In the year 1588 soon after his second commitment to close prison, he began to fast three days every week, Mondays, Wednesdays and Fridays, and in them

[ate] neither flesh nor fish: But finding by experience that his body was not able to endure so much, he altered it in this manner. That his one meal on Mondays was of flesh: on Wednesdays of fish: on Fridays of neither flesh nor fish, and abstaining also from all whitemeats and wine. And this manner he observed constantly both before and after his arraignment (excepting only the Wednesday immediately following it, wherein he did eat some small thing for supper having then some special need thereof) until he was prescribed by his physicians to alter that course, which was not long before his death. Many time he used also the same abstinence upon Thursdays as upon Mondays with only one meal of flesh. And upon some special days he abstained wholly from all kinds of Sustenance either meat or drink. These were the vigils of the feasts of Corpus Christi, of the Ascension of our Saviour, of All Saints, as also the eves of the feasts of the Blessed Virgin, to whom he was particularly devout.

Source: Caraman, 1960: 169

Document 17

A bequest for the Jesuits and other Catholic causes

The English missionary priests depended to a large extent for their finance on the bequests of the English Catholic laity. But such bequests had to be left in a discreet manner to avoid falling foul of the law. The need for such 'discretion' was a factor in gentry opposition to secular clergy's proposal that a new English bishop should supervise the finances of the mission. Here William Blundell relates how his sister did this in a letter written in 1640.

Emelia Blundell, my unmarried sister, died at my house, Crosby in Lancashire, on 29 of August 1640. Some few days before her death, she made a Will of which she named me the sole Executor, and did give me thereby all her monies, Bonds and other worldly Goods. (This Will was afterwards attested at Chester, and there I suppose it remaineth still recorded.) But after she had done and that the Witnesses were retired, she told me it was her desire that I should send one hundred pounds to Our Lady's of Loreto and give £100 to the Society of Jesus, and several other sums to other charitable uses: so that it was believed ... that she did prudently disguise her piety by colour of such a will, as knowing well that our laws did not favour such kind of gifts.

Source: Blundell, 1933: 7–8

Document 18

Fear of Catholicism

Fear of Catholicism grew in the seventeenth century and rumours of papist plots tended to circulate during times of political crisis. By the 1640s, on the eve of the English Civil War, and then during the war itself, the belief in papist plots became far more widespread, and fear of Catholicism became a potent political factor.

The 16th of November, 1641, there was a cruel and wicked plot discovered about the city of London, which was intended against some of the chief members of the High Court of Parliament, and brought to light by a religious man. Therefore it was commanded by the House of Commons that great search should be made for the finding out of two Frenchmen, who were supposed to be the chief agents in this wicked design ... they intended the murder of many Protestant Lords, with many other gentlemen, such as Mr Pym and the like, and the papists in Wales intended to seize into their hands all the strongholds of Cheshire and Lancashire, with the adjacent parts, And that in that hurly burly and combustion, the plot was laid and contrived that by the papists at the same instance, the City of London should have been surprized, and all the Protestants' throats cut.

A Plot against Norwich to burn the City

Upon the 27 day of November [1645] there was a great uproar in Norwich concerning the Papists arising there, they being intended to burn the whole city without any remorse, two being appointed privily for the same purpose, one to begin at one end of the City, and the second at the other end. The one was discovered being about to set fire to a thatched house, the other he set the house on fire joining to high Bridge street, which was burnt to the ground to the great astonishment of the whole City.

Source: Wallington, 1869: 44–8

Document 19

John Pym's anti-Catholicism in the Short Parliament, April 1640

John Pym was the key MP leading the attack on Charles I, and the main instrument of that attack was 'anti-popery'. Charles's failure to defeat the Presbyterian Scots, with whom Pym was clearly closely allied, exposed the monarchy to a frontal attack for its supposedly lenient policies towards Catholics throughout the 1630s. By the standards of Pym's attacks in the Long Parliament, this speech was in fact quite restrained.

The second generall head is of those grievances that concerne Religion, established by the Lawe of God and man,

1. The encouradgm[en]te given to them of the Popish Religion; divers of them might be of themselves I confesse of peaceable disposicions and good natures, but wee must not looke upon them [as] they are in their natures for the planetts of themselves are of a slowe and temperate motion, weare they not hurried about by the rappid motions of the spheares, and they carryed about by the violence of the primum mobile; soe are all these Papists at the Popes command at any tyme, who onely waytes for blood. I may Instance in Hen. 3 and 4 of France, that were both taken away for alloweinge of Protestants. I desire noe

newe lawes, nor a rigid execucon of these wee have but onely soe far forth as may tend to the safetye of his Majestye. 2dly I observe a suspension of those lawes made against the Papists which are not either executed at all, or are onely so farre used as to make a proffitt by them whereas the said lawes were not made for the Kings revenue, but for distinction.

3dly There is an unrestrayned and mutuall communication of o[u]r Consell with them [such as at Court].

4thly They are encouradged by admittinge them to greate places of trust in the church and commonwealth (I crave pardon for the last slippe of my tongue), but I wish with all my heart that it neither be soe nowe nor at any tyme hereafter.

5thly The employm[en]t of a Nuncio from Rome, whose Councell and businesse is to reduce our land to the Pope.

2 The second head of the second Generall is an Applying of us towards a conversion to Rome.

First by the printing and publishing of many ill Popish bookes with priviledg; the publishing and preachinge [of] many Popish poynts in Pulpitts and disputed in schooles in the Universityes and there maynteyned for sownd Doctrine.

2dly The introduccon of Popish Ceremonyes such I meane not as the Constitucon since the Reformed Religion continued onto us; But we must introduce againe many of the superstitions and infirme cermonyes of the most decreppid age of Poperye, as the setting up Altars, boweing to them, and the like.

3. Next I shall observe the dayly discouradgement of those that are the best professors of o[u]r Religion, for not doinge something that were against their consciences. The manner of howse of Commons usually hath been to reconcile men of nice Consciences to their B[isho]pps, thereby to hide the weaknesses of others, but this was a meanes [to publish] the disgrace yt may be to all the world, as these good men for the most part feele.

Now Ceremonyes as boweing at the name of Jesus [and] rising up at Gloria Patri are imposed upon the consciences of men and required as dutye and the omission thereof punish without all grownd. And many Ministers likewise without any ground of Lawe questioned [for not reading] the Booke of Libertyes on the Saboth a booke which I must needs affirme hath many thinges faultye. And for not doing of it have beene deprived of their livings, etc. This is a very greate greivance being ag[ains]t the foundacon of gover[n]m[en]t.

Source: Coates, 1977: 254–60

Guide to further reading

The volumes in the Catholic Record Society's Records Series, published from 1905 onwards, are among the most accessible ways of accessing primary sources relating to the English Catholic community in the entire period covered by this book. At the time of writing, past volumes up to 2006 are available to read free online at https://issuu.com/tcrs.

Chapters 1 and 2

On Elizabeth's own policy and motivations, the work of Susan Doran is indispensable, especially in *Elizabeth I and her Circle* (2015) and *Monarchy and Matrimony* (1996), the latter dealing with the projected Anjou match. Sandeep Kaushik's work on loyalist Catholicism, especially his 1996 article 'Resistance, Loyalty and Recusant Politics' is important for understanding the motivations of Sir Thomas Tresham and other recusants in supporting the Elizabethan regime. The work of Katy Gibbons, especially her book *English Catholics in Late Sixteenth-Century Paris* (2011), is essential to the study of the first wave of English Catholic expatriates on the Continent.

Chapters 3 and 4

Jessie Childs's *God's Traitors* (2014) offers important insight into the recusant community, while Alexandra Walsham's classic study *Church Papists* (1999) remains essential reading on those Catholics who were not recusants. The competing interpretations of John Bossy and Christopher Haigh regarding the extent to which Elizabethan Catholicism was a largely new creation or largely the persistence of traditional faith can be found in Bossy's *The English Catholic Community* (1975) and Haigh's *Reformation and Resistance in Tudor Lancashire* (1975), and these differing approaches remain seminal. Gerald Kilroy's recent work on the mission of Edmund Campion (*Edmund Campion: Memory and Transcription* [2005] and *Edmund Campion: A Scholarly Life* [2015]) is an important contribution to our understanding of the Elizabethan English mission, while Michael Questier's editions of and commentary on correspondence relating to the Archpriest Controversy and related issues are comprehensive and crucial. The works of

Alexandra Walsham represent one of the most important contributions to the study of post-Reformation Catholic culture and devotional practices.

Chapter 5

On Catholicism in the reign of James I, Michael Questier's *Catholicism and Community in Early Modern England* (2006) and *Dynastic Politics and the British Reformations* (2019) are two important works, along with older work by A. J. Loomie on Anglo-Spanish relations in James's reign in studies such as *Spain and the Early Stuarts 1585–1655* (1996). David L. Smith's study of Edward Sackville (1991) provides a good example of the ambiguity of religious convictions in the period.

Chapter 6

The work of Richard Cust on Charles I in *Charles I: A Political Life* (2007) and other writings is important for the study of Charles's character and motivations. Michael Questier's *Newsletters from the Caroline Court, 1631–1638* (2005) chronicles the ecclesiastical policy of the Catholic church in Caroline England and the growth of court Catholicism. Arthur Marotti's studies of anti-Catholicism, especially his *Religious Ideology and Cultural Fantasy* (2005), are excellent for understanding the phenomena of anti-popery and anti-Catholic prejudice, alongside the older work of Robin Clifton, and Peter Lake's seminal article 'Antipopery: The Structure of a Prejudice' (1989). John Walter's *Understanding Popular Violence in the English Revolution* (1999) remains essential to appreciating the role of anti-Catholicism in the slide towards Civil War in the early 1640s. Eilish Gregory's *Catholics during the English Revolution, 1642–61* (2021) will no doubt become the standard work on the period immediately after that covered by this book.

Bibliography

Albion, G., *Charles I and the Court of Rome*, Burns & Oates, 1935.
Alford, S., *The Early Elizabethan Polity: William Cecil and the British Succession Crisis, 1558–1569*, Cambridge U.P., 1998.
Allison, A.F., 'A Question of Jurisdiction. Richard Smith, Bishop of Chalcedon, and the Catholic Laity, 1625–31', *Recusant History*, 16, 1982: 111–145.
Álvarez-Recio, L., *Fighting the Antichrist: A Cultural History of Anti-Catholicism in Tudor England*, Sussex Academic Press, 2018.
Aveling, J.C.H., *Northern Catholics: The Catholic Recusants of the North Riding of Yorkshire, 1558–1790*, Chapman, 1966.
Aveling, J.C.H., *Catholic Recusancy in the City of York*, Catholic Record Society, 1970.
Aveling, J.C.H., *The Handle and the Axe: The Catholic Recusants in England from Reformation to Emancipation*, Blond & Briggs, 1976.
Bainbridge, V., 'Propaganda and the Supernatural: The Bridgettine Nuns of Syon Abbey in Exile, c. 1539–1630' in *Women on the Move: Refugees, Migration and Exile*, 25–42, ed. F. Reid and K. Holden, Cambridge Scholars Publishing, 2020.
Bartlett, K., 'Papal Policy and the English Crown, 1563–1565: The Bertano Correspondence', *Sixteenth Century Journal*, 23, 1992: 643–659.
Basset, B., *The English Jesuits*, Burns & Oates, 1967.
Basset, B., *The English Jesuits from Campion to Martindale*, Gracewing, 2004.
Bastow, S.L., 'Aspects of the Catholic Gentry of Yorkshire from the Pilgrimage and Grace to the First Civil War', PhD, University of Huddersfield, 2002.
Binczewski, J., 'Power and Vulnerability, Widows and Priest Holes in the Early English Catholic Community', *British Catholic History*, 35, 2020: 1–24.
Bindoff, S.T., *The House of Commons, 1509–1558*, History of Parliament Trust, 1982.
Blundell, M., ed., *Letters of William Blundell to his Friends 1620–1648*, Longman, 1933.
Borges, C.J. (2004) 'Stephens, Thomas (1549–1619)', in *Oxford Dictionary of National Biography*. Available at: https://doi.org/10.1093/ref:odnb/26393 (Accessed 18 October 2020).
Bossy, J., 'English Catholics and the French Marriage', *Recusant History*, 5, 1959: 1–16.
Bossy, J., 'The English Catholic Community 1603–1625' in *The Reign of James VI and I*, 91–105, ed. A.G R. Smith, MacMillan, 1973.
Bossy, J., *The English Catholic Community 1570–1850*, Darton, Longman and Todd, 1975.
Bossy, J., 'The Heart of Robert Persons' in *The Reckoned Expense: Edmund Campion and the English Jesuits*, 142–158, ed. T.M. McCoog, Institutum Historicum Societatis Jesu, 1996.

Bossy, J., *Under the Molehill: An Elizabethan Spy Story*, Yale U.P., 2001.
Brigden, S., 'Youth and the English Reformation', *Past & Present*, 95, 1982: 37–67.
Butler, C., *Additions to the Historical Memoirs Respecting the English, Irish and Scottish Catholics*, vol. 4, John Murray, 1821.
Caraman, P., *The Other Face: Catholic Life under Elizabeth I*, Sheed & Ward, 1960.
Caraman, P., *Henry Garnet, 1555–1606 and the Gunpowder Plot*, Longman, 1964.
Carleton, K. (2011) 'Watson, Thomas (1513–1584)', in *Oxford Dictionary of National Biography*. Available at: https://doi.org/10.1093/ref:odnb/28865 (Accessed 13 October 2020).
Childs, J., *God's Traitors: Terror and Faith in Elizabethan England*, The Bodley Head, 2014.
Cliffe, J.T., *The Yorkshire Gentry: From the Reformation to the Civil War*, Athlone, 1969.
Clifford, H., *The Life of Jane Dormer, Duchess of Feria*, ed. E.E. Estcourt and J. Stevenson, Burns & Oates, 1887.
Clifton, R., 'Popular Fear of Catholicism during the English Civil War', *Past and Present*, 52, 1971: 23–55.
Clifton, R., 'Fear of Popery' in *The Origins of the Civil War*, 144–167, ed. Conrad Russell, 1973.
Coates, S., ed., *Proceedings of the Short Parliament*, Camden Society, 1977.
Cogswell, T., 'England and the Spanish Match' in *Conflict in Early Stuart England: Studies in Religion and Politics 1603–1642*, 107–133, ed. R. Cust and A. Hughes, Longman, 1989.
Cogswell, T., Cust, R. and Lake, P., eds, *Politics, Religion and Popularity: Early Stuart Essays in Honour of Conrad Russell*, Cambridge U.P., 2002.
Collinson, P., *From Cranmer to Sancroft: Essays on English Religion in the Sixteenth and Seventeenth Centuries*, Hambledon Continuum, 2006.
Connelly, R., *Women of the Catholic Resistance in England, 1540–1680*, Pentland Press, 1997.
Cooper, T. (rev. T.H. Clancy) (2004), 'Gilbert, George (d. 1583)', in *Oxford Dictionary of National Biography*. Available at: https://doi.org/10.1093/ref:odnb/10689 (Accessed 14 October 2020).
Cooper, T. (rev. T. McCoog) (2007), 'White, Andrew (1579–1656)' in *Oxford Dictionary of National Biography*. Available at: https://doi.org/10.1093/ref:odnb/29236 (Accessed 18 October 2020).
Corens, L., *Confessional Mobility and English Catholics in Counter-Reformation Europe*, Oxford U.P., 2019.
Coward, B. and Gaunt, P., *The Stuart Age: England 1603–1714*, Routledge, 2017.
Cressy, David, 'The Fifth of November Remembered' in *Myths of the English*, 68–90, ed. R. Porter, Polity, 1992.
Croft, P., 'The Catholic Gentry, the Earl of Salisbury and the Baronets of 1611' in *Conformity and Orthodoxy in the English Church, c. 1560–1660*, 262–282, ed. P. Lake and M. Questier, Boydell, 2000.
Cunningham, A. and Grell, O.P., *The Four Horsemen of the Apocalypse: Religion, War, Famine and Death in Reformation Europe*, Cambridge U.P., 2000.
Cust, R., 'Charles I and Popularity' in *Politics, Religion and Popularity: Early Stuart Essays in Honour of Conrad Russell*, 235–258, ed. T. Cogswell, R. Cust and P. Lake, Cambridge U.P., 2002.
Cust, R., *Charles I: A Political Life*, Routledge, 2007.

Debe, D.D. and Menard, R.R., 'The Transition to African Slavery in Maryland: A Note on the Barbados Connection', *Slavery and Abolition*, 32, 2011: 129–141.

Dickens, A.G., 'The First Stages of Romanist Recusancy, 1560–1590', *Yorkshire Archaeological Journal*, 35, 1943: 157–181.

Dietz, F.C., *English Public Finance, 1558–1641*, Century, 1943.

Dijkgraaf, H., *The Library of a Jesuit Community at Holbeck, Nottinghamshire (1679)*, LP Publications, 2003.

Dillon, A., *The Construction of Martyrdom in the English Catholic Community 1535–1603*, Ashgate, 2002.

Dolan, F.E., *Whores of Babylon: Catholicism, Gender and Seventeenth-Century Print Culture*, Cornell U.P., 1999.

Doran, S., *Monarchy and Matrimony: The Courtships of Elizabeth I*, Routledge, 1996.

Doran, S., 'The Queen' in *The Elizabethan World*, 35–58, ed. S. Doran and N. Jones, Routledge, 2011.

Doran, Susan, *Elizabeth I and her Circle*, Oxford U.P., 2015.

Duffy, E., *The Stripping of the Altars: Traditional Religion in England, 1400–1580*, Yale U.P., 1992.

Duffy, E. (2008), 'Allen, William (1532–1594)' in *Oxford Dictionary of National Biography*. Available at: https://doi.org/10.1093/ref:odnb/391 (Accessed 16 October 2020).

Duffy, E., *Fires of Faith: Catholic England under Mary Tudor*, Yale U.P., 2009.

Duffy, E., 'Praying the Counter-Reformation' in *Early Modern English Catholicism: Identity, Memory and Counter-Reformation*, 206–225, ed. J. Kelly and S. Royal, Brill, 2016.

Duffy, E., *Reformation Divided: Catholics, Protestants, and the Conversion of England*, Bloomsbury, 2017.

Duffy, E., *A People's Tragedy: Studies in Reformation*, Continuum, 2020.

Dures, A., *English Catholicism 1558–1642*, Longman, 1983.

Dures, A., 'The Emergence of The Catholic Community in London', *South-Eastern Catholic History*, forthcoming.

Durston, C. and Eales, J., eds, *The Culture of English Puritanism, 1560–1700*, Palgrave, 1996.

Edwards, J., *Archbishop Pole*, Ashgate, 2013.

Fincham, K., *The Early Stuart Church 1603–42*, Stanford U.P., 1993.

Fletcher, A., *The Outbreak of the English Civil War*, Hodder Arnold, 1981.

Fletcher, A. and MacCulloch, D., *Tudor Rebellions*, 5th edn, Pearson, 2008.

Foley, H., *Records of the English Province of the Society of Jesus*, vol. 3, Burns & Oates, 1878.

Freist, D., '"Popery in Perfection": The Experience of Catholicism: Henrietta Maria between Private Practice and Public Discourse' in *The Experience of Revolution in Stuart Britain and Ireland*, 33–51, ed. M.J. Braddick and D.L. Smith, Cambridge U.P., 2011.

Gerard, John, *John Gerard the Autobiography of an Elizabethan*, ed. P. Caraman, Family Publications, 2006.

Gibbons, K., 'Saints in Exile: The Cult of St Thomas of Canterbury and Elizabethan Catholics in France', *Recusant History*, 29, 2009: 315–324.

Gibbons, K., *English Catholics in Late Sixteenth-Century Paris*, Boydell & Brewer, 2011.

Gillett, C.P., 'Probabilism, Pluralism, and Papalism: Jesuit Allegiance Politics in the British Atlantic and Continental Europe, 1644–50' in *Jesuit Intellectual and Physical Exchange between England and Mainland Europe, c. 1580–1789: 'The World is our House?'*, 235–262, ed. J. Kelly and H. Thomas, Brill, 2019.

Graffius, J., 'Relics and Cultures of Commemoration in the English College of Saint Omers in the Spanish Netherlands' in *Jesuit Intellectual and Physical Exchange between England and Mainland Europe, c. 1580–1789: 'The World is our House?'*, 113–132, ed. J. Kelly and H. Thomas, Brill, 2019.

Green, M.E., ed., *Calendar of State Papers Domestic 1591–94*, Her Majesty's Stationery Office, 1867.

Green, M.E., ed., *Calendar of State Papers Domestic Additional 1580–1625*, Her Majesty's Stationery Office, 1872.

Gregory, E., *Catholics during the English Revolution, 1642–61: Politics, Sequestration and Loyalty*, Boydell & Brewer, 2021.

Guy, J., *My Heart is My Own: The Life of Mary Queen of Scots*, Harper Perennial, 2004.

Haigh, C., *Reformation and Resistance in Tudor Lancashire*, Cambridge U.P., 1975.

Haigh, C., 'The Fall of a Church or the Rise of a Sect? Post-Reformation Catholicism in England', *The Historical Journal*, 21, 1978: 181–186.

Haigh, C., 'From Monopoly to Minority: Catholicism in Early Modern England', *Transactions of the Royal Historical Society*, 31, 1981: 129–147.

Haigh, C., 'The Recent Historiography of the English Reformation', *The Historical Journal*, 25, 1982: 995–1007.

Haigh, C., *The Plain Man's Pathways to Heaven: Kinds of Christianity in Post-Reformation England, 1570–1640*, Oxford U.P., 2007.

Harmsen, Theodor (2004), 'Weston [alias Edmunds, Hunt], William (1549/50–1615)', in *Oxford Dictionary of National Biography*. Available at: https://doi.org/10.1093/ref:odnb/29137 (Accessed 14 October 2020).

Haugaard, W.P., *Elizabeth and the English Reformation*, Cambridge U.P., 1968.

Havran, M.J., *The Catholics in Caroline England*, Oxford U.P., 1962.

Havran, M.J., *Caroline Courtier: The Life of Lord Cottington*, MacMillan, 1973.

Hibbard, C.M., *Charles I and the Popish Plot*, U. of North Carolina P., 1983.

Hilton, J.A., 'The Catholic Poor: Paupers and Vagabonds 1580–1780' in *English Catholics of Parish and Town 1558–1778*, 115–129, ed. M.B. Rowlands, Catholic Record Society, 1999.

Holmes, P., *Resistance and Compromise: The Political Thought of the Elizabethan Catholics*, Cambridge U.P., 1982.

Houliston, V., *Catholic Resistance in Elizabethan England: Robert Persons's Jesuit Polemic, 1580–1610*, Ashgate, 2007.

Huxley, G., *Endymion Porter: The Life of a Courtier 1587–1649*, Chatto & Windus, 1959.

Jones, N., 'Elizabeth, Edification, and the Latin Prayer Book of 1560', *Church History*, 53, 1984: 174–186.

Kaushik, S., 'Resistance, Loyalty and Recusant Politics: Sir Thomas Tresham and the Elizabethan State', *Midland History*, 21, 1996: 37–72.

Kelly, J.E., 'Counties without Borders: Religious Politics, Kinship Networks and the Formation of Catholic Communities', *Historical Research*, 91, 2018a: 22–38.

Kelly, J.E., 'The Contested Appropriation of George Gervase's Martyrdom: European Patronage and Controversy over the Oath of Allegiance', *Journal of British Studies*, 57, 2018b: 253–274.

Kesselring, K.J., *The Northern Rebellion of 1569: Faith Politics and Protest in Elizabethan England*, Palgrave MacMillan, 2007.

Kilroy, G., *Edmund Campion: Memory and Transcription*, Ashgate, 2005.

Kilroy, Gerard, *Edmund Campion: A Scholarly Life*, Ashgate, 2015.
Krugler, J.D. (2010), 'Calvert, George, first Baron Baltimore (1579/80–1632)' in *Oxford Dictionary of National Biography*. Available at: https://doi.org/10.1093/ref:odnb/4420 (Accessed 19 October 2020).
La Rocca, J., 'James I and his Catholic Subjects, 1606–1612: Some Financial Implications', *Recusant History*, 18, 1987: 251–262.
Lake, P., 'Antipopery: The Structure of a Prejudice' in *Conflict in Early Stuart England: Studies in Religion and Politics 1603–1642*, 72–106, ed. R. Cust and A. Hughes, Longman, 1989.
Lake, P., *Bad Queen Bess? Libels, Secret Histories, and the Politics of Publicity in the Reign of Queen Elizabeth I*, Oxford U.P., 2016.
Lake, P. and Questier, M., 'Prisons Priest and People' in *England's Long Reformation 1500 to 1800*, 195–234, ed. C. Tyacke, Routledge, 1998.
Lake, P. and Questier, M., *All Hail to the Archpriest: Confessional Conflict, Toleration, and the Politics of Publicity in Post-Reformation England*, Oxford U.P., 2019.
Lewycky, N. and Morton, A., eds., *Getting Along? Religious Identities and Confessional Relations in Early Modern England – Essays in Honour of Professor W.J. Sheils*, Routledge, 2016.
Lindley, K.J., 'The Lay Catholics of England in the Reign of Charles I', *Journal of Ecclesiastical History*, 22, 1971: 199–221.
Lindley, K.J., 'The Impact of the 1641 Rebellion upon England and Wales', *Irish Historical Studies*, 18, 1972: 143–176.
Lockyer, R., *James VI and I*, Longman, 1998.
Longueville, T., *A Life of Archbishop Laud*, Kegan Paul, 1894.
Loomie, A.J., *Guy Fawkes in Spain, the 'Spanish Treason' in Spanish Documents*, Institute of Historical Research, 1971.
Loomie, A.J., *Spain and the Jacobean Catholics*, Volume 1: *1603–1612*, Catholic Record Society, 1973.
Loomie, A.J., 'London's Spanish Chapel before and after the Civil War', *Recusant History*, 18, 1987: 402–417.
Loomie, A.J., *Spain and the Early Stuarts 1585–1655*, Routledge, 1996.
Lunn, D., *The English Benedictines 1540–1688: From Reformation to Revolution*, Burns and Oates, 1980.
Lux-Sterritt, L., 'Virgo Becomes Virago: Women in the Accounts of Seventeenth Century English Catholic Missionaries', *Recusant History*, 30, 2011: 537–550.
MacCaffrey, W.T., *Elizabeth I*, Edward Arnold, 1993.
McClain, L., *Lest We be Damned: Practical Innovation and Lived Experience among Catholics in Protestant England 1559–1642*, Ashgate, 2004.
McCoog, T.M., '"The Slightest Suspicion of Avarice": The Finances of the English Jesuit Mission', *Recusant History*, 19, 1988: 103–123.
McCoog, T.M., *The Reckoned Expense: Thomas Campion and the Early Jesuits*, Boydell, 1996.
McCoog, T.M., *The Society of Jesus in Ireland, Scotland, and England, 1598–1606: 'Lest Our Lamp be Entirely Extinguished'*, Brill, 2017.
McDermott, J., *England and the Spanish Armada: The Necessary Quarrel*, Yale U.P., 2005.
McGrath, P., *Papists and Puritans under Elizabeth I*, Blandford Press, 1967.
McGrath, P. and Rowe, J., 'The Marian Priests under Elizabeth I', *Recusant History*, 17, 1984: 103–120.

Manning, R.B., *Religion and Society in Elizabethan Sussex*, Leicester U.P., 1969.

Marcombe, D., 'A Rude and Heady People: The Local Community and the Rebellion of the Northern Earls' in *The Last Principality: Politics, Religion and Society in the Bishopric of Durham, 1494–1660*, 117–151, ed. David Marcombe, U. of Nottingham, 1987.

Marotti, A.F., *Religious Ideology and Cultural Fantasy: Catholic and Anti-Catholic Discourses in Early Modern England*, U. of Notre Dame P., 2005.

Marshall, Peter, 'Confessionalisation and Community in the Burial of English Catholics, c. 1570–1700' in *Getting Along? Religious Identities and Confessional Relations in Early Modern England – Essays in Honour of Professor W.J. Sheils*, 57–76, ed. N. Lewycky and A. Morton, Routledge, 2012.

Marshall, P., *Heretics and Believers: A History of the English Reformation*, Yale U.P., 2017.

Marshall, R.K. (2008), 'Cornwallis, Anne, countess of Argyll (d. 1635)', in *Oxford Dictionary of National Biography*. Available at: https://doi.org/10.1093/ref:odnb/68036 (Accessed 9 January 2021).

Milton, A., *Catholic and Reformed: The Roman and Protestant Churches in English Protestant Thought 1600–1640*, Cambridge U.P.,1995.

Muller, A., 'The Agnus Dei, Catholic Devotion and Confessional Politics in Early Modern England', *British Catholic History*, 34, 2018: 1–28.

Mullett, M., '"So They Become Contemptible": Clergy and Laity in Missionary Territory' in *Catholic Communities in Protestant States: Britain and the Netherlands c.1570–1720*, 33–47, ed. B.J. Kaplan, R. Moore, H. Van Nierop and J. Pollmann, Manchester U.P., 2009.

Murphy, G.M. (2004), 'D'Almeida, João (c. 1572–1653)', in *Oxford Dictionary of National Biography*. Available at: https://doi.org/10.1093/ref:odnb/418 (Accessed 18 October 2020).

Newton, D., *The Making of the Jacobean Regime: James VI and I and the Government of England, 1603–1605*, Boydell & Brewer, 2005.

Nicholls, M., *Investigating the Gunpowder Plot*, Manchester U.P., 1991.

Nicholls, M., 'Treason's Reward: The Punishment of Conspirators in the Bye Plot of 1603', *The Historical Journal*, 38, 1995: 821–842.

Okines, A.W.R.E., 'Why Was There So Little Government Reaction to Gunpowder Plot?', *Journal of Ecclesiastical History*, 55, 2004: 275–292.

Ornsby, G., ed., *Selections from the Household Books of Lord William Howard of Naworth Castle*, The Surtees Society, 1878.

Palmes, W., *Life of Mrs. Dorothy Lawson*, George Richardson, 1851.

Patterson, W.B., *King James VI and the Reunion of Christendom*, Cambridge U.P.,1997.

Petti, A.G., ed., *Recusant Documents from the Ellesmere Manuscripts*, Catholic Record Society, 1968.

Pritchard, A.G., *Catholic Loyalism in Elizabethan England*, U. of North Carolina P., 1979.

Pursell, B., 'The End of the Spanish Match', *The Historical Journal*, 45, 2002: 699–726.

Questier, M., *Conversion, Politics and Religion in England 1580–1625*, Cambridge U.P., 1996.

Questier, M., 'Loyalty, Religion and State Power in Early Modern England: English Romanism and Jacobean Oath of Allegiance', *The Historical Journal*, 40, 1997, 311–329.

Questier, M., ed., *Newsletters from the Archpresbyterate of George Birkhead*, Royal Historical Society, 1998.

Questier, M., 'Conformity, Catholicism and the Law' in *Conformity and Orthodoxy in the English Church, c. 1560–1660*, 237–261, ed. P. Lake and M. Questier, Boydell, 2000.

Questier, M., ed., *Newsletters from the Caroline Court, 1631–1638: Catholicism and the Politics of Personal Rule*, Royal Historical Society, 2005.
Questier, M., *Catholicism and Community in Early Modern England*, Cambridge U.P., 2006.
Questier, M., ed., *Stuart Dynastic Policy and Religious Politics, 1621–5*, Cambridge U.P., 2009.
Questier, M., *Dynastic Politics and the British Reformations, 1558–1630*, Oxford U.P., 2019.
Rapple, R. (2008), 'Stanley, Sir William (1548–1630)', in *Oxford Dictionary of National Biography*. Available at: https://doi.org/10.1093/ref:odnb/26283 (Accessed 17 January 2021).
Redworth, G., *The Prince and the Infanta: The Cultural Politics of the Spanish Match*, Yale U.P., 2003.
Renold, P., ed., *The Wisbech Stirs (1595–1598)*, Catholic Record Society, 1958.
Rice, D.W., *The Life and Achievements of Sir John Popham 1531–1607: Leading to the Establishment of the First English Colony in New England*, Rosemont, 2005.
Rodriguez-Salgado, M.J. (2006), 'Suárez de Figueroa [née Dormer], Jane, duchess of Feria in the Spanish nobility (1538–1612)'. Available at: https://doi.org/10.1093/ref:odnb/7836 (Accessed 9 January 2021).
Rowe, J. and Young, F., 'East Anglian Catholics in the Reign of Elizabeth, 1559–1603' in *Catholic East Anglia: A History of the Catholic Faith in Norfolk, Suffolk, Cambridgeshire and Peterborough*, 37–60, ed. F. Young, Gracewing, 2016.
Rowlands, M.B., 'Recusant Women 1560–1640' in *Women in English Society 1500–1800*, 149–166, ed. M. Prior, Routledge, 1985.
Rowlands, M.B., 'Hidden People: Catholic Commoners, 1558–1625' in *English Catholics of Parish and Town 1558–1778*, 10–35, ed. M.B. Rowlands, Catholic Record Society, 1999.
Rowlands, M.B., 'Harbourers and Housekeepers: Catholic Women in England 1570–1720' in *Catholic Communities in Protestant States: Britain and the Netherlands c.1570–1720*, 200–215, ed. B.J. Kaplan, R. Moore, H. Van Nierop and J. Pollmann, Manchester U.P., 2009.
Russell, C., *Unrevolutionary England, 1603–1642*, Hambledon Continuum, 1990.
Russell, C., *The Fall of the British Monarchies, 1637–1642*, Oxford U.P., 1991.
Schofield, N., 'A Church without Bishops: Governance of the English Catholic Mission, 1594–1685', *Ecclesiastical Law Journal*, 19, 2017: 156–168.
Scott, J. (2015), 'Percy [née Somerset], Anne, countess of Northumberland (1536–1591)', in *Oxford Dictionary of National Biography*. Available at: https://doi.org/10.1093/ref:odnb/107539 (Accessed 9 January 2021).
Sharpe, K., *The Personal Rule of Charles I*, Yale U.P., 1992.
Sheils, W., 'Catholics and their Neighbours in a Rural Community: Egton Chapelry 1590–1780', *Northern History*, 34, 1995: 109–133.
Sheils, W., 'Household, Age and Gender among Jacobean Yorkshire Recusants' in *English Catholics of Parish and Town 1558–1778*, 131–152, ed. M.B. Rowlands, Catholic Record Society, 1999.
Sheils, W., '"Getting On" and "Getting Along" in Parish and Town: Catholics and their Neighbours in England' in *Catholic Communities in Protestant States: Britain and the Netherlands c.1570–1720*, 67–83, ed. B.J. Kaplan, R. Moore, H. Van Nierop and J. Pollmann, Manchester U.P., 2009.
Sheils, William, 'The Catholic Community' in *The Elizabethan World*, 254–269, ed. S. Doran and N. Jones, Routledge, 2011.
Sheils, W., 'Catholics and their Protestant Neighbours' in *The Oxford History of British and Irish Catholicism, Volume 1: c.1540–1640*, ed. J.E. Kelly and J. McCafferty, Oxford U.P., forthcoming.

Shell, A., '"Furore Juvenilis": Post-Reformation English Catholicism and Exemplary Youthful Behaviour' in *Catholics and the 'Protestant Nation': Religious Politics and Identity in Early Modern England*, 185–206, ed. E. Shagan, Manchester U.P., 2005.

Shell, A., *Oral Culture and Catholicism in Early Modern England*, Cambridge U.P., 2007.

Smith, F.E., 'The Origins of Recusancy in Elizabethan England Reconsidered', *The Historical Journal*, 60, 2017: 301–332.

Smith, F.E., 'Life after Exile: Former Catholic Émigrés and the Legacy of Flight in Marian England', *The English Historical Review*, 133, 2018: 806–834.

Smith, D.L., 'Catholic, Anglican or Puritan? Edward Sackville, Fourth Earl of Dorset and the Ambiguities of Religion in Early Stuart England', *Transactions of the Royal Historical Society*, 2, 1991: 105–124.

Smith, D.L., *The Stuart Parliaments 1603–1689*, Hodder, 1993.

Sommerville, J.P., 'Papalist Political Thought and the Controversy over the Jacobean Oath of Allegiance' in *Catholics and the 'Protestant Nation': Religious Politics and Identity in Early Modern England*, 162–184, ed. E. Shagan, Manchester U.P., 2005.

Streete, A., *Apocalypse and Anti-Catholicism in Seventeenth Century English Drama*, Cambridge U.P., 2017.

Temple, L., *Mysticism in Early Modern England*, Boydell & Brewer, 2019.

Thomas, H., 'The Society of Jesus in Wales, c. 1600–1679: Rediscovering the Cwm Jesuit Library at Hereford Cathedral', *Journal of Jesuit Studies*, 1, 2014: 572–588.

Trimble, W.J.R., *The Elizabethan Catholic Laity*, Harvard U.P., 1964.

Tutino, S., *Thomas White and the Blackloists: Between Politics and Theology during the English Civil War*, Ashgate, 2008.

Underwood, L., 'Recusancy and the Rising Generation', *Recusant History*, 31, 2013: 511–533.

Underwood, L., *Childhood, Youth and Dissent in Post-Reformation England*, Palgrave MacMillan, 2014.

Underwood, L., 'Persuading the Queen's Majesty's Subjects from Their Allegiance: Treason, Reconciliation and Confessional Identity in Elizabethan England', *Historical Research*, 89, 2016: 247–267.

Von Klarwill, V., ed., *Queen Elizabeth I and Some Foreigners*, John Lane, 1928.

Walker, C., 'Priests, Nuns, Presses and Prayers: The Southern Netherlands and the Contours of English Catholicism' in *Catholic Communities in Protestant States: Britain and the Netherlands c.1570–1720*, 139–155, ed. B.J. Kaplan, R. Moore, H. Van Nierop and J. Pollmann, Manchester U.P., 2009.

Walker, C., 'Continuity and Isolation: The Bridgettines of Syon in the Sixteenth and Seventeenth Centuries' in *Syon Abbey and its Books: Reading, Writing and Religion, c. 1400–1700*, 155–176, ed. E.A. Jones and A. Walsham, Boydell, 2010.

Wallington, N., *Historical Notices of the Reign of Charles I*, vol. 2, Richard Bentley, 1869.

Walsham, A., *Church Papists: Catholicism, Conformity and Confessional Polemic in Early Modern England*, Boydell, 1999.

Walsham, A., '"Yielding to the Extremity of Time": Conformity, Orthodoxy and the Post-Reformation Catholic Community' in *Conformity and Orthodoxy in the English Church, c. 1560–1660*, 211–236, ed. P. Lake and M. Questier, Boydell, 2000.

Walsham, A., *Charitable Hatred: Tolerance and Intolerance in England, 1500–1700*, Manchester U.P., 2006.

Walsham, Alexandra, 'Beads, Books and Bare Ruined Choirs: Transmutations of Catholic Ritual Life in Protestant England' in *Catholic Communities in Protestant*

States: Britain and the Netherlands c.1570–1720, 103–122, ed. B.J. Kaplan, R. Moore, H. Van Nierop and J. Pollmann, Manchester U.P., 2009.

Walsham, A., *The Reformation of the Landscape: Religion, Identity and Memory in Early Modern Britain and Ireland*, Oxford U.P., 2011.

Walsham, A., 'Supping with Satan's Disciples: Spiritual and Secular Sociability in Post-Reformation England' in *Getting Along? Religious Identities and Confessional Relations in Early Modern England – Essays in Honour of Professor W.J. Sheils*, 29–56, ed. N. Lewycky and A. Morton, Routledge, 2012.

Walsham, A., 'In the Lord's Vineyard: Catholic Reformation in Protestant Britain' in *Catholic Reformation in Protestant Britain*, 1–49, ed. A. Walsham, Ashgate, 2014.

Walsham, A., 'Luis de Granada's Mission to Protestant England: Translating the Devotional Literature of the Spanish Counter Reformation' in *Publishing Subversive Texts in Elizabethan England and the Polish-Lithuanian Commonwealth*, 129–154, ed. T. Bela, C. Calma and J. Rzegocka, Brill, 2016.

Walsham, A., 'Relics, Writing, and Memory in the English Counter-Reformation: Thomas Maxfield and his Afterlives', *British Catholic History*, 34, 2018: 77–105.

Walter, W., *Understanding Popular Violence in the English Revolution: The Colchester Plunderers*, Cambridge U.P., 1999.

Weston, W., *William Weston: The Autobiography of an Elizabethan*, ed. P. Caraman, Longmans Green, 1955.

White, Jason, *Militant Protestantism and the British Identity 1603–42*, Routledge, 2012.

Wiener, C.Z., 'The Beleaguered Isle: A Study of Elizabethan and Early Jacobean English Catholicism', *Past & Present*, 51, 1971: 27–62.

Williams, M.E. (2004), 'Gifford, William [name in religion Gabriel of St Mary] (1557/8–1629)' in *Oxford Dictionary of National Biography*. Available at: https://doi.org/10.1093/ref:odnb/10668 (Accessed 16 October 2020).

Williams, R.L., 'Cultures of Dissent: English Catholics and Visual Arts' in *Catholic Communities in Protestant States: Britain and the Netherlands c.1570–1720*, 230–248, ed. B.J. Kaplan, R. Moore, H. Van Nierop and J. Pollmann, Manchester U.P., 2009.

Willson, D.H., *King James VI and I*, Cape, 1966.

Wooding, L., 'Professor John Bossy FBA (1933–2015)', *British Catholic History*, 33, 2016: 1–8.

Worthington, D., *British and Irish Experiences and Impressions of Central Europe, c. 1560–1688*, Routledge, 2012.

Young, F., 'The Shorts of Bury St Edmunds: Medicine, Catholicism and Politics in the 17th Century', *Journal of Medical Biography*, 16, 2008: 188–194.

Young, F., *English Catholics and the Supernatural, 1553–1829*, Ashgate, 2013.

Young, F., 'The Bishop's Palace at Ely as a Prison for Recusants, 1577–97', *Recusant History*, 32, 2014: 195–218.

Young, F., *The Gages of Hengrave and Suffolk Catholicism, 1640–1767*, Catholic Record Society, 2015.

Young, F., ed., *Rookwood Family Papers, 1606–1761*, Suffolk Records Society, 2016.

Young, F., *Magic as a Political Crime in Medieval and Early Modern England: A History of Sorcery and Treason*, I.B. Tauris, 2017.

Young, F., *Edmund: In Search of England's Lost King*, I.B. Tauris, 2018.

Young, F., 'Sir Thomas Tresham and the Christian Cabala', *British Catholic History*, 35, 2020: 145–168.

Younger, N., 'How Protestant was the Elizabethan Regime?', *English Historical Review*, 133, 2018: 1060–1092.

Index

Abbot, George, archbishop of Canterbury 89, 91, 93, 100
Abbot, Robert, bishop of Salisbury 111
Acquaviva, Claudio 38, 39
Agnus Dei (consecrated object) 50, 64–5
Alba, duke of 20
Alban, St 66
Albert, archduke of Austria 88
Allegiance, Oath of 45, 46, 56, 73, 75, 85–8, 92, 93, 94, 95, 99, 104, 106, 127–8, 129–30
Allen, Edward 6
Allen, William, cardinal 22, 24, 27, 28, 29, 30, 31, 32, 33, 35–7, 38, 39, 40, 41, 44, 45, 49, 63, 66, 67, 122, 125–6
Allen's Island, Canada 51
Allensore, Herefordshire 62
Amsterdam, Netherlands 111
Anglo-Spanish Peace (1604) 81, 82, 86
Anne of Denmark, queen of England 79, 93
anti-Catholicism 3, 10, 16, 24, 48, 57, 78, 84, 88, 95, 96, 98, 106–13, 116, 117, 118, 133–4 *see also* anti-popery
anti-popery 2, 19, 77, 95, 107, 109, 110, 111–12, 116, 118, 133 *see also* anti-Catholicism
Antichrist 6, 21, 71, 105, 106–7, 109, 110, 111, 112
Antwerp, Belgium 36, 49, 64, 65
Appellants 26, 31, 32, 39, 40, 45, 46, 47, 76, 80
aristocrats 9, 16, 18, 21, 22, 29, 49, 53, 71, 106
Armada, Spanish 4, 25, 29–31, 40, 75, 108–9, 110, 123
Arminianism 115, 120, 124
armsbearing 104, 122, 126, 136
'Army Plot' 125

Arundel, earl of 10, 13, 17, 74, 115
Arundell, Charles 22, 23, 29–30, 31
Arundell, John 55
Arundell, Thomas, baron Wardour 51, 79, 83
Association, Bond of (1584) 24–5
Augustinians 32
Avalon colony, Canada 51
Aylmer, John, bishop of London 23

Babington, Anthony 22
Babington Plot 20, 22–3, 25, 31, 55
Bacon, Francis 91
Bacon, Nicholas 18
Bagshawe, Christopher 45
Baille, Robert 114, 115
Ballard, John 22
Bampton, Cumbria 73, 130
Bancroft, Richard, archbishop of Canterbury 26, 46, 76, 81
Barnard Castle, Co. Durham 15
baptisms 56, 57, 60, 62, 74, 103
Barberini, Francesco, cardinal 103, 104, 115
Barlow, Ambrose 61
baronetcies, sale of 90
Barrow, Henry 26
Bavard, John 40
Becket, Thomas, St 66
Bedford, earl of 102
Bell, Thomas 40, 41, 61, 109
Bellarmine, Robert 87
Bellingham, James 131
Benedictines 32–3, 43, 47, 48, 49, 60–1, 104
Bennet, Edward 77, 94
Bennet, John 76
Bennet, Robert, bishop of Hereford 81
Bergen-op-Zoom, Netherlands 33

Bernard, Richard 110
Berwick-on-Tweed 73
Berwick, Truce of (1639) 116
Biblical studies 36
Birkhead, George, archpriest 46, 47, 88
Bishop, William, bishop of Chalcedon 46–7, 111
Bishops' War, Second 113, 116
Blackwell, George, archpriest of England 46, 80, 87, 129
Blois, Treaty of (1572) 19
Blount, Richard 47
Bluet, Thomas 45
Blundell family 54
Blundell, William 54, 132
Bohemia 56, 61, 91, 111
Bold, Richard 60
Boleyn, Anne, queen of England 11
Bonner, Edmund, bishop of London 33
Bonnington, Lincolnshire 7
books 36, 41, 50, 56, 57, 65–6, 68, 92, 101, 107, 112, 134; burning of 15
booksellers 57
Boste, John 66
Boteler, lord 104
Bradford, Yorkshire 118
Bramston, Thomas 43, 124–5
Brazil 51
Bridgettines 32
Bristol 113, 116
Bristow, Richard 27
Brome, Suffolk 70
Brome, Bridget 66
Brome, Elizabeth 66
Brookesby, Eleanor 57
Brookesby, Robert 39
Browne family 53, 55, 75
Browne, Francis 39
Brudenell, Thomas 90
Bruges, Belgium 36, 49
Bruges, Cornelius 117
Buckhurst, lord *see* Dorset, earl of
Buckinghamshire 32, 113
burials 56, 62–3, 100
Burnham, Buckinghamshire 32
Bury St Edmunds, Suffolk 54, 119
Bush, Nicholas 9
Bye Plot 32, 80–1, 83, 86
Byrd, William 60

Cabalism, Christian 65
Caetani, Enrico, cardinal 46
Calais, France 36, 37

Calvert, Cecilius, 2nd baron Baltimore 51, 52
Calvert, George, 1st baron Baltimore 51, 52
Calvin, John 14
Calvinism 3, 12, 78, 89, 98, 100, 112, 114
Cambridge, Cambridgeshire 7
Camden, William 108
Campion, Edmund 22, 30, 35, 37–9, 44, 45, 58, 66, 109, 121–3; 'Campion's Brag' 38
Canisius, Peter 36
Canterbury, Kent 10, 66, 124
Capuchins 33, 102
Carier, Benjamin 93
Cash, Katherine 57
catacombs, Roman 66
Catesby, Robert 32, 74, 82, 83, 90
Catesby, William 39, 51
Catholic League 22, 24, 26
Caussin, Nicolas 101
Cecil, John 66
Cecil, Robert, earl of Salisbury 46, 56, 58, 75, 80–1, 82–3, 84, 85, 86, 90
Cecil, William (Lord Burghley) 5, 10, 11, 12, 13, 16, 17, 18, 19, 20, 25, 28, 29, 56, 73, 74, 123, 124
Champney, Anthony 78, 115
Charles I, king of England 51, 52, 75, 77, 89, 90, 111, 113, 114–15, 116, 119, 133; court of 100–6; journey to Spain 92–3; religious policy 95–100
Charles, archduke of Austria 10, 12
Charles de Bourbon ('Charles X') 24
Cheshire 29, 37, 71, 77, 133
Chester, Cheshire 132
Chester, Edward 59
children 14, 26, 41–2, 59, 62, 68, 70, 74, 95, 99, 103
Childwall, Lancashire 63
Cholmley family 54
Cholmley, Richard 71
Christchurch, Hampshire 63
church papists 1, 5, 27, 41–2, 43, 49, 56, 59, 62, 69, 70–1, 72, 73, 74, 75, 85, 90, 125, 126
Circignani, Niccolo 66
Civil War, English 1, 3, 4, 24, 43, 69, 73, 95, 109, 112, 118, 119, 133
Clement VIII, pope 84
Cletheray, Thomas 62
Clifford, Henry, earl of Cumberland 15
Clitheroe, Margaret 67
Clotworthy, John 117

Clynnog, Morgan 62
Coke, Edward 88, 110
Coke, John 96
Colchester, Essex 113, 116, 118
Coldham Hall, Suffolk 47, 54
Colton, Robert 60
compounding 97, 99–100
Con, George 78, 102, 103–4, 105, 106, 113–14, 115
confession, sacrament of 24, 41, 47–8, 60, 61, 109, 122, 125
conformists, occasional 1, 27, 40, 41, 42, 70, 73, 74
Constantine, emperor 108
Contarini, Alvise 99
convents *see* women religious
conversion 1, 23, 27, 43, 44, 45, 49, 50, 51, 57, 59, 69, 76, 87, 93, 101, 102, 104–5, 107, 131, 134
Copley, Robert 8, 14
Copley, Thomas 51
Cordell, William 21
Cork, Ireland 36
Cornwallis, Anne, countess of Argyll 33
Cornwallis, Thomas 55, 70
Cottington, Francis 99, 102, 103, 104–5, 114
Counter-Reformation 2, 4, 14, 30, 33, 35, 36, 43, 49, 50, 51, 60, 64, 66, 68, 109
court Catholicism 3, 77, 100–6, 112, 113, 115
courts, ecclesiastical 48, 97
Covenanters 3, 106, 113–15, 116
Coventry, Warwickshire 92
Cranach, Lucas 107
Creswell, Joseph 31
Croft, James 17
Croncke, Peter 63
crypto-Catholics 1, 21, 90, 91, 93, 99, 102, 104, 114, 115
Cumberland 12, 15, 73, 130
Cumbernauld Bond 116
Curwen, Henry 131
Cuthbert, St, banner of 15
Cwm, Herefordshire 47

Dacre, Leonard 14, 15
Dacres, Henry 131
Darcy, Elizabeth, countess Rivers 119
Deene, Northamptonshire 90
Dekker, Thomas 111
Dent, Arthur 110
Derby, earl of 77
Derbyshire 22, 39, 53, 61, 62, 70, 116

Digby, Everard 104
Digby, John 91, 92
Digby, Kenelm 78, 104, 117
Dimley, George 70
Dominicans 11, 66, 100, 103
Dormer, Jane, duchess of Feria 33
Douai, France 26, 27, 32, 35–6, 37, 41, 42, 43, 45, 54, 59, 68
Douai Bible 36
Douce, Ann 57
Dover, Kent 122
Drury family 44
Drypool, Yorkshire 62
Dudley, Robert, earl of Leicester 10, 13, 20, 21, 22, 23, 28, 29, 123
Dunkirk, France 36, 37
Durham, Co. Durham 14–15
Durham, Co. 14, 41, 50, 73, 131

East Anglia 40, 44, 54, 55, 59, 70, 76
Edinburgh, Scotland 80, 113
Edmondes, Thomas 82
Edmund, St 66
education 32, 33, 42, 54, 59, 70, 73, 95, 124–5
Edward VI, king of England 2, 6, 32, 124
Egton, Yorkshire 54, 72
Eliot, John 96
Elizabeth I, queen of England 2, 9, 11, 13–14, 15–16, 17, 18, 19, 23, 24, 25, 26, 27, 28, 29, 30, 31, 33, 34, 46, 59, 73, 74, 76, 80, 81, 83, 89, 108; accession 1, 4, 5–7, 120; excommunication of 11, 15–16, 28, 64; marriage negotiations 12, 20–3; progress in East Anglia 27; religious views 5–7, 9, 10, 12, 16; succession to the throne 3, 79
Elizabeth, queen of Bohemia 75, 89, 98
Elliot, Thomas 88
Ellis, John 120
Ely, Cambridgeshire 29, 65
embassy chapels 9, 44, 56, 60, 91, 103, 105, 111–12, 116, 117
Emerson, Ferdinand 97
Emerson, Ralph 39, 122
émigrés 32–4
Englefield, Francis 20
Essex 9, 12, 49, 53, 55, 75, 77, 110, 18–19
Essex, earl of 74
Essex Rebellion 31–2, 83
Etwall, Derbyshire 70
Eure, lord 73
'evil counsellors' 18, 28, 31
Exchequer 24, 70, 85, 95, 96, 97

excommunication (as penalty for recusancy) 62, 128, 129
executions 15, 17, 19, 21, 23, 25, 26, 27, 29, 38, 40, 44, 48, 57, 66–7, 76, 81, 83, 100, 101
exile 11, 14, 20, 24, 27, 29, 31, 32–3, 35, 37, 50, 102, 104, 127
exorcism 67, 69, 131
Eyre family 53

Fairfax, Thomas 73
Fairhair, Elizabeth 62
fasting 59, 67–8, 117, 131
Fawkes, Guy 74, 82, 92, 110, 126–7
Feckenham, John 125
Fenn, John 64
Ferdinand I, emperor 11, 12, 120
fines *see* recusancy, penalties for
Fishbourne, Sussex 59
Fisher, George 59
Fisher, John, bishop of Rochester 66
Fitch, Benet ('Benet of Canfield') 33
Fitzgerald, James Fitzmaurice 37
Fitzherbert family 33
Flanders 82–3, 84, 86, 88, 115
Flinton, George 65
forced loan 75, 77
Fortescue, John 59
Fowler, John 65
Foxe, John 66, 107–8
François, duke of Anjou 20–1, 24, 37
Frankfurt, Germany 5
Frederick of the Palatinate 75, 89, 91, 98, 111
Frier, Dr 130

Garnet, Henry 40–1, 44, 57, 58, 63–4, 66, 67, 68, 72, 79, 83
Garrat, Henry 62
Gee, John 57
Gell, John 116
Geneva, Switzerland 5, 14
gentry 15, 25, 27, 30, 38, 39–40, 41, 42, 43–4, 47, 48, 49–50, 53–4, 55, 56, 57, 61, 68, 71, 72, 73, 85, 88, 90, 119, 125, 131, 132
Gerard, John 31, 40, 42, 44, 50, 57, 58, 60, 66, 70, 79, 90
Gerard, Nicholas 70
Gerard, Thomas 90
Germany 11, 66, 89
Gervase, George 48
Gifford, William Gabriel, archbishop-duke of Rheims 48

Gilbert, George 38
Gilling, Yorkshire 73
Gilsland, Cumbria 131
Golborne, Lancashire 63
Goldwell, Thomas, bishop of St Asaph 11
Gondomar, count 56, 89, 106, 111
Goring, George 117
Grand Remonstrance 106
Grant, John 83
Gravelines, France 36
Great Ashby, Leicestershire 58
Greenwood, John 26
Gregory XIII, pope 28, 64
Grey Plot 80, 82
Griffith, Ambrose 70
Grimstone, Harbottle
Grindal, Edmund, archbishop of Canterbury 55
Grosmont Priory, Yorkshire 37, 41
Grove, John 70
Guest, Edmund, bishop of Rochester 12
Guildford, Surrey 118
Guise, duke of 22, 23
Gunpowder Plot 3, 4, 32, 58, 67, 69, 74, 82–3, 85, 86, 87, 88, 90, 93, 100, 103, 104, 108, 110, 113, 127; commemoration of 118

Halifax, Yorkshire 118
Halley's Comet 111
Hamilton, marquess of 114
Hampshire 7, 19, 63
Hartburn, Richard 15
Hartlepool, Co. Durham 15
Hastings, Henry, earl of Huntingdon 26, 55
Hathersage, Derbyshire 62
Hazlewood Castle, Yorkshire 71
Helffstein, Count 5, 120
Hengrave, Suffolk 54
Henry, prince of Wales 89
Henry II, king of England 66
Henri III, king of France 24
Henri IV, king of France (Henry of Navarre) 24, 26, 87, 88, 89
Henrietta Maria, queen of England
Henry VII, king of England 11
Henry VIII, king of England 2, 5, 6, 11, 32, 35, 64, 66, 108
Hereford, Herefordshire 7, 8–9, 53, 120
Herefordshire 38, 47, 62, 82
heresy 5, 25, 28, 37, 70, 72, 87, 121, 131
Heskins, Thomas 65
Heyricke, Richard 113

Higgons, Theophilius 111
Hinlip Hall, Worcestershire 40
Hintlesham, Suffolk 70
historiography 1, 2
Hobblethorne, lady 9
Hodgson, John 54
Holbeck House, Nottinghamshire 47
Holderness, Yorkshire 7
Holland, earl of 102
Holtby, Richard 40–1
Hopton, Derbyshire 116
Horne, Robert, bishop of Winchester 119
Hospitaller, Knights 33
Howard, Henry 21, 22
Howard, Philip, lord 68, 131–2
Howard, William, lord 53, 73, 130–1
Huguenots 19, 21, 24, 79
Hull, Yorkshire 36
Hungary 66
Hutton, Matthew, archbishop of York 81
Hyde, Edward, earl of Clarendon 98, 118

India 37, 50, 51
influenza 7
Ingatestone, Essex 75
Ipswich, Suffolk 111, 112
Ireland 2–3, 13, 20, 36, 37, 89, 90, 110, 114, 115, 116, 118, 122
Irish Rebellion (1641) 117–18
Irnham, Lincolnshire 54

Jackson, Christopher 15
James VI and I, king of Scotland and England 2, 3, 22, 23, 28, 30, 31, 55, 73, 75, 82, 94, 99, 100, 111, 127; accession in England 42, 46, 79–80, 110; foreign policy 91–3, 111; reaction to Gunpowder Plot 83–6; religious policy 81–2, 87–90
James, Henry 69
Jerningham, Edward 59
Jerningham, George 59
Jesuits 20, 22–3, 25, 28, 30–1, 35, 36, 37–40, 45, 46, 47, 48, 49, 50–1, 53, 55, 57–8, 60, 62, 64, 65, 66, 67–8, 69, 70, 75–6, 78, 79, 80, 82, 83, 87, 88, 90, 96, 99, 101, 102, 112, 117, 125, 130, 131, 132; stereotypes of 109, 110, 113
Jones, Inigo 103
Jones, Leander 48, 104
Jordan, Ignatius 107
Juan de Mariana 88
Jülich-Cleves crisis 89, 110

justices of the peace (JPs) 9, 72, 73, 75, 86, 123
Juxon, William, archbishop of Canterbury 112

Katherine of Aragon, queen of England 11
Kensington, lord 93
Kent 39, 44, 55, 73, 92
Kirkby Hatton, Northamptonshire 57
Kitchin, Anthony, bishop of Llandaff 6
Kraków, Poland 51

La Rochelle, France 36
Lancashire 7, 8, 9, 27, 29, 37, 41, 42, 43, 44, 54, 60, 61, 63, 70, 73, 117, 132, 133
Lancaster, Lancashire 81
Lane, Ann 59
Lane, John 59
Lane, Thomas 59
Langdale, Alban 41
Langford family 53
Laud, William, archbishop of Canterbury 77, 97, 100, 101, 103, 104–5, 112, 113, 116
Laudianism 48, 99, 101, 104, 107, 112–13
Lawshall, Suffolk 44, 54
laws, penal see legislation, anti-Catholic
Lawson, Dorothy 57, 60, 63
legislation, anti-Catholic 16, 26, 34, 35, 68, 80, 88, 89, 90, 92, 95, 96, 97, 98, 132; Act of supremacy (1558) see Settlement, Elizabethan; Act of uniformity (1558) see Settlement, Elizabethan; Act to retain the queen's majesty's subjects in their due obedience (1581) 23–4, 25, 26, 124; Act against Jesuits, seminary priests and such other like disobedient persons (1585) 25, 124; Act against popish recusants (1587) 24, 27, 42, 97; Act against popish recusants (1593) 26; Act for the better discovering and repressing of popish recusants (1606) 84–5, 86; Act to prevent and avoid dangers which may grow by popish recusants (1606) 84; Act for the administration of the Oath of Allegiance and the reformation of married women recusants (1610) 56, 88, 90
Leicestershire 39, 58
Lenthall, William 70
Leslie, John, bishop of Ross 17
Levellers 113
lieutenant, lords 75, 81
Lincoln, Robert 59

Lincolnshire 7, 53
Lisbon, Portugal 32
Little Crosby, Lancashire 54, 132
Lloyd, George, bishop of Chester 88
Loarte, Gaspar 64, 66
London 27, 84; Arundel House 116; Clerkenwell 53, 55, 96; East Ham 58; Hackney 55; Holborn 55, 57; Hoxton 39, 55; Inns of Court 55; St Paul's Cross 88; Shoreditch 55; Smithfield 38; Somerset House 60, 101, 102, 103, 116; Southwark 38, 39, 74, 116; Tower of 14, 68, 83, 125; Tyburn 38, 48, 67, 101; Westminster Abbey 43; Westminster, Palace of 82, 125
Long Melford, Suffolk 119
Louis XIII, king of France 101
Louvain, Belgium 5, 7–8, 15, 32, 33, 49, 64, 65
Louvain exiles 7–8, 9, 11, 14, 16, 27, 43
Lovett, Drew 56
loyalism, Catholic 2, 20, 22, 26, 27, 31–2, 46, 76, 87, 96, 130
Low Countries 2, 22, 30, 33, 50, 83, 113
Luis de Granada 66, 68
Luther, Martin 8
Lutheranism 2, 6, 107
Lyford Grange, Berkshire 38

MacDonnell, Randal, earl of Antrim 114–15
Machiavellianism 17, 109
Madrid, Spain 91, 92
magistrates *see* justices of the peace
Main Plot 80, 82
Malpas, Cheshire 71
Malta 33
Malton, Yorkshire 73
Margam, Glamorgan 62
Marian priests 8–9, 14, 41, 43, 45, 60, 74, 120
Markenfield, Thomas 14, 16
Markham, Gavin 83
marriage, clerical 15
Marshall, Stephen 118
Martin, Gregory 35, 36, 41
Martinengo, Hieronimo 11
martyrdom 1, 4, 38, 48, 50, 66–7, 101, 122–3, 126
Mary, queen of Scots 2, 10, 11, 12–14, 16–18, 19, 20, 22–3, 24, 25, 28, 33, 74, 106
Mary I, queen of England 2, 5, 6, 11, 14, 30, 32, 33, 35, 36, 41, 66, 106, 108, 124
Maryland 51

mass 7, 9, 12, 15, 17, 37, 43, 44, 50, 54, 60–1, 65, 68, 79, 85, 102, 103, 107, 122, 124
Matthew, Toby, archbishop of York 89, 110
Matthew, Toby (convert to Catholicism) 69
Maximillian, emperor 16
Maxwell, Robert, earl of Nithsdale
Maxwell, Thomas 67, 114
Mayne, Cuthbert 66
Mead, John (João D'Almeida) 51
medicine (profession) 54, 56, 84, 130, 132
Mercurian, Everard 37, 38
Methley, Yorkshire 71
Meymelle family 71
Middelburg, Netherlands 40
Middleton, William 71, 88
midwives 57
mission, Catholic 3, 35–52, 109
Monmouthshire 73, 81
Montague, Magdalen 44, 60, 63, 68
Montague, viscount 10, 18, 21, 23, 30, 39, 41, 49, 62, 74–5, 76, 81, 83, 88
Montagu, Wat 78, 104, 117
Montagu, Richard 103
Montrose, earl of 116
Moore, John 56
Moray, earl of 13, 14
Mordaunt, lord 83
More, Thomas 66
Morgan family 53
Morren, John 7–8
Morton, Thomas, bishop of Durham 100
Mount Grace, Yorkshire 63
Monteagle, lord 90
Mush, John 40, 67

Nanfan, Giles 62
Nantes, France 36
naturalisation 32, 33, 34
Naughton, Robert 91
Naworth Castle, Cumbria 73
Necolalde, Juan de 103
Neile, Richard, archbishop of York 77, 97
Nero, emperor 106
Netherlands *see* Low Countries
Neville, Charles, 5th earl of Westmorland 14, 15
New World 45, 50, 51, 52 *see also* Maryland
Newcastle-upon-Tyne 37, 63, 116
Newcomen, Matthew 113
Newport, lady 104

Nicodemism *see* church papists
Norfolk 39, 100
Norfolk, duke of 10, 12, 13–14, 16–17, 19, 20, 21, 74, 76
North, Council of the 55, 73, 91, 93, 97
North Kilvington, Yorkshire 71
North Leigh, Oxfordshire 70
Northampton, Northamptonshire 79, 113
Northampton, earl of 83, 93, 110
Northamptonshire 38, 57, 72, 90
Northern Rebellion (1569) 9, 12–18, 27, 33, 108
Northumberland, earl of *see* Percy, Thomas, 7th earl of Northumberland
Norton, Francis 14
Norton, Richard 14
Norton, Thomas 14
Norton, Thomas (Protestant writer) 16, 17
Norumbega, New England (proposed colony) 51
Norwich, Norfolk 99, 116, 118, 133
Nowell, Alexander 10, 12, 108, 121
nuns *see* women religious

O'Connell, Terence 103
O'Connor, William 117
Oglethorpe, Owen, bishop of Carlisle 6
Oldcorn, Edward 40
Olivares, count-duke of 29
Oratorians 101
Owen, Hugh 82, 88
Oxford, Oxfordshire 36, 65, 92
Oxford, earl of 21, 22
Oxfordshire 38, 70

Paget, Thomas, lord 38
Palmes, William 57
Panzani, Gregorio 103–4
Parham, Edward 86
Paris, France 93, 104
Parker, Matthew, archbishop of Canterbury 10, 19
Parliament (Commons, Lords, lower house, upper house) 6, 10, 16–17, 18, 19, 21, 25, 33, 48, 61, 72, 74, 75, 77, 81, 83, 84, 85, 88, 91, 92, 93, 94, 95, 96–7, 98, 101, 105, 110, 115–16, 118, 119, 121, 123, 125, 129, 133; Irish 89; Long Parliament 116–17, 133; Short Parliament 116, 133
Parr, Katherine, queen of England 6
Parry, Thomas 85
Parry Plot 30

Paternoster plays 54
Paul V, pope 84, 87
Pembroke, earl of 10, 13, 17
Percy, Anne, countess of Northumberland 33
Percy, Charles 82
Percy, Henry (alleged plotter) 117
Percy, Henry, 8th earl of Northumberland 22
Percy, Henry, 9th earl of Northumberland 83
Percy, Thomas, 7th earl of Northumberland 14
Percy, Thomas (Gunpowder plotter) 83
Perkins, William 71, 107
Perry, John 26
Persons, Robert 22, 28–9, 30–1, 35, 37–40, 41, 44, 45, 48, 49, 58, 74, 76, 79, 83, 87, 109, 122
Petre family 49, 53, 75
Petre, John 75
Petre, William, 2nd baron Petre 49, 75, 77
Petworth, Sussex 22
Philip II, king of Spain 10, 11, 13, 16, 22, 23, 26, 29, 30
Philip III, king of Spain 82
Phillip, Robert 104
physicians *see* medicine (profession)
Piers, John, bishop of Salisbury 109
pilgrimage 32, 44, 63, 67, 101
Pilkington, James, bishop of Durham 9, 14–15
Pilkington, Katherine 15
Pius IV, pope 7, 11
Pius V, pope 11, 15, 18, 64 *see also Regnans in Excelsis*
Pole, Reginald, cardinal archbishop of Canterbury 32
poor relief 72
Popham, John 27
Porter, Endymion 102, 104, 115
Porter, Olive 104
Porter, Tom 104
Pory, John 101
Pounde, Thomas 81
Poznán, Poland 51
praemunire 86
Prayer Books: 1549 6; 1552 6; 1559 7; 1637 (Scottish) 113
presbyterianism 2, 133
Preston, Thomas 48
printing 39, 61, 64, 65, 68, 111, 118, 134
prisons 9, 12, 25, 27, 29, 30, 38, 39, 40, 44, 45, 48, 50, 55, 60, 61, 62, 65, 67, 68, 83, 84, 85, 86, 88, 92, 97, 100, 111, 122–3, 131; Clink 61, 65; Fleet 9, 74; Marshalsea 61; New Prison 61; Newgate 61, 100

Privy Council 9, 10, 11, 24, 27, 48, 54, 64, 73, 77, 88, 89, 95, 120
Probin, Marjorie 59
Probin, Mary 59
proclamations, royal 24, 26, 80, 81, 82, 92, 93, 95, 96, 99, 105
Prynne, William 101, 102–3, 105–6, 112–13
Pudsey, Yorkshire 118
Puritans 2, 21, 26, 31, 65, 76–7, 78, 80, 81, 83, 92, 96, 97, 98, 99, 102, 105, 109, 111, 112, 115, 116–17
pursuivants 58, 97, 100
Pym, John 2, 96, 116, 117, 118, 133–4

Radford, John 61
Ranters 113
Ravaillac, François 88
reconciliation (of conformist Catholics) 14, 16, 23–4, 57, 65, 125, 134
recusancy 1, 5, 7, 8–9, 16, 23, 26–7, 35, 36, 38–9, 41–3, 53–4, 55, 56, 57, 59–60, 63, 65, 69–70, 71, 72–4, 75, 80, 81, 86, 87, 88, 89, 90, 92, 93, 95, 96–8, 99–100, 105, 124, 125, 130; penalties for 24, 30, 62, 71, 82, 84–5, 88, 90, 93, 96, 110, 115, 126
Redondela, Spain 67
Regnans in Excelsis (1570) 12, 15–16, 27, 108
relics 50, 57, 65, 66, 67, 68
resistance, Catholic 1, 8, 11, 15, 27–8, 29, 30, 31, 76 *see also* Gunpowder Plot; Northern Rebellion
Restoration of the Monarchy 119
Revelation, Book of 107, 108
Rheims, France 32, 36, 39, 41
Ridolfi, Roberto 16
Ridolfi Plot 19
Rigby, Alexander 117
Rigby, John 23, 25
Rigge, Richard 131
Right, Petition of 77
Rio da Janeiro, Brazil 51
Ripon, Yorkshire 7, 8, 15
Ripon, Treaty of (1640) 116
Rochdale, Yorkshire 118
Roe, Thomas 99
Rogers, Thomas 109
Rome, Italy 20, 29, 46, 66, 76–7, 84, 104, 108, 110, 118, 134; English College at 26, 32, 59, 66, 79
Rookwood, Edward 27
rosary 50, 63–4, 68

Rossetti, Carlo 116, 117
Rossingham, Edward 102
Rouen, France 39, 65
Rudyard, Benjamin 92
Rushton, Northamptonshire 65, 72
Russell, John 110

Sackville, Edward, earl of Dorset (Lord Buckhurst) 62, 73, 74, 101
Sackville, Thomas 75
St Bartholomew's Day Massacre 19, 21
St Omer, France 36, 59, 122
St Osyth, Essex 119
Saffron Walden, Essex 44
Salisbury, Wiltshire 116
Salkeld, Hugh 131
Salkeld, Thomas 131
Salvetti, Amerigo 115, 116, 118
Sander, Nicholas 5, 7–8, 14, 16, 27, 37, 65
Sandys, Edwin, bishop of Worcester 8, 108
Santiago de Compostella, Spain 67
Savage, Thomas, viscount Savage 77, 102
Sayer, Gregory 33
Scandinavia 2
schism 8, 23, 41, 72, 127
schools *see* education
Scory, John, bishop of Hereford 7, 8, 120
Scotland 2, 3, 11, 13, 15, 18, 20, 22, 23, 28, 31, 46, 76, 79, 110, 113, 114, 115, 116, 129
Scrope, lord 91, 99
secular priests *see* seminary priests
Sedgefield, Co. Durham 15
Selden, John 96
seminaries 32, 35, 36, 39, 41, 44, 45, 54, 59, 72
seminary priests (seculars) 22, 25, 26, 27, 28, 29, 30, 31, 35, 38, 39, 40, 41, 43, 44, 45–6, 48–9, 50, 53, 55, 57, 61, 62, 63, 64, 65, 67, 68, 75, 76, 78, 80, 88, 94, 96, 100, 102, 109, 115, 116, 124, 125, 132; chapter of 47, 78, 115
separatists, Protestant 26, 31 *see also* Puritans
sequestration 24, 84, 85, 90, 96, 119
Settlement, Elizabethan 3, 5, 9–10, 12, 32, 36, 119
Seville, Spain 32, 36, 46
Shaftesbury, Dorset 79
Shanne, Richard 71
Sheffield, lord 91
Shelley, Jane 57, 85
Sherland, Christopher 96

Shrewsbury, earl of 53, 96
Sibbes, Richard 112
Sidney, Henry 17
Skeffling, Yorkshire 71
slavery 51
Smith, Francis 102
Smith, Richard, bishop of Chalcedon 47–8, 68, 88, 100, 115
sodalities 50, 64
Somerset, Edward, 4th earl of Worcester 49, 53, 75, 81–2
Somerset, Henry, 5th earl of Worcester 78, 116, 117
Somerset, Katherine 49, 75
South Shields, Co. Durham 40–1
Southcote, John 49, 100
Southerne, William 91
Southwell, Robert 23, 25, 31, 40, 44, 60, 62, 63, 67, 68
Spain 12, 19, 24, 25, 32, 33, 36, 37, 50, 76, 83, 84, 86, 89, 91, 92–3, 96, 98–9, 102, 105, 108, 109, 110, 111, 114, 118, 126, 127
'Spanish marriage', the 76–7, 90–1, 93, 111
Spes, Guerau de 13
Spiller, Henry 85
Stanley, William 33
Stanney, William 61
Stanningfield, Suffolk see Coldham Hall, Suffolk
Stapleton, Thomas 8, 31, 33
Star Chamber, Court of 70, 81–2
Starkey, Oliver, prior of England 33
Stephens, Thomas 51
Stevens, Christian 63
Stockeld, Yorkshire 71
Stonor, Cecilia 43
Story, John 33–4
Stourton, lord 83, 90
Strasbourg, France 5
Stuart, Mary see Mary, queen of Scots
Stubbs, John 21
Suárez, Francisco 87
Suffolk 44, 47, 54, 55, 70, 73, 77, 98, 109, 119
Supremacy, Oath of 7, 10
Sussex 7, 9, 22, 29, 42, 53, 55, 57, 59, 60, 73, 75
Sussex, earl of 12, 17, 20, 74

Taylor, James 55
Thames, River 55
Thimelby family 54
Thirty Years' War 91, 98, 99, 105, 110, 111

Thornley, Co. Durham 41
Throckmorton, Francis 22, 28
Throckmorton, Nicholas 5, 11, 13
Throckmorton Plot 20, 24, 28, 55
Timperley, Nicholas 70
toleration 3, 20, 30, 42, 46, 51, 76, 77, 79–80, 81, 82, 83, 90–4, 96, 99, 100, 110, 130
Topcliffe, Richard 56
treason 10, 16, 17, 23, 25, 30, 33, 64, 85, 103, 110, 111, 113, 114, 128
Trent, Council of 4, 7, 11, 35, 36, 47, 61
Tresham, Francis 83, 90
Tresham, Mary 90
Tresham, Thomas 30, 39, 43, 55, 65, 72, 76, 79, 80, 124, 125
Tudor, Margaret, queen of Scots 11
Tunstall, Cuthbert 66
Tynley, Robert 88
Tyrrell, Antony 69

Ulster, plantation of 90
Uvendale, William 57

vagrants 54
Valladolid, Spain 26, 32, 36, 46, 59, 102
Vaux, Ann 50, 57, 58
Vaux, Elizabeth 57
Vaux, Laurence 8, 11, 60, 61
Vaux, William, lord 30, 39–40, 55, 57
Vavasour, Dorothy 62
Vavasour, John 71
Vavasour, Thomas 57, 62
Vavasour, William 88
Velasco, Juan Fernández de 82, 127
Vereept, Simon 65
Vicars, John 110
Vienna, Prague 51
Villiers, George, duke of Buckingham 92, 93, 101, 102, 104, 111, 113, 115
Vilnius, Lithuania 51
Vondeville, Jean de 36

Waferer, Arden 55
Wales 2, 53, 62, 69, 72, 78, 81, 94, 117, 115, 116, 118, 133
Walsingham, Francis 17, 20, 21, 22–3, 31
Wandesford, Christopher 97
Ward, Samuel 111
Warwick, earl of 102
Warwickshire 22, 58
Waterford, Ireland 36
Watson, William 32, 46, 80, 83
Waymouth, George 51

Wellington, Alice 62
Wentworth, Thomas, earl of Strafford 96, 97–8, 99–100, 114, 115, 116–17
Westmorland 73, 130, 131
Weston, Richard, 1st earl of Portland
Weston, William 102
White, Andrew 51
Whitford, Richard 66
Whittingham, William 14–15
widows 54, 56, 57–8, 85, 115
Wilbram, Owen 71
Wilford, William 39
William of Orange 24, 28
Wilmot, Henry 117
Windebank, Francis 99, 102–3, 114
Winter, Thomas 83
Wintringham, Thomas 71
Winwood, Ralph 91
Wisbech Castle, Cambridgeshire 39, 45, 50, 59
Wiseman family 44, 55

Wiseman, Thomas 118
women, role in the English Catholic community 33, 55, 56–8, 63, 67, 72, 104, 105, 109
women religious 32, 49, 58, 59, 64, 101
Woodford, Elizabeth 32
Worksop, Nottinghamshire 110
Wotton, lord 93
Wren, Matthew, bishop of Norwich 99, 113
Wright, John 82
Wright, Thomas 31–2, 79, 83
Wycliffe, Yorkshire 54

yeomen 50, 54, 55, 71
York, Yorkshire 13, 14, 54, 57, 61, 62, 66, 81, 88, 116
Yorkshire 7, 8, 9, 15, 37, 40, 42, 49, 54, 63, 71, 72, 73, 88, 97, 99, 118
Young, Robert 54

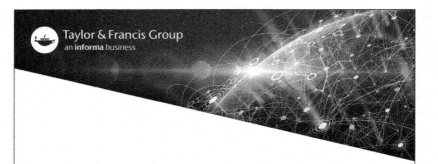